the politics of
migration&
immigration
in europe

SAGE was founded in 1965 by Sara Miller McCune to support the dissemination of usable knowledge by publishing innovative and high-quality research and teaching content. Today, we publish over 900 journals, including those of more than 400 learned societies, more than 800 new books per year, and a growing range of library products including archives, data, case studies, reports, and video. SAGE remains majority-owned by our founder, and after Sara's lifetime will become owned by a charitable trust that secures our continued independence.

Los Angeles | London | New Delhi | Singapore | Washington DC | Melbourne

the politics of
migration &
immigration
in europe

2nd edition

andrew geddes
& peter scholten

Los Angeles | London | New Delhi
Singapore | Washington DC | Melbourne

Los Angeles | London | New Delhi
Singapore | Washington DC | Melbourne

SAGE Publications Ltd
1 Oliver's Yard
55 City Road
London EC1Y 1SP

SAGE Publications Inc.
2455 Teller Road
Thousand Oaks, California 91320

SAGE Publications India Pvt Ltd
B 1/I 1 Mohan Cooperative Industrial Area
Mathura Road
New Delhi 110 044

SAGE Publications Asia-Pacific Pte Ltd
3 Church Street
#10-04 Samsung Hub
Singapore 049483

Editor: Natalie Aguilera
Assistant editor: George Knowles
Production editor: Katie Forsythe
Copyeditor: Christine Bitten
Indexer: David Rudeforth
Marketing manager: Sally Ransom
Cover design: Stephanie Guyaz
Typeset by: C&M Digitals (P) Ltd, Chennai, India
Printed by CPI Group (UK) Ltd, Croydon, CR0 4YY

Library of Congress Control Number: 2015959158

British Library Cataloguing in Publication data

A catalogue record for this book is available from
the British Library

ISBN 978-1-84920-467-5
ISBN 978-1-84920-468-2 (pbk)

At SAGE we take sustainability seriously. Most of our products are printed in the UK using FSC papers and boards.
When we print overseas we ensure sustainable papers are used as measured by the PREPS grading system.
We undertake an annual audit to monitor our sustainability.

Contents

List of Figures and Tables

Figures

Tables

About the Authors

Andrew Geddes is Professor of Politics and Co-Director of the Faculty of Social Sciences Migration Research Group at the University of Sheffield. He was awarded a European Research Council Advanced Investigator grant for 2014–19 to analyse the drivers of global migration governance through comparison of Europe, North America, South America and Asia-Pacific.

Peter Scholten is Associate Professor of Public Policy and Politics at Erasmus University and Director of IMISCOE, Europe's largest research network on international migration, integration and cohesion. Peter is also Editor-in-Chief of the journal *Comparative Migration Studies*, and member of the editorial board of the *Journal of Comparative Policy Analysis*. At Erasmus University he co-ordinates the MSc programme on the Governance of Migration and Diversity.

List of Acronyms

A2	Refers to Bulgaria and Romania that joined the EU in 2007
A8	Eight countries in Central and Eastern Europe that joined the EU in 2004 (Czech Republic, Estonia, Latvia, Lithuania, Slovenia, Slovakia, Poland and Hungary)
ACSE	Agence pour la cohesion sociale et l'egalite des chances (Agency for Social Cohesion and Equality of Opportunities)
AKP	Adalet ve Kalkınma Partisi (Justice and Development Party, Turkey)
AMIF	Asylum, Migration and Integration Fund
BAMF	Bundesamt für Migration und Flüchtlinge (Federal Office for Migration and Refugees)
CDA	Christen Democratisch Appel (Christian Democrat Party)
CDU	Christlich Demokratische Union (Christian Democrat Union, Germany)
CEAS	Common European Asylum System
CEC	Commission of the European Communities
CEE	Central and East European
CJEU	Court of Justice of the European Union
CRE	Commission for Racial Equality
EASO	European Asylum Support Office
ECSC	European Coal and Steel Community
EHRC	Equality and Human Rights Commission
EMN	European Migration Network
ERF	European Refugee Fund
EURODAC	European Dactyloscopy

EUROSUR   European Border Surveillance System

FASILD   Fonds d'action sociale pour l'integration et la lute contre les dis-
           criminations (Social fund for integration and anti-discrimination)

FN   Front National (National Front)

FNPS   Fondo Nazionale per le Politiche Sociali (National Fund for Social
           Policies)

FRONTEX   European Agency for the Management of Operational Co-operation
           at the External Borders of the Member States of the European
           Union

GAMM   Global Approach to Migration and Mobility

HALDE   Haute Authorité de Lutte contre les Discriminations et pour l'Egalité
           (the High Authority for the Fight Against Discrimination and for
           Equality)

HCI   Haut Conseil à l'Integration (High Council for Integration)

HSMP   High Skilled Migrants Programme (UK)

IOM   International Organisation for Migration

LAOS   Popular Orthodox Rally (Greece)

LPF   Lijst Pim Fortuyn (Pim Fortuyn Party)

MIPEX   Migrant Integration Policy Index

NIO   Swedish Integration Board

OFPRA   Office français de protection des réfugiés et des apatrides (French
           Office for the Protection of Refugees and Stateless Persons)

ONI   Office national d'immigration (National Office of Immigration)

PASOK   Panhellenic Socialist Movement (Greece)

PEGIDA   Patriotische Europäer gegen die Islamisierung des Abendlandes
           (Patriotic Europeans Against the Islamisation of the West)

PvdA   Partij van de Arbeid (Labour Party, Netherlands)

PVV   Partij voor de Vrijheid (Freedom Party)

QMV   Qualified Majority Voting

SAP   Sveriges socialdemokratiska arbetareparti (Swedish Social Democrat
           Party)

SCP   Sociaal en Cultureel Planbureau (Social and Cultural Planning Office)

SD	Sweden Democrats
SIS	Schengen Information System
SPD	Sozialdemokratische Partei Deutschlands (Social Democrat Party Germany)
TCN	Third Country Nationals (Non-EU nationals)
UKIP	United Kingdom Independence Party
VIS	Visa Information System
VVD	Volkspartij voor Vrijheid en Democratie (People's Party for Freedom and Democracy)
WRR	Wetenschappelijke Raad voor het Regeringsbeleid (Dutch Scientific Council for Government Policy)
ZUS	Zones urbanes sensibles (sensitive urban zones)

Analysing the Politics of Migration and Immigration in Europe

Introduction

This book analyses and compares responses by European countries to international migration in its various forms and examines collective responses at European Union (EU) level. We assess why, how and with what effects European countries have developed policies that seek to regulate entry to their territory (immigration policies); what it means when they then seek to 'integrate' these migrant newcomers (immigrant policies); and the causes and effects of common EU migration and asylum policies.

Debates in Europe about migration have been profoundly influenced by the refugee crisis. In 2015, 1,003,124 people were reported by the International Organization for Migration (IOM) to have arrived in the EU via Mediterranean maritime routes with 3771 people reported dead or missing (IOM, 2016). Following their arrival in Europe – with the IOM reporting that 845,852 people arrived in Greece in 2015 – hundreds of thousands of men, women and children then began journeys across Europe via countries such as Macedonia, Serbia, Slovenia, Hungary and Austria, with Germany often the preferred final destination. By the end of 2015, there were estimates of up to 1 million people in Germany seeking refuge. This disorderly, dangerous and mass movement of people with its associated horrifying death toll opened the eyes of many people to the tragic effects of conflict and economic inequalities that underpin much international migration. Syria, Iraq, Afghanistan and Eritrea were all key origin countries.

For other people, the refugee crisis demonstrated a need for much greater effort to secure the borders of EU states in the face of what were seen as unmanageable flows and threats to security. Whether or not a stronger and more collective EU migration and asylum policy can be developed also formed part of this debate. In September 2015, EU member states agreed to a scheme to relocate up to 160,000 asylum seekers from Greece, Hungary and Italy, but there were tensions within the EU. The Czech Republic, Hungary, Slovakia and Romania opposed the scheme but were outvoted, and it also raised major implementation challenges (CEC, 2015). The EU's Schengen system of passport free travel – with compensating security measures – came under close scrutiny, which intensified after the terror attacks in Paris on November 2015 in which 130 people were murdered. Prior to the Paris attacks, border control efforts had already been reinforced. In summer 2015 Hungary constructed a fence at its borders with Serbia and Croatia to stop onward movement of migrants who had entered the EU in Greece. In December 2012, the Greek government completed a 12.5 km-long fence at their land border with Turkey. The Spanish had already intensely fortified their borders with Morocco in the Spanish enclaves of Ceuta and Melilla (Andersson, 2014). The port of Calais had for more than 10 years become a high security zone with extensive fencing to stop migrants making irregular crossings from France to the UK. It wasn't just new fences that were popping up all over Europe. Germany, Sweden and France all reinstated temporary border checks during 2015 in an attempt to control refugee and migrant flows.

While the refugee crisis has been at the top of the European agenda since 2014, this book makes the point that we need to see it as a manifestation of a much broader and complex debate about how international migration in its various forms (to work, to join family, to seek refuge and to study being four key motives) affects European politics and societies and how these countries and societies themselves affect and shape migration. While the focus was on refugee flows, channels for labour and family migration remained the main routes for entry to Europe while hundreds of thousands of international (non-EU) students arrive each year to study at colleges and universities in Europe. Mobility within the EU by EU citizens with free movement rights has also increased, particularly from new member states such as Poland, Hungary and Romania, but also from economic crisis-hit Greece, Italy and Spain. More than ever before, migration and mobility became central to the debate about Europe's future.

The wider point, as this book shows, is that European countries have long histories of immigration and emigration, which means that the day-to-day business of living together in European countries has been shaped by migration and has become part of everyday life, potentially holding both positive and negative connotations for societies and political systems. To take one example, the causes and effects of immigration-related diversity have long been debated across European societies that are undoubtedly more socially, ethnically, religiously and linguistically diverse. Immigration clearly plays a part in this diversity. For many people these changes are viewed as positive and as providing economic, social and cultural enrichment. For others they are viewed more negatively as a cost and burden. Immigration-related diversity means that European societies have become more multicultural, but there is a difference between a society being multicultural and a government pursuing multicultural policies. In 2011 the leaders of Germany, the UK and France all claimed that so-called 'multicultural' policies had failed because of their over-emphasis on difference and diversity and too little emphasis on commonalities. Austria, France, Greece, Italy, Hungary, the Netherlands, Sweden and the UK all saw increased support for anti-immigration and anti-EU political parties that oppose immigration and multiculturalism.

How then to make sense of these dynamics? How can we understand contemporary developments while still being sensitive to historical factors and influences?

Since the 1990s, there has been a huge increase in resources devoted to categorising, regulating and trying to 'manage' migration and migrants, including at EU level. There has, for example, been an increase in migration that falls into categories defined by state policies as 'illegal' or 'irregular', i.e. migration that is not authorised by migration laws and policies in destination countries (Jordan and Düvell, 2002). One unintended effect of this has been to direct migrants towards more dangerous routes of entry and to provide a powerful stimulus to the people-smuggling industry, as well as to government departments, international organisations, civil society groups, businesses, media organisations and researchers that all become involved in various ways in what Andersson calls 'Illegality Inc' (Andersson, 2014).

Geo-politically, the impact of international migration has widened since the 1990s from a group of 'older' immigration countries in North West Europe to include newer immigration countries, newer EU member states and non-EU member states in Southern and Central Europe, such as Greece, Hungary, Italy, Poland, Spain and Turkey. International migration now forms an important part of the relations between European countries and surrounding states and regions, including in Eastern Europe, North Africa, the Middle East and countries in the Horn of Africa such as Somalia and Eritrea.

This book analyses the political causes and consequences of international migration to Europe. We also suggest an alternative way of thinking about these causes and consequences. Often the focus is on the ways in which international migration 'challenges' nation states. Thought about in analytical terms, this means seeing international migration as a challenge to the nation state and means understanding it as an independent variable that can then help explain various social and political changes in European countries.

As we argue in this book, it can be equally – if not more – useful to reverse the analytical focus and explore the ways in which European countries (as well as changed relations between European states), play a key role in producing and shaping understandings of international migration (Geddes, 2005b). In these terms, territorial borders as well as important forms of social organisation within states, such as their labour markets and welfare states, play a central role in the constitution of immigration as a social and political issue (Bommes and Geddes, 2000; Ireland, 2004; Carmel et al., 2011). Put another way, these boundaries shape how we 'see' and understand immigration (as a challenge, threat, opportunity, benefit, cost etc.). Immigration also interacts with 'conceptual' boundaries of membership, belonging and entitlement that mediate relations between 'us' and 'them' (Anderson, 2013). Our approach means seeing international migration as a dependent variable that acquires meaning when it meets the borders (territorial, organisational and conceptual) of destination states. International migration is, by definition, made visible by the borders of states. If there were no such things as states then there would be no such thing as international migration (Zolberg, 1989). As such, international migration is defined by the categorisations and classifications that occur at Europe's borders. These differences between categories have hugely important effects because being labelled a 'high skilled migrant' leads to an entirely different relationship to the host society compared to that experienced by an 'asylum seeker' or 'refugee'.

Thought about in such terms, whether international migration is viewed as a 'good' or 'bad' thing is heavily dependent on decisions made in destination countries and, as Zolberg (1989: 406) evocatively put it, the walls that these countries build and the small doors that they open in these walls. This metaphor becomes more powerful in light of the efforts by European countries such as Britain, France, Greece, Hungary and Spain to literally build walls and fences to prevent migrants entering their territory. By shifting the analytical focus in this way and concentrating on the shaping effects of borders, we account for the ways in which the actions, inactions, inclusions, omissions and world-views of institutions and organisations in destination countries shape perceptions of and responses to international migration and migrants (Geddes, 2005b).

This tallies with the need to view international migration as related to underlying structural factors that play a key role in its generation. Chief among these are effects of global economic inequalities in the form of relative income and wealth inequalities plus the role played by conflicts, demographic change and environmental factors that can also cause people to move to another country (Black et al., 2011).

In such terms, international migration can be understood as epiphenomenal, i.e. it occurs as a result of something else happening such as economic inequalities and conflict. It also means that immigration policies can be after-the-fact reactions to the underlying factors that drive international migration and limits

the extent to which immigration policies provide 'solutions' to the more fundamental aspects of the global politics such as inequality, conflict, demographic
patterns or environmental and climate change.

An important implication of this is that it's not so much the personality or
character of the individual migrant – for example, an asylum seeker or a high
skilled labour migrant – that matters in immigration policy, but rather the
ways in which they are viewed by institutions and organisations in the countries to which they move. These can then shape wider social perceptions of
the 'value' of migration and migrants irrespective of the actual qualities, skills
and attributes that they possess.

It is also important to think about the issue of 'who decides'. Decisions about
law and policy are still quite strongly focused at the national level, although the
EU does play an increased role (Geddes, 2008a; Acosta and Geddes, 2013). It is,
however, crucial to note that EU member states decide on the numbers of
migrants from non-EU member states (known as third country nationals (TCNs))
to be admitted. In contrast, citizens of the EU's 28 member states can move freely
within the EU. This highlights a point that is central to the analysis that follows.
The EU promotes economic liberalisation and free movement but seeks to strictly
regulate entry by non-EU citizens. In this way European integration changes the
meaning of borders both 'internally' within the EU and 'externally' in terms of
relations with countries that are not EU member states. This became manifest
again in response to the refugee crisis in 2015 and 2016 when, as mentioned
earlier, *ad hoc* border controls were reinstated between EU member states in order
to control or prevent onwards movement by refugees. By 2016, questions were
being raised about the sustainability of the EU's Schengen system of passport free
travel covering 26 European countries. Former French President Nicolas Sarkozy
stated that 'Schengen is dead' while Dutch Prime Minister Mark Rutte stated that
border controls at the EU's external frontiers were imperative if Schengen were to
survive. Yet, for hundreds of thousands of EU citizens, passport free travel has
become part of their daily lives with many commuting across borders for work.
Hungarian Prime Minister, Viktor Orban, usually renowned for his Euroscepticism,
said that for Hungarians Schengen was freedom (*The Guardian*, 2016).

Why do people move? Explaining mobility and immobility

International migration is linked to underlying features of global politics,
particularly inequalities between richer and poorer countries as well as the
effects of factors such as political repression and conflict. Focusing on these
and their effects can help to avoid a destination country bias focused only on
the 'problems' for European countries and allow appreciation of the factors
that cause people to migrate to Europe.

The term international migration might seem relatively straightforward: movement by people across state borders that leads to permanent settlement. This movement is then viewed by receiving states as immigration. It is in these terms – as immigration and permanent settlement in a world of nation states – that the politicisation of immigration has occurred across Europe. But it is not as straightforward as this. There are, in fact, many types of movement by people that cross state frontiers and each are 'capable of metamorphosing into something else through a set of processes which are increasingly institutionally driven. What we then choose to define as migration is an arbitrary decision, and may be time-specific' (Dobson et al., 2001: 25). Migration can be short-term or long-term. Migrants could live in one country and work in another. There can also be movement back and forth between sending and receiving countries.

Defining immigration and immigrants are political matters. Some governments distinguish between people of national descent 'returning' to their 'home' country after several generations (such as ethnic German *Aussiedler* or Dutch 'repatriates') and those who are 'immigrants' of non-national descent with implications for the policy developed towards such people and their treatment. A more recent manifestation is the debate about intra-EU free movement. EU institutions tend not to use the term 'migrant' because such people are mobile EU citizens making use of the possibilities that free movement offers. In political debate, however, intra-EU 'mobility' swiftly turns into 'migration' when permanent settlement in another EU state occurs and can raise concerns about issues such as housing, health care and education.

People movement from one country to another is primarily driven by relative inequalities of income and wealth. These can be thought of as powerful economic drivers of migration, but this does not mean that international migration or EU free movement are subject to simple push–pull pressures as migrants move for economic reasons from poor countries to richer ones. In addition to relative inequalities of income and wealth, other factors include:

- the effects of political change, including conflict;
- the operation and effects of migrant networks connecting potential migrants to kith and kin that have already moved and that can be facilitated by new information and communication technologies;
- the effects of population structure on people's ability to move with younger adults generally being more able to move than older people;
- the effects of environmental change on peoples' livelihoods.

It is also important to note that all of these factors – economic, political, social, demographic and environmental – can be reasons why people don't or are unable to move. If people lack resources (economic, physical, social) or are fearful of the effects of conflict then they may not be able to move or may even be trapped in areas that threaten their livelihoods and lives. Evidence suggests that the effects of conflict can be to push people to simply the next safe place, which meant in the case of the Syrian conflict that, by summer 2015, upwards of 4.5 million Syrians had fled to Turkey, Lebanon and Jordan.

For destination countries, it is important to specify what actually is meant by the term immigration and how this turns into policy categories such as labour migrant, asylum seeker, family migrant and international student. The underlying assumptions informing definitions can have very powerful effects. Take, for example, the categories 'voluntary' economic migrant and 'forced' refugee. These tend to be defined from the vantage point of receiving states and can also be redefined by these states. Forced migrants are those fleeing persecution who are offered protection on the basis of the 1951 Geneva Convention on the rights of stateless people to which all EU member states are signatories. Only a small proportion of international migrants fall within the remit of this convention. Are migrants voluntary or forced if they leave their countries because of unemployment or poverty? Voluntarism would tend to be the supposition in receiving countries, which then legitimates restriction on this migration because it is defined as motivated by economic reasons. Instead, it has been argued that the voluntary/involuntary distinction is better viewed as a continuum reflective of the varying degrees of choice or freedom available (Faist, 2000: 23).

If the term international migration is unclear, then there are likely to be some difficulties enacting policies to establish authoritative capacity in order to manage and regulate it. Governments often make claims to be able to plan, regulate and even to control international migration, but, by doing so, it is assumed that the phenomena associated with international migration are relatively knowable and to some extent predictable. Yet, more often than not, migration policy can seem like reactive muddling through in the face of unpredictable migration pressures. For example, no-one predicted the scale of the refugee crisis that hit Europe in the 2010s. Migration policy is also made within institutional settings that do not always facilitate the translation of policy objectives into policy outcomes (Sciortino, 2000). One reason for this is that between the formulation of policy objectives and their implementation, there is the political process of decision-making during which countervailing and sometimes contradictory dynamics can affect migration policy (Boswell and Geddes, 2011). During elections there might be 'tough' rhetoric about controlling immigration, but, in government, other pressures such as the interest of the business community can lead to more expansive labour migration policies (Freeman, 1995; Geddes, 2008b).

A brief history of European migration

The main focus of this book is on events after the end of the Cold War in 1989, although there is also reference to earlier patterns of migration and their legacies.

The end of the Cold War fundamentally reshaped the EU leading to the collapse of the Soviet Union, German reunification and a wave of new countries joining the EU (16 between 1989 and 2013 when Croatia joined).

This wave of 'new', post-1989 migration does require some historical contextualisation. International migration is at a lower level in this contemporary era of 'globalisation' than in the late nineteenth and early twentieth centuries when millions of Europeans left for the US or moved from colonising to colonised parts of the world (Moch, 1992). In 2015, around 3.5 per cent (around 244 million people) of the world's population were international migrants meaning they were born outside of the country in which they reside (UNFPA, 2015). Of these around 10 per cent have moved to Europe. Most originate from certain countries and even from particular towns and villages in those countries (OECD, 2014).

When looking at post-war migration to Western Europe we can see that it was powerfully structured by links between sending and receiving countries and by the development of the European economy that generated demand for migrant workers. Migration to countries such as France, the Netherlands and the UK was shaped by colonialism and into West Germany (as it then was) by guestworker recruitment agreements. Those migrants that settled then increased their level of engagement with the institutions of the host societies, particularly the labour market, welfare state and political system. Migration since the end of the Cold War in 1989 has not been so powerfully structured by post-colonial ties or guestworker recruitment.

Trends in post-war migration

Immigration into Western Europe during the 1950s and 1960s was central to economic reconstruction. There was, however, a lurking assumption that labour migration was temporary and migrants would return to their countries of origin when economic conditions changed. This assumption was misplaced: the guests stayed (Rogers, 1985). Labour migration peaked in the 1960s and ended with the recruitment-stop following economic slowdown and the oil price rises of 1973–4 before increasing again in the 2000s. By the late 1970s it was clear that supposed temporary migration had turned for many into permanent settlement. The immigrant-origin communities changed in profile to include more women, younger and older people. This meant increased engagement with key social institutions, particularly welfare states.

The door was closed to large-scale labour migration in the early 1970s, but migration by family members continued and became the main form of immigration to Europe. While labour migrants in the 1950s and 1960s were typically represented as being male, there were also female labour migrants

(Phizacklea, 1983). Family reunion led to a further feminisation of international migration, as well as bringing more children and older people. The origins of migrants also differed. Some migrants arrived from former colonies, holding the passport and nationality of the country to which they moved, and thus with the same formal rights as other citizens (Britain, France and the Netherlands all stand out in this respect). Meanwhile, non-national migrants such as guestworkers in Germany were granted legal rights and welfare state membership in accordance with what Hammar (1990) calls 'denizenship'. This status can be understood as legal and social rights linked to legal residence falling short of full citizenship. The transformation of the incomplete membership status of denizenship into full citizenship would then depend upon naturalisation laws.

The decision to restrict labour migration did not lead to the end of immigration. It did not even lead to the end of labour migration. Rather, the labour migration channel was narrowed to allow mainly high skilled immigrants to enter while there was still scope for family migration. Much of the political debate about immigration in the 1970s, 1980s and 1990s centred on family migration and the implications of permanent settlement.

A 'third wave' of migration developed in the aftermath of the end of the Cold War in 1989–90 with a particularly noticeable increase in asylum-seeking migration and migration defined by state policies as 'illegal' or 'irregular'. This has contributed both to a diversification in terms of the countries of origin of migrants and the numbers of European countries affected by international migration. This phase is closely associated with the development of common EU migration and asylum policies since the 1990s that were then tested by the refugee crisis and huge scale movement towards Europe that plunged the EU asylum, migration and border control system into crisis. Table 1.1 provides an overview of Mediterranean arrivals and fatalities in the EU during 2015 and shows that the vast majority occurred in Greece.

Analytical themes

This chapter now introduces three themes that help develop these points and that will then be the basis for the comparative analysis in the chapters that follow: immigration policies, immigrant policies and the impact of European integration. The European societies upon which this book focuses can be understood as both structures and actors. As structures we are interested in the characteristics of their institutions and organisations, or put another way, their practices. As actors we pay attention to the understandings and ideas that animate these practices. The ways in which these organisations view the world plays an important part in the production of migrant categories and thus

Table 1.1 Mediterranean migration flows to Europe: Arrivals and fatalities in 2015

Fatalities by month in 2015 (compared to 2014)

	Jan		Feb		March		April		May		June		July		August		Sept		Oct		Nov		Dec		Total	
	2014	2015	2014	2015	2014	2015	2014	2015	2014	2015	2014	2015	2014	2015	2014	2015	2014	2015	2014	2015	2014	2015	2014	2015	2014	2015
	12	82	24	346	10	61	50	1244	95	329	10	318	230	864	616	686	813	268	126	432	22	106	95	205	3279	3771

Total arrivals in Greece and Italy 2015

	Number
Italy	153,052
Greece	845,852

Top five origin countries in 2015 for Italy and Greece

To Italy		To Greece	
Eritrea	37,882	Syria	455,363
Nigeria	20,171	Afghanistan	186,500
Somalia	11,242	Iraq	63,421
Sudan	8,766	Pakistan	23,318
Syria	7,837	Iran	19,612

Source: IOM Missing Migrants Project, January 6 2016.

shapes responses to international migration in its various forms. Organisational practices concern, for example:

- procedures governing legal residence and the rights associated with this status;
- citizenship, naturalisation and nationality laws;
- access to the labour market and welfare state (health care, education, housing, etc.);
- political rights;
- anti-discrimination and laws to tackle racism and xenophobia;
- policies that can seek to change, promote, preserve or protect aspects of immigrants' social and cultural identities.

These are all informed by ideas about membership, entitlement and belonging. A central aspect of political activity is the attempt to control shared meaning and, as such, debates about immigration's effects on European countries are good examples of conflict over the concepts used in framing political judgements on social problems and public policies (Edelman, 1988).

Theme 1: Explaining immigration policies

Immigration policies concern themselves with conditions regulating territorial access by non-nationals and access to key social institutions such as the labour market and welfare state. A state's power, authority and capacity to regulate access to its territory are important indicators of its sovereign authority.

EU member states have become increasingly open to free movement of goods, capital and services as part of the EU's Single Market, but have been more resistant to free movement of people. Hollifield (2000a) calls this a 'liberal paradox' of open markets and relatively closed states. European states devote immense resources to the regulation of immigration and to efforts at control. As Brubaker (1994: 230) argues: 'True, states are open at the margins to citizens of other states, but only at the margins. Seen from outside, the prosperous and peaceful states of the world remain powerfully exclusionary'.

This leaves us with a puzzle referred to earlier: since at least the 1970s, European countries have declared their intention to strictly regulate immigration but have continued to accept migrants. To address this puzzle, it has been argued that we need to analyse the *form* that immigration politics takes and the institutional venues where decisions are made. Gary Freeman (1995) has argued that immigration policies in liberal states such as European countries are inherently expansive in terms of numbers of migrants admitted and inclusive in terms of the rights that are extended. This seemingly counter-intuitive argument draws from studies of the politics of regulation, which identifies the role that small groups, with high stakes in a given policy area can play when trying to maximise the political benefits from a particular policy (Stigler, 1971). Freeman analyses the form of immigration politics that arises as a result of the distribution of costs and benefits. He argues that the concentrated beneficiaries (business and pro-migrant groups) have a greater incentive to organise than the diffuse bearers of costs (the general public). The result, Freeman argues, is 'client politics' and expansive and inclusive immigration policies that reflect business and pro-migrant NGO interests. Freeman focuses on the groups that have a stake in policy and presents a counter-argument to 'fortress Europe' style accounts of contemporary European migration politics. He offers a theoretically grounded account of an empirically observable phenomenon; namely that rhetorical commitments to control have been difficult to put into practice.

Similarly, Hollifield et al. (2014) identify a systematic gap in all the world's major destination countries between the rhetorical commitment to control and the reality of continued immigration that has emerged because of the role of courts as guarantors of the rights of both nationals and non-nationals in liberal states. Since the 1970s, courts have offered protection to immigrant newcomers with the effect that the liberalness of liberal states constrains the restrictive urges of politicians (Hollifield, 1992; Guiraudon, 1998; Joppke, 1998, 1999). Brian Barry (1996: 538) wrote that the basic idea of liberalism is to create a set of rights under which people are treated equally in certain respects, and in the past 200 years, western societies have been transformed in accordance with the precept of equal treatment. The generality of liberal institutions, with courts as defenders of rights, has been seen as leading to the development of 'rights-based politics' linked to what Ruggie (1983) characterised as the 'embedded liberalism' of the post-Second World War international order. Hollifield (1992) writes that this has helped to open 'social and political spaces' for migrants and their descendants in European states, with, for instance, courts defending the right to family life for national and non-national migrants in accord with national and international laws.

This presents a quite rosy picture of expansive policies and immigrant inclusion based on a universalistic ethic of inclusion that over-rides communitarian or nationalistic ethics of closure. Yet, these values are used to justify the exclusion of immigrants on the grounds that the moral relevance of community membership supersedes the openness of liberal universalism (Boswell, 1999, 2000). This can justify exclusion on the basis of protecting welfare states. Mann argues (1995, 1999) that there was a 'dark side' to the foundation of many European states based on ethno-cultural nationalism and racism rather than liberal universalism.

While not arguing that courts have always (and at all times) been progressive bastions of migrants' rights, recently judicial cool heads have tempered restrictive policies that contravened legal or constitutional provisions. It has also been argued that the changes in the EU system arising from the Treaty of Lisbon (2009) have given a greater role to the CJEU and that this has led to decisions that affect expulsion, family migration and integration (Acosta and Geddes, 2013).

These arguments about expansiveness and inclusivity have been challenged by those who argue that there is a rights versus numbers trade-off in admissions policies, which means that greater openness to the admission of migrants entails more restrictiveness in terms of the rights that are offered to them (Ruhs, 2013). The rights–numbers trade-off argument suggests that expansiveness and inclusivity do not go hand-in-hand. EU states, it could be argued, offer fairly extensive rights to those that are 'in', but they also make it increasingly difficult for people to get 'in'.

While there is some variation between European countries in citizens' attitudes to immigration, survey research in 2014 showed a general tendency to oppose current levels and also to see immigration as a burden rather than an opportunity, in terms of its impacts on labour markets and welfare states. As Figures 1.1 and 1.2 show this is particularly evident in Greece and Italy that both experienced relatively high immigration and suffered the consequences of austerity and economic crisis. As Figure 1.2 shows, there are interesting aspects to these attitudes that confound the notion of uniform hostility. For example, most British and German respondents thought that there should be fewer immigrants, but also recognised the contributions that immigrants made through their work and talents.

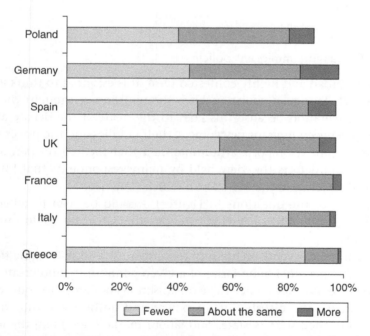

Figure 1.1 Percentage of the population saying their country should allow fewer/about the same/more immigrants

Source: Pew Research Centre, 2014

Note: Excludes data for those who answered 'don't know'

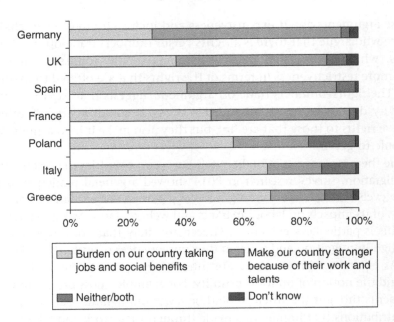

Figure 1.2 Percentage of the population saying immigrants are a burden or make country stronger

Source: Pew Research Centre, 2014

Theme 2: Explaining immigrant policies

While a very broad and highly contested term, it is essential to think about the ways in which European countries have thought and re-thought the issue of immigrant integration because this goes to the heart of the debate about the relationship between migrant newcomers, their families and the places to which they move. Figure 1.3 reports attitudinal data that focused on perceptions of assimilation and detects the view held by many respondents that immigrants want to be distinct from the societies in which they live.

The framing of the questions in Figure 1.3 could be seen to reflect a turn towards assimilation and away from the idea that diversity could intrinsically be good thing.

Immigrant policies mark an attempt to re-organise and re-imagine the organisational and conceptual boundaries of a given community and create capacity to include or exclude newcomers. The organisations of European countries (their political systems, the distribution of power and authority within them, the organisation of their welfare states and labour markets, etc.) and the ideas that animate these practices (about the nation and about membership of the imagined national community) are of central importance. Here too we can see how the forms taken by national and local politics have shaped immigrant integration processes thus showing how the organisation of the political system, and

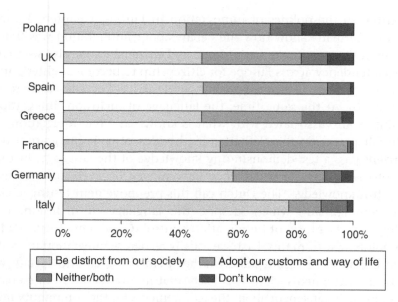

Figure 1.3   Attitudes to integration: immigrants in our society want to ...

Source: Pew Research Centre, 2014

broader societal reflections on national identity and social cohesion, have shaped immigrant integration processes as much as the other way around.

This suggests strong associations between immigrant policies in European countries and the regulation of entry to the territory (sovereignty) and membership of the community (citizenship) in these nation states. This also means that the vocabulary of integration becomes heavily imprinted with historical, political and social processes associated with the nation state and national self-understanding (Brubaker, 1992).

The term 'integration' looms large in this debate, but it needs to be borne in mind that a social expectation of integration affects everyone and the costs of failure – social exclusion – are high for the individual and society. Integration in these terms can be linked to core nation state principles and associated with the ideas of T.H. Marshall (1964) who saw modern citizenship as a vehicle for the building of a national community based on the extension of legal, political and social rights (in that order). Marshall wrote before the arrival of large numbers of immigrants. Responses to immigration upset Marshall's categorisation in the sense that non-citizen immigrants accessed legal and social rights but acquired political rights more slowly. Hammar (1990) then understood the status of non-national immigrants as 'denizenship' meaning legal and social rights falling short of full citizenship because of the absence of political rights. The various meanings of citizenship – as a status, as a relationship between the citizen and political authority and as a process of inclusion and exclusion – have been central to the politics of immigration in Europe. Chapters 3 and 4 on France and Germany show how the debate about immigration was framed by debate about the meaning of nationhood and citizenship. We also see that there has been a tendency across Europe for citizenship to become 'lighter', meaning that fewer rights are associated with it while it has become easier to obtain (Joppke, 2010). At the same time, the language of inclusion, integration and citizenship is also associated with what is known as 'civic integration'. As we show in Chapter 5 on the Netherlands, the idea of civic integration requires that citizens pass a test demonstrating knowledge of the language, history and culture of the country to which they have moved or, even, prior to moving, showing this knowledge. The Dutch call this pre-movement testing 'civic integration from abroad', which, despite the language of inclusion, is more accurately seen as a form of immigration control (Goodman, 2010, 2014).

Four points arise from this. First, we usually recognise integration in its absence as social exclusion or disintegration rather than being able to specify what is meant by an integrated society. It is likely that in any room full of co-nationals there would be disagreement about the requirements for the community membership that they hold in common. Second, the integration of immigrants can be linked to discussion of the supposed racial, ethnic, religious or cultural differences of immigrants as though these could be barriers to inclusion or, alternatively, could be vehicles for creation of a more progressive multicultural society. Clearly, the absence of knowledge about the society to which a person moves – such as the inability to speak the language – can work against inclusion; but to emphasise supposed racial, ethnic, religious and cultural differences can create social chasms between newcomers and their new country. Third, citizens tend to look to the state to guarantee integration. If the state won't or can't, then this can swiftly become a legitimacy problem for governments. While debates about the 'integration' (or lack thereof) of immigrants often focus on supposed racial, ethnic, religious or cultural traits of newcomers, these debates are also, if not more, about the capacity of European countries to secure social inclusion or social integration in the face of factors such as immigration, as well as welfare state and labour market changes that can affect the state's capacity to perform this role. Fourth, the content, meaning and practice of citizenship itself as a manifestation of integration has been redefined and changed by immigration.

Just as for immigration policy, the ways in which migrants are understood and represented is highly significant. In Britain and the Netherlands immigrants and their children have been referred to as 'ethnic minorities', in Germany immigrants have been defined mostly based on their national origin (such as 'Turks') and in France, officially at least, there is a preference not to speak of immigrant minorities at all as it would conflict with the idea of the 'one and indivisible' French Republic. Distinctions between 'migrants' or 'minorities' and 'us' or 'natives' is also becoming increasingly complex as the descendants of migrants blend into society over several generations meaning that terms such as 'majority' and 'minority' can become unclear in what have been labelled as 'superdiverse' cities such as London and Amsterdam (Vertovec, 2007).

Theme 3: Explaining the effects of EU integration

No account of European immigration politics could be complete without factoring-in the EU's role, but, at the same time, strong foundations need to be put in place before the EU's role can be assessed in order to balance either neglecting the impacts of the EU or overstating them. Put another way, the politics of migration and immigration in Europe is not a story of various national excep-tionalisms or of countries just doing their own thing. There are close ties between European countries as a result of European integration. However, this does not mean that European countries are locked into a trajectory that will inevitably transport them to some kind of federal Europe.

The EU can lurk in the background of analyses of European immigration politics either as the repressive 'fortress Europe' or as a potentially progressive source of post-national rights. Both these perspectives pay too little attention to the form and content of EU migration policy. The basic analytical problem is that while it is clear that the EU's importance has grown, it's not always clear how and why this has been the case and what have been European integration's effects on immigration and immigrant policies. The EU is not a nation state and there is no reason to assume that European integration can be likened to a nation-state building process.

EU migration policy has three main elements, which will be analysed more closely in Chapter 7:

- Free movement laws for (mainly) EU citizens within the single market.
- Migration and asylum provisions that have developed since the mid-1980s and are related to a number of factors such as the implications of single market integration for immigration and asylum coupled with the growing awareness of domestic legal and political constraints on immigration control.
- Immigrant policies that offer some legal, social and political rights to legally resident non-EU citizens, or TCNs.

The unevenness of European commonality across migration policy sectors (with some sectors such as asylum and irregular migration being more common than others such as admissions policy and integration), and the unevenness of effects (with some member states more affected than others) means that we need to assess both the reasons for the shift to the EU and the effects on member states and on surrounding states and regions. We should also avoid ascribing political and institutional changes to the impact of the EU without first being sure that it was actually the EU that drove these changes rather than domestic or other international factors. The congruence of EU developments does not make the EU a cause of all change in the member states. It is easy to overstate the EU's influence, but at the same time, the sources of legal, material and symbolic power associated with it need to be carefully analysed. European integration profoundly changes the strategic context for policy-shaping and making while having substantial effects on both member states and non-member states. The EU is a regional bloc comprising rather resilient nation states that have moved towards a highly developed form of market integration and common currency (for some, but not all member states) that extends rights to its citizens under the banner of EU citizenship while building barriers between themselves and surrounding states and regions. As the EU response to the refugee crisis shows there are still highly significant national sensitivities at play, which mean that movement to a common EU policy is far from assured.

Comparing European immigration countries

Focusing entirely on national differences between countries and on the particularities of debates within these countries could lead to the conclusion that national particularities are the key element of immigrant policies in Europe. This would diminish the opportunities for comparison. In fact, many studies of migration, and of migrant integration in particular, have tended to focus on the national specificities of migration and integration regimes. Yet, we are analysing responses in European countries to ostensibly similar phenomena associated with international migration while inclusion and exclusion are mediated in arenas (i.e. nationality laws, welfare states, labour markets) that display some broad similarities in both their structure and exposure to pressures. While there are clear national particularities, there are also crosscutting factors presenting similar dilemmas to European countries of immigration. One of the purposes of this book is to uncover how different European countries have responded to these dilemmas and to find explanations for these country responses by looking at a country's historical and institutional settings as well as to more crosscutting factors such as levels of politicisation of immigration, the effects of Europeanisation and the influence of factors such as the organisation of welfare states.

Another challenge to a state-centred emphasis on national cases and national political processes has come from those who argue that rights and identities have become decoupled and that forms of 'post-national membership' change the position of migrants and their descendants in European countries. Soysal (1994) argues that a universalised discourse of entitlement derived from international human rights standards underpins claims for social and political inclusion made by migrants and their descendants. Thus the incomplete membership status of denizenship (rights short of full citizenship) is recast as a progressive model for new forms of post-national belonging that no longer take the nation state as their frame of reference. For example, EU citizenship could be construed as a significant 'post-national' development that defies narrow state-centrism by offering scope for free movement and 'rights beyond borders' that could signify the decline of national citizenship (Jacobson, 1996).

A further challenge to the state-centric approach to integration stresses the local dimension of migration and integration. This is not necessarily incompatible with the key role of national governments, but, instead, emphasises the importance of local politics, particularly at city level, in many EU states. Rather than nationally distinct integration philosophies, integration policies can be shaped by local conditions with different local approaches in different towns and cities. This is reflected in a growing local political leadership visible in towns and cities across Europe. It is also reflected in the growing importance of networks of cities for the exchange of knowledge and ideas about immigrant integration, such as the 'EUROCITIES' and 'Intercultural Cities' networks.

While this book focuses on different European countries it does not take national approaches to migration and integration (or 'national models') as its point of departure. Rather, we study the institutional conditions that frame policy responses at the country level while also taking into account relevant developments at the sub-national and EU levels. Our objective is not to find what is specific to the countries discussed in this book, but rather to examine how and why they have responded to similar challenges under specific institutional conditions.

Some of these factors will be pursued throughout the book and reflected upon in the conclusions. Within the book's focus on the politics of migration, this search for factors involves more than recounting different migration histories that may account for policy differences. One key factor is the role of the welfare state in European countries in shaping immigrant policies given the different organisational form that they take. Another factor is the degree of politicisation of immigration with one indicator being the growth or resurgence of populist and anti-immigrant parties throughout Europe.

The widening of migration

A drawback with analyses of European immigration politics can be a focus only on 'older' immigration countries in North Western Europe with less attention paid to the experiences of 'newer' immigration countries in Central, Eastern and Southern Europe. In fact, to label countries in Southern Europe as 'new' immigration countries is to misuse the word. For example, Greece, Italy and Spain have been experiencing immigration for more than 25 years while Turkey has a complex migration history that can also belie the word 'new'. The geographical focus needs to be widened if genuine elements of novelty in European immigration politics and policy are to be properly captured. This book thinks beyond the EU's current members to also consider Turkey, which has, over the past decade, experienced growing levels of immigration. Turkey was also central to the European refugee crisis both as a major destination for around 2 million people displaced by the Syrian conflict but also because relations with Turkey were central to EU responses to attempt to deal with these complex issues. Debate about Turkish membership of the EU has been dominated by fear in some member states about large-scale emigration by Turks towards the EU, but Turkey has also experienced rapid economic growth and become an immigration country. Chapter 10 shows that, while Turkey is not an EU member state, its policy responses have been shaped by the EU while the refugee crisis also became part of the debate about EU–Turkey relations.

By focusing on the wider Europe and beyond the usual suspects in North West Europe, this book also highlights issues around policy implementation. Policy implementation is difficult because it depends upon decisions made by one group of people at a particular point in time and in a particular place being implemented by another group of people, at a different point in time and at a different place. We should, perhaps, be more surprised when policies are actually implemented. This dilemma is particularly important for the EU as it relies on member states to implement its legislation. We will see that the making of a formal policy commitment at national or EU level does not mean that this commitment will be fulfilled if legal, bureaucratic and administrative resources are lacking. In the case of restrictive immigration policies, we have already seen that in 'older' immigration countries there has been continued immigration despite restrictive policies. Constraints may arise because of implementation dilemmas such as the costs of control and the lack of well-developed bureaucratic or administrative resources. Control capacity can also be hindered if policy is not based on a valid theory of cause and effect. For example, if there is a continued demand for migrant labour in some economic sectors and well-entrenched economic informality that provides a context for the economic insertion of irregular migrants then the discussion of internal controls and the regulatory capacity of states is also important, as shown in the cases of Italy, Greece and Spain (Chapters 8 and 10).

Plan of the book

This book's analysis of European migration politics is organised at two levels.

- A horizontal dimension compares responses in European countries. To what extent is European immigration politics characterised by distinct national responses to international migration? How have national responses changed over time and what factors have underpinned these changes? Where are the points of convergence and the points of divergence between European countries? If there is convergence, then what causes this?

- A vertical dimension analyses the impact of European integration. We can assess both the institutionalisation of Europe (the development of common institutions and policies) and the Europeanisation of institutions (the impact on member states of EU integration, including at local or city level).

These two dimensions can then be connected to explore the extent to which it makes sense to talk of a politics of migration and immigration in Europe with linkages at both horizontal and vertical level.

The horizontal and vertical analytical dimensions are analysed in relation to the two themes discussed in this introductory chapter.

- Immigration policies to regulate and manage international migration.
- Immigrant policies that centre on the development of a social and political response to the presence of immigrant newcomers and their descendants.

We now take these ideas forward and apply them in Britain (Chapter 2), France (Chapter 3), Germany (Chapter 4), the Netherlands (Chapter 5) and Sweden (Chapter 6). Chapter 7 examines the development of EU responsibilities. This is followed by consideration of the politics of migration in Italy and Spain (Chapter 8) and in Central and Eastern Europe (Chapter 9). Chapter 10 extends the analysis into South East Europe by looking at Greece and Turkey.

The aim is then to highlight divergence and convergence, while seeking explanations for these when and where they arise. The book demonstrates both the conceptual (new types of migration and new types of response) and geo-political (more countries) widening of the migration issue in contemporary European politics as well as their effects.

2

Britain: The Unexpected Europeanisation of Immigration

Introduction

If we judge British immigration politics by the buzzwords used to characterise them then the country has moved from 'zero immigration' in the 1970s and 1980s to 'managed migration' under New Labour from 1997–2010, then to 'good immigration, not mass immigration' with the creation of a 'hostile environment' for 'unwanted immigrants' under the Conservative–Liberal Democrat Coalition government 2010–15 and Conservative government after 2015. The context for this has been steep growth in immigration to the UK with net migration (the balance between immigration and emigration) estimated at 330,000 in 2015, the highest level since 2005. These numbers include EU citizens using free movement rights, non-EU migrants moving in particular into higher skilled employment, family migrants and around 200,000 international students. The Conservative Party had pledged to reduce net migration to the tens of thousands.

There was, in the 2000s, a dramatic return of the immigration issue to the very top of the British political agenda when a series of events challenged previous understandings of British immigration and immigrant politics. The immigration issue also became entangled with debate about Britain's EU membership because of the steep increase in EU citizens moving to the UK, particularly after 2004. The Conservative government elected in 2015 sought a renegotiation of the terms of EU membership including restrictions on access to welfare benefits by citizens of other EU member states living in the UK.

Between 1993 and 2012, the foreign-born population in the UK increased from 3.8 million to 7.7 million with estimates that by 2015 it had topped 8 million. Figure 2.1 shows the salience of immigration as a political issue in Britain between 1997 and 2014. As will be seen, growth in public concern about immigration coincides with the growth in numbers that has occurred since the 2000s. More recent times have also seen strong growth in support for the United Kingdom Independence Party (UKIP), which topped the polls at the 2014 European Parliament elections – the first time since 1906 that a party other than Conservative or Labour had 'won' a national election.

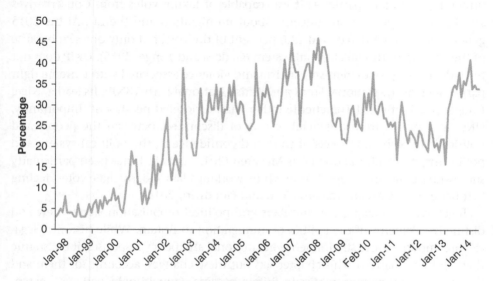

% mentions of immigration/race relations as the most important/another important issue July 1997–May 2014

Figure 2.1   The salience of the immigration issue in Britain 1997–2014

Comparing British immigration politics

Immigration politics in Britain were seen as standing apart from those evident in other European countries. A strong executive branch of government and relatively weak courts enabled strict immigration controls in the 1960s and 1970s as part of a rapid retreat from the immigration consequences of colonialism. During the 1980s and early 1990s immigration was a low priority issue, but a lot has changed since the mid-1990s. One key change – particularly since 2004 – is the impact of EU free movement both in terms of EU citizens moving to Britain and on the politics of immigration. Despite the tendency of UK governments to lack enthusiasm for the 'European project', immigration policy and politics in Britain have been extensively Europeanised, largely – but not only – because of free movement. The extent of the Europeanisation of migration politics was unexpected and, for some, unwanted. The British government may not have intended to stimulate large-scale movement from other EU member states, but that was the effect of their decision taken in 2004 to allow free access to the labour market for citizens of the so-called A8 countries (the eight Central and East European countries that joined the EU in May 2004).

The populist right were very marginal in Britain, but that has also changed. UKIP has performed well in second-order elections – particularly those for the European Parliament where after the 2014 elections it was the largest UK party – while unnerving the main parties as it was capable of taking votes from Conservatives and Labour by playing on concerns about immigration and the EU. At the 2015 general election, UKIP received 12.6 per cent of the vote, but only one seat because of the non-proportional electoral system (Geddes and Tonge, 2015). UKIP does not have the baggage of extremism, fascism and violence associated with extreme right parties such as the National Front and British National Party (BNP). Its leader, Nigel Farage, is a disaffected Thatcherite rather than a closeted neo-fascist. Importantly, UKIP also profits from a general feeling of disconnect between the people and politics marked by low levels of trust and confidence in the political system and politicians, or a 'cultural divide' as McLaren (2012) puts it. It has been particularly successful in drawing support from white, working class, elderly male voters feeling 'left behind' by societal changes (Ford and Goodwin, 2014).

Together, these changes in numbers and political mobilisation signify new and distinctive elements of the politics of immigration in Britain. While historical legacies are important and still influence institutional and policy responses, it is also true that a lot has changed. This chapter sets out these changes, accounts for them and shows how immigration politics in Britain became – unwittingly, perhaps – extensively Europeanised. From the mid-1990s onwards the effects of European integration and free movement have been woven into the fabric of British immigration politics.

Immigration policy

To understand the extent to which things have changed it is initially important to explore the origins of post-war immigration policy and politics in Britain, which (as is also the case in France and the Netherlands) were shaped by imperialism. From an expansive, imperial notion of citizenship that gave all subjects of the crown the right to enter Britain – formalised by the 1948 British Nationality Act – there was swift movement towards restriction between 1962 and 1971 with the 'imperial citizenship' downsized to a more restricted understanding based on descent (Hansen, 2000).

Post-imperial downsizing

Why did Britain move swiftly to controls in the 1960s? One school of thought emphasises state racism and the 'whitewashing' of Britain that unleashed racist hostility to immigrants from Africa, Asia and the Caribbean and underpinned stringent immigration legislation (Paul, 1997). A counter argument is that British immigration and citizenship policy can better be understood as public-driven rather than state-led, where advocates of strict controls were appeased while space was also created for the anti-discrimination legislation that laid the foundations for the British version of multiculturalism (Hansen, 2000). This latter interpretation echoes the point made by Freeman (1994) who argued that British immigration policy was an example of 'responsible issue management' by government in the face of public hostility to immigrant newcomers. From this perspective, public opinion has played an important part in shaping government responses to immigration.

Between 1948 and 1962 Britain had an open migration regime. The 1948 British Nationality Act formally gave all subjects of the Crown in Britain and its empire the right to move to Britain. People from the colonies and the commonwealth could state *civis Britannicus sum* (I am a British citizen) and access the same formal legal, social and political rights as other subjects of the crown. This created a potentially enormous pool of would-be migrants, although it would be a mistake to think that anything more than a small proportion of would-be post-imperial migrants – totalling up to 800 million people – would be actual migrants.

The British Nationality Act did not intend to create post-war migration to Britain because when it was drafted such immigration could not have been foreseen. There were, however, strong pull factors at work in the 1950s with active recruitment of migrant workers for employment work in public transport, the newly created National Health Service and the textile and car industries.

Immigration in the 1950s was largely unplanned and there was no direct preference for people from former colonies. Indeed, their arrival was met in official circles with suspicion and sometimes with racist hostility. Those who focus on state racism would contend that the open migration regime that existed until 1962 actually hung by a thread and was continually questioned on racist grounds at elite governmental level (Paul, 1997). Hansen (2000), on the other hand, has identified debates at the highest levels of government about the desirability of continued immigration in which there were both pro- and anti-immigration voices but with a bi-partisan consensus between the Labour and Conservative parties and an attachment to a post-imperial Commonwealth ideal.

Restrictions came more squarely onto the political agenda in the late 1950s as a result of so-called 'race riots' – actually racist attacks on immigrants by white youths and neo-fascist organisations – in the West London district of Notting Hill and the East Midlands city of Nottingham (Pilkington, 1988). These disturbances helped transform migration from a regional into a national issue (Hansen, 2000: 82). This coincided with the rise to prominence of a populist wing of the Conservative Party, which became less upper class and paternalistic and more middle class and populist (Rich, 1986). Grassroots pressure from backbench MPs combined with anti-immigration groups outside the Party such as the Birmingham Immigration Control Association and the Southall Residents Association. However, Hansen (2000: 96) argues that the key development was a Whitehall turf war between the anti-restriction Colonial Office and the pro-restriction Ministry of Labour, which the Ministry of Labour won as the Commonwealth ideal faded and limits to economic growth began to set in in the late 1950s.

Racialised controls and the 'colour problem'

The rationale for the control legislation introduced by the Conservative government rested in part on the exaggerated idea that all those who could potentially move to Britain would actually do so. The Home Secretary of the time, R.A. Butler, claimed that around 800 million people were entitled to move to Britain. The chances of 800 million people moving to the UK were about the same as the Conservative government of the day admitting the real reason for introducing the legislation: concerns about the 'racial' character of some immigrants.

The Labour Party's initial opposition to restriction faded when the electoral potency in key marginal constituencies of anti-immigration sentiment became clear. Labour opposed the 1962 Act, which its Home Affairs spokesman Patrick Gordon Walker described in the House of Commons as 'bare-faced, open race discrimination'. These words came back to haunt him at the 1964 general election when he lost his seat in the industrial West Midlands constituency of Smethwick to a Conservative candidate, Peter Griffiths, whose supporters used the racist slogan 'If you want a nigger for a neighbour vote Liberal or Labour'. Griffiths won Smethwick with a pro-Conservative swing against a more general pro-Labour swing at the 1964 general election (Deakin, 1964). The Labour leadership was aware, as one Cabinet minister put it, 'that immigration can be the greatest potential vote loser for the Labour party' (Crossman, 1977: 149–50).

Immigration became salient at a time when there was actually net emigration from, not immigration to, the UK. In 1964, 211,000 people immigrated to Britain, but 271,000 left (Office for National Statistics, 2013). It was not until 1979 that the number of people entering Britain exceeded the number emigrating (and then only by 6,000). This provides a contrast with events in the 2000s and 2010s when there was relatively large-scale net immigration. This further highlights the way in which debate in Britain in the 1950s and 1960s was 'racialised', that is, it was represented socially and politically as involving race (Miles, 1993).

The 1962 Commonwealth Immigrants Act distinguished between citizens of the UK and its colonies, and citizens of independent Commonwealth countries. The latter became subject to immigration controls via the issue of employment vouchers. The mechanism for control was fairly straightforward. In 1963, 30,130 of these vouchers were issued. In 1972, only 2,290 were issued. Between 1963 and 1972, 20 per cent of these permits were issued to women. Immigration law was based on the assumption that men were the breadwinners and women were dependants who would follow their husbands. This was then the foundation for the British government's attempts to prevent women migrants from enjoying the same family reunification rights as men. When in 1985 the European Court of Human Rights (ECtHR) ruled against this discriminatory practice, the response of the UK government was to introduce new regulations in 1988 to hinder both male and female family reunion (Kofman, 1999: 276). In 1980 the Conservative government introduced the 'primary purpose' rule that gave the immigration authorities the power to probe the 'real' status and reasons for an application to enter the UK for purposes of marriage. The Labour government elected in 1997 fulfilled a pledge to abolish this rule although restrictions on family migration remain tight and became more restrictive under the Coalition and Conservative governments after 2010.

The effectiveness of controls

The controls instigated by the 1962 legislation provided mechanisms to regulate primary, labour migration, but family migration by dependants (such as parents, wives, husbands and children) continued. Family migration became the main target for restriction from the mid-1960s. Those who argue that 'rights-based politics' based on the role of courts have played a key role in opening social and political spaces for migrants in Europe (Hollifield, 1992) have faced difficulties when applying their arguments to the UK. There was no constitutional protection of the rights of the family as there was in other European countries because there is not a formal, written UK constitution. Family migration was provided for by statute. This changed in 1999 when the Labour government introduced the Human Rights Act incorporating the European Convention on Human Rights (ECHR) into British law.

By the mid-1960s the outline of an immigration policy consensus had emerged that rested on two pillars: tight restriction of immigration coupled with anti-discrimination legislation that was introduced in three 'race relations' acts of 1965, 1968 and 1976 (discussed more fully below). Labour politician Roy Hattersley summed up the resultant policy mix: 'Without integration limitation is inexcusable, without limitation integration is impossible' (Hansen, 2000: 26).

Despite the ordering of Hattersley's maxim, the underlying logic flowed in the opposite direction: integration was predicated on the tight control of immigration; integration would be jeopardised by large-scale immigration.

The way in which immigration and race were presented in public debate shaped public understandings of a 'colour problem'. There were, for example, concerns in the early- to mid-1960s that anti-immigration sentiment could damage the Labour Party (Hansen, 2000). The Labour government elected in 1964 and re-elected in 1966 reduced the number of work permits available under the 1962 Act. In 1968, a second Commonwealth Immigrants Bill was introduced. This removed the right to enter the UK from British citizens of Indian origin facing persecution as a result of 'Africanisation' policies in Kenya and Uganda. The 1968 legislation was a kneejerk response to the sudden influx of 13,000 people of Asian origin. Legislation rushed through Parliament in only three days made these East African Asians subject to immigration controls on the basis of a patriality rule stipulating that for anyone to enter the UK they needed to have one parent or grandparent born, adopted or naturalised as a British citizen.

The restrictive legislation culminated with the 1971 Immigration Act, introduced by Edward Heath's Conservative government. All preceding legislation was replaced by one statute that distinguished between citizens of the UK and its colonies who were patrial (essentially, the 'one grandparent' rule introduced by the 1968 Act) who could enter and settle in the UK, and citizens of independent Commonwealth countries who could not. For non-patrials, work permits, to be renewed annually, replaced vouchers. The exceptions to this were nationals of EC member states. UK accession on 1 January 1973 meant that workers from other member states and their dependants could move to and reside in the UK. This has since developed into a generalised right of free movement for EU citizens.

As leader of the opposition (1975–79), Margaret Thatcher resuscitated some Powellite themes to create a dividing line between her Conservative Party and the governing Labour Party. As Conservative leader she was in a more powerful position than Powell, but was ultimately also more constrained by the realities of practical politics. In an April 1978 interview given to the TV programme *World in Action* she stated that she could understand peoples' fears of being 'swamped' by what she called 'alien cultures'. Thatcher expressed concern that people might be attracted by the political message of the extreme right-wing National Front (NF) and that it was her duty to address the concerns of people attracted by right-wing extremism. This could be construed as an attempt to play the 'race card' at the 1979 general election. Yet, once the electoral victory had been secured there were constraints on the Conservative Party's capacity to further restrict immigration beyond the tight controls already introduced.

The final piece of the jigsaw was the amendment of nationality law to reflect Britain's post-imperial downsizing and the idea of patriality. The Labour government in 1977 had already proposed changes in a Green (discussion) Paper.

Margaret Thatcher's first Conservative government developed these proposals to introduce the British Nationality Act (1981). This created three types of British citizen:

- full British citizenship for those with close ties, i.e. that were patrial;
- British Dependent Territories Citizenship for people living in dependent territories, i.e. Gibraltar, the Falkland Islands and Hong Kong;
- British Overseas Citizenship, a residual category to which almost no rights were attached. This category was designed to encourage East African Asians and Malaysians to acquire citizenship in their country of residence.

The effect was that millions of people found their citizenship status amended to deny them access to the country of which ostensibly they had been citizens. The British government had been able to implement tight controls and redefine national citizenship, stripped of post-colonial implications.

Tight immigration controls meant that there was little political space for the extreme-right NF, which (although it acquired some notoriety and a lot of publicity in the 1970s) never won a seat on a local council never mind in the House of Commons. The UK's 'first past the post' electoral system played a key part in this as too did Margaret Thatcher's harder line on immigration. These factors were compounded by the violence associated with the NF and left-wing counter mobilisations by the Anti-Nazi League and Rock Against Racism, which were particularly effective in their use of popular music to spread the anti-racist and anti-fascist message among young people.

The return of immigration

Much has changed in British immigration politics since the mid-1990s. First, there has been relatively large-scale immigration. Second, much of this so-called immigration is actually EU free movement, guaranteed and protected by EU law. Third, there have been high levels of public concern about immigration. And, fourth, UKIP has risen to prominence appealing to anti-immigration sentiment. These four factors are compounded by a more general disconnect between the people and politics marked by low levels of trust and confidence in politicians and the political system. The Labour Party was particularly associated with this changed approach to immigration, but its initial enthusiasm for labour migration between 1997 and 2001 was soon tempered by a more cautious approach. By the 2010 general election, Labour's record on immigration was a key reason why it lost support, even more so than the effects of the financial crisis. The financial crisis was widely seen as global, while immigration was still seen as an issue in the hands of the British government (Evans and Chzhen, 2013).

To give some indication of the influence of these four factors, Figure 2.2 shows immigration, emigration and net migration since 1982. During the 1980s and early 1990s, there was effectively a balance between immigration and emigration. From the mid-1990s onwards there was a significant growth in immigration. Between 1997 and 2010 when Labour was in government, there was positive net migration to the UK of 2.76 million people. These numbers include EU citizens using free movement rights to move to the UK. Figure 2.2 shows levels of net EU free movement between 2004 and 2013. These figures were revised when the Office for National Statistics realised after the publication of the 2011 census that there was an under-estimate by an estimated 346,000 of movement to Britain by EU citizens from A8 states because of the numbers of people travelling with low cost airlines through smaller regional airports that were not being picked up by the International Passenger Survey (the main method of monitoring migration flows). Between 1997 and 2003 an average of 67,000 EU citizens moved to Britain each year. This increased to an average of 170,000 a year between 2004 and 2013.

Net migration remained positive under the Coalition government elected in 2010. In 2014, for example, 641,000 (up from 526,000 people in 2013) moved to the UK (including EU and non-EU citizens) while 323,000 people emigrated (314,000 in 2013). This left a positive net migration figure of 318,000 (211,000 in 2013), which was significantly above the Coalition government's migration target to reduce net migration from the 'hundreds of thousands' to the 'tens of thousands'.

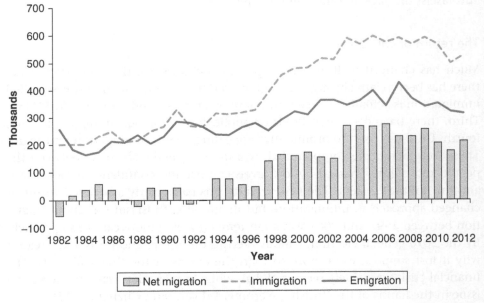

Figure 2.2 Net migration to Britain 1982–2013

Source: Office for National Statistics (2013)

The net migration target had been an important aspect of the Coalition agreement when the Conservative–Liberal Democrat coalition was established in 2010. The Coalition agreement stated that:

> The Government believes that immigration has enriched our culture and strengthened our economy, but that it must be controlled so that people have confidence in the system. We also recognise that to ensure cohesion and protect our public services, we need to introduce a cap on immigration and reduce the number of non-EU migrants. (HM Government, 2010)

Unsurprisingly, the Conservative Manifesto for the 2015 general election reaffirmed the intention to get immigration to the tens of thousands albeit as an 'aspiration' rather than a 'target', but by 2015 estimated net migration was running at 330,000.

The populist challenge to mainstream politics was made clear across the EU, but in the UK the shock to mainstream parties was that in the 2014 European Parliament elections UKIP secured 27.5 per cent of the vote (with a dismal 34 per cent turnout), winning 24 seats and was the leading UK party in the European Parliament. UKIP's campaign was almost entirely focused on the effects of EU open borders. There had previously been some signs of growing support for the extreme right BNP in towns such as Burnley, Oldham, Stoke-on-Trent as well as parts of East London such as Barking and Dagenham. In the 2009 European Parliament elections, the BNP secured 2 seats in what, at the time, was seen as a major breakthrough. Of its two MEPs, one soon defected and by 2015, the BNP had disintegrated as an organisation and its vote totally collapsed with UKIP replacing them as the challenger from the right. UKIP is a party of the Eurosceptic right, but did not have the BNP's reputation for violence, racism, homophobia, Islamophobia and anti-Semitism. It has been argued that UKIP's roots in Euroscepticism rather than neo-fascism provide it with a 'reputational shield' against accusations of prejudice and hate (Ivarsflaten, 2006). This shield was dented by a series of incidents that saw UKIP members, for example, blame flooding in southern England on gay marriage, call for the repatriation of one of Britain's most popular TV actors (although he was born in England's West Midlands) while the party leader, Nigel Farage, said that he would not be happy if Romanians moved in next door to him. While profiting from anti-immigration and anti-EU sentiment, UKIP was also strengthened by more general disaffection from the political system and the mainstream parties. Politicians are often held in low esteem, but the poor reputation of politicians allowed UKIP to sharpen its message about the 'political class' being in it for themselves.

In May 2014, the polling organisation Ipsos MORI in its regular survey of people's attitudes to key issues asked respondents to identify the most important issues facing the country: the top concern was the economy identified by 36 per cent, but, just behind, on 34 per cent, was immigration and race relations. The 2014 British Social Attitudes Survey (Park et al., 2014) showed that 77 per cent of respondents wanted immigration to be reduced either 'a little' or 'a lot', although with important variations both spatially (London is more pro-immigration) and socially (people in lower social classes and with lower educational levels tend to be more anti-immigration while those in higher social groups and the more highly educated are more likely to be positive about immigration).

It is important to drill down into data on attitudes to immigration for these reasons. There is significant social and spatial variation, as already shown, while there is also evidence that many people don't see immigration as a cause of social conflict where they live. To take another example, the 2007–8 Citizenship Survey found that 85 per cent of people reported that in the area in which they lived people of diverse backgrounds got along well. The perceived economic contribution of migrants can also make a difference. Figure 2.3 shows that people are more likely to oppose reductions in the numbers of skilled migrant workers compared to those that are unskilled.

Accounting for change

Explanations for the changes identified above zoom in on the first New Labour government (1997–2001) led by Tony Blair, when a distinctly more liberal

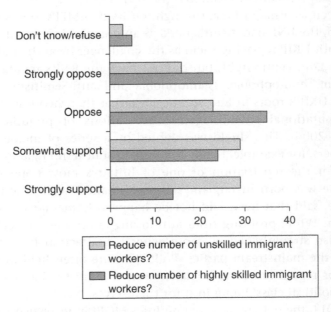

Figure 2.3 Attitudes to skilled immigration

Source: IPSOS MORI, 2014

approach to labour migration became evident in both openness to skilled labour migration and the incorporation of the ECHR into British law by the Human Rights Act of 1998.

Using the language of historical institutionalism, the period between 1997 and 2001 has been identified as a 'critical juncture' when previous 'structural constraints' on policy-making were relaxed. This means that policy and institutions could break free from previous 'path dependencies' and a new policy path could be taken (Consterdine and Hampshire, 2014). Reasons for this included: economic growth and labour market gaps; the role of new actors (within and outside government) in shaping more positive perceptions of immigration; New Labour's idea that Britain should embrace globalisation and pursue international competitiveness and that being more positive about labour migration was part of this; and, finally, the crushing parliamentary majority enjoyed by Labour after its 1997 landslide victory.

After 2004, EU free movement became part of the debate about immigration. The right to free movement did, of course, exist prior to the 2004 'big bang' enlargement that saw ten new member states enter the EU, but the key decision was that of the British government to allow free access to Britain for citizens of the ten new member states – including the so-called A8 of Central and East European countries – that joined on 1 May 2004. This was a hugely important decision for the future shape of both migration/free movement flows and migration politics, but the key point is that such flows cannot be controlled, as they are a right guaranteed by EU law. Migration from other EU member states using the right to free movement became a subject of intense debate in the run-up to the 2015 general election. In November 2014 Prime Minister Cameron outlined plans to restrict access for EU migrants to welfare state benefits for four years. Shortly before Cameron outlined his plans, the Labour Party had proposed that the restriction be set at two years. This bidding war between the two main parties was driven by their desire to respond to the UKIP challenge.

2.1 IMMIGRATION AND INTEGRATION IN SCOTLAND

The United Kingdom is a unitary state, but has devolved significant competencies to Scotland in particular, and in some areas also to Wales and Northern Ireland. It is important to note that immigration policy is not amongst the devolved policy areas. This has, however, led to tensions between the Westminster and Scottish governments. Scotland advocates a more open immigration policy linked to the revitalisation of the Scottish economy and to combat the effects of population ageing.

(Continued)

(Continued)

Various projects have been developed to attract asylum migrant families and to incentivise student migrants to settle in Scotland. The Scottish government also actively lobbied the UK government for a relatively open approach toward migration from Central and East European countries.

Immigrant policy is a devolved policy area with the result being that Scottish immigrant policies have developed very differently than those in England. The 'community cohesion' discourse that developed after urban unrest in English towns in the 2000s did not 'travel' to Scotland, where the focus has remained much more on race equality and a more open acceptance of pluralism. Scotland is also one of the very rare cases where a nationalist party, the Scottish National Party (SNP), is an advocate of more open immigration policies and professes to welcome immigration-related diversity.

Asylum and the reassertion of controls

By 2015, the immigration debate centred on EU free movement and the Mediterranean refugee crisis. Fifteen years earlier the focus was on asylum and provides a demonstration of how the British state asserted control over this form of migration. Asylum became a political obsession for the second New Labour government led by Tony Blair between 2001 and 2005. To give an indication of its centrality, more meetings were held to discuss the asylum issue between 2001 and 2004 than on any other subject except Iraq (Spencer, 2011: 359). In the mid-1990s the numbers of asylum seekers began to increase, reaching a peak of 84,132 in 2002. In the year leading up to March 2014, there were 23,731 asylum applications made in the UK, compared to 22,630 in the preceding year. These lower numbers compared to the 2002 figures are not because the world became a safer place and people no longer needed to seek refuge from war, persecution and human rights abuses. In 2014, there were more refugees globally than at any time since the Second World War: 51.2 million, according to the United Nations High Commissioner for Refugees. The real story in British asylum politics was about the reassertion of controls by the British government, both domestically through tougher controls and changes to procedures, and through EU co-operation. Reducing the numbers of asylum applicants was the policy aim and, in these terms, it succeeded. The EU's role in this was important with Prime Minister Tony Blair calling this combination of domestic and EU measures 'getting the best of both worlds' (Geddes, 2005a).

Britain does not have dedicated asylum legislation, but has amended the 1971 Immigration Act to introduce new rules designed to curb asylum-seeking migration. Broadly speaking, there have been three types of measures:

- control of external frontiers that had both domestic and EU components;
- controls at key organisational borders of the welfare state and labour market that made it more difficult for asylum seekers to access welfare benefits while excluding them from the labour market while claims are processed;
- speeding up the legal process.

External controls have expanded to include private actors such as airlines, ferry companies, truck drivers, employers and private landlords with fines for those who bring in, employ or house people without the appropriate documentation.

Internal controls have focused on exclusion from the welfare state and the labour market. The argument used to legitimate these exclusions from work and welfare was that not all asylum seekers were 'genuine' because they were really disguised economic migrants trying to circumvent immigration controls. The 'bogus asylum seeker' became a powerful component in the debate about asylum. Labour governments after 1997 wanted to be seen as tough on the asylum issue. In a February 2002 interview on the BBC Radio 4 Today programme, the then Labour Home Secretary David Blunkett claimed that the children of asylum seekers were 'swamping' local schools and should be educated separately from other children in special asylum seeker accommodation centres. The basic rationale was that any chance for social integration would be removed if asylum seekers' contact with wider society was minimised (Geddes, 2000). There have also been efforts to strengthen internal controls with, for example, universities required to monitor attendance by international students.

Controlling access to welfare state benefits was the target of legislation introduced by the Conservative and Labour governments in 1996, 1999 and 2002. The Conservative government's 1996 Asylum and Immigration Act removed access to welfare benefits for 'in-country' asylum applicants, as opposed to applications made at the point of entry such as an air or seaport. The effect was the risk of destitution for thousands of in-country applicants. The courts intervened to determine this could lead to homeless and hungry asylum seekers, and that such an outcome would be barbaric and that it could not have been the legislation's intention.

Asylum seekers have been the responsibility of local authorities since the 1948 National Assistance Act. The Court of Appeal upheld this act in February 1997. The effects were that the costs of caring for asylum seekers fell on a relatively small number of local authorities, such as London boroughs, or seaside resorts with plenty of accommodation that housed the majority of asylum seekers. In the seaside towns of southern England resentment among some local people to asylum-seeking migration was most evident (Geddes, 2000). It was the 1999 Immigration and Asylum Act that introduced vouchers for asylum seekers in place of cash paid welfare benefits and set up a national dispersal system to reduce the concentration of asylum seekers in London and the South East.

Measures have also sought to speed up the asylum system, further driven by the idea propagated extensively by the government that many asylum claims were bogus and that individuals were thus abusing the system. For example, the right to in-country appeal for certain categories of asylum applicant was removed, legal aid was reduced and this all expedited the process for cases that were seen as likely to be assessed as unfounded (Gibney, 2008). After 2010, the Conservative-led Coalition government maintained a focus on restricting asylum with efforts focused on speeding up the process through the 'Asylum Operating Model' introduced in April 2013.

Taken together, external controls, internal controls and changes to asylum procedures have helped to reduce the number of people making claims for asylum in Britain. Numbers have fallen not because the world is a safer place, but because the British government has been able to impose fairly stringent controls. The British government has also opted out of the second phase in the development of the Common European Asylum System (CEAS) and was not bound by EU plans agreed in September 2015 to relocate up to 160,000 asylum applicants from Greece, Italy and Hungary. Instead, the UK government in 2015 announced a separate scheme to resettle 20,000 Syrians over a five-year period.

New openings to labour migration

New Labour in power between 1997 and 2010 were 'hyperactive' on immigration with ten pieces of asylum and immigration legislation introduced during their time in office. Labour sought to shift the rationale for policy from immigration control to 'managed migration' (Consterdine and Hampshire, 2014). This approach was supported by research conducted within government; particularly the analysis conducted for the Cabinet Office entitled *Migration: An Economic and Social Analysis* (Gott et al., 2001) that concluded that 'migration has the potential to deliver significant economic benefits'. In 2001 the government introduced the High Skilled Migrant Programme (HSMP), a points-based system that allowed entry to the UK in relation to factors such as high levels of education and earnings. In 2003 Home Secretary Blunkett said in a TV interview that he saw no obvious upper limit to the numbers of skilled migrants that could be admitted.

The decision to allow free access to citizens of new EU member states had a fundamental impact on both migration flows and policy. Only Britain, Ireland and Sweden of the then 15 member states decided not to impose controls. The British decision was motivated by three factors. First, there were labour market shortages in key economic sectors. Second, Britain had long been an advocate of a 'wider' EU, which it was hoped would diminish federal impulses and therefore sought to build bridges to new member states. Third, openness to labour migration fitted with a more general ideological commitment to ensuring competitiveness in the global economy. Aside from these three countries, all other member states used transitional controls lasting for up to seven years (i.e. the end of May 2011 for the countries that joined in 2004). Research commissioned by the Home Office, based on the (flawed at it turned out) assumption that other member states would allow free movement, estimated the scale of movement from new member states at 5,000–13,000 a year. Between 2004 and 2012, an average of 170,000 people moved to the UK from new EU member states.

At the 2005 General Election the Conservative party sought to tap into rising public concern about immigration. One of the party's campaign posters stated that: 'it's not racist to impose limits on immigration'. The Conservatives lost the 2005 election, but the Labour government was becoming aware of the potential effects of anti-immigration sentiment on its support. The rhetoric from government became less open to new immigration, although the large inflows continued. In 2008, Blair's successor, Gordon Brown, introduced a five-tier system for labour migration as follows:

Tier 1 – highly skilled migrants targeted at very high skilled or high earning employment;

Tier 2 – replacing the work permit system for medium to high skilled workers;

Tier 3 – never opened, but designed for low skilled and temporary employment. EU free movement addressed such labour market needs;

Tier 4 – students;

Tier 5 – youth mobility.

Brown's period as Prime Minister saw a distinct cooling of the rhetoric on immigration. In a 2007 speech, he said that his government would seek to provide 'British jobs for British workers'. There were two problems with this. First, the phrase is a perennial slogan of extreme right political parties. Second, the promise was unrealisable because of EU free movement rules. Brown's miserable time as Prime Minister was compounded during the 2010 General Election campaign when, unaware that a microphone was still live, he criticised a woman he had met in the street while campaigning in the northern town of Rochdale who had complained about migration by people from Eastern Europe as 'that bigoted woman' (Carey and Geddes, 2010).

The Coalition government and the return of Conservative government

After its formation in May 2010, the Coalition government introduced a cap on non-EU migration with, for the first time, a net migration target, although this was specified somewhat vaguely as being in the 'tens of thousands'. This target proved unattainable because EU citizens moving to the UK were counted within the immigration figures, but controls could not be imposed on EU free movement, aside from temporary transitional restrictions lasting for up to seven years on new member states. For tiers 1, 2 and 4, there was a strong economic case for continued entry, plus lobbies from well-organised business (284,000 people from outside the UK came for employment purposes in 2014) and universities (around 200,000 students came to the UK in 2014). The government conceded to pressure from business to remove 'intra-corporate transferees' from the target while universities also protested about moves that could restrict their ability to recruit international students who were a lucrative income source. In the education sector, there was a clamp down on colleges providing courses to prepare for university entry with the suspicion that some were abusing the student visa system for people who were really coming to work in the UK. Universities were also required to monitor attendance by non-EU students.

Family migration was also a target for government action. In 2012, new rules came into force that British citizens or settled persons wishing to sponsor a national EEA partner to join them needed an annual income of at least £18,600 a year with foreign spouses/partners required to wait five years (up from the previous two) before they could apply for permanent settlement. The immigration authorities were also required to focus on the 'genuineness' of marriages.

The Coalition government was in a dilemma. It had announced a target (which was popular with the general public), but was unable to attain its objective (because of EU free movement and pressure from key interests such as business and universities). Caps were introduced on entry by non-EU migrants with annual quotas for Tier 1 'exceptional talent' set at 1,000 a year with a further 1,000 for Tier 1 'Graduate Entrepreneurs'. The number of people who could enter under Tier 2 for non-EEA workers with a firm job offer was set at 20,700 annually (Hampshire and Bale, 2015: 154). The front page of the *Financial Times* on 3 July 2014 (*FT*, 2014a) reported business concerns that an arbitrary limit frustrated their ability to recruit top talent, showing the resonance of Freeman's (1995) point about the potential influence on policy of concentrated and well-organised beneficiaries, such as business (see also Somerville and Goodman, 2010). In June 2015, Prime Minister Cameron asked the government's Migration Advisory Committee to examine how to reduce demand for non-EU migration. Given that low skilled routes were already closed off, this could only realistically be done by reducing higher skilled (Tier 2) migration or by restricting entry for international students. Both options would be likely to lead to conflict with business and universities while the economic growth models developed by the Treasury relied on relatively high net migration. The debate about immigration remained a key issue for the Conservative government elected in 2015 with scope for tension between the Home Office pursuing restriction in line with manifesto commitments to reduce immigration to the tens of thousands and the Treasury – backed by key business interests – which saw the benefits of economic migration.

One of the first measures introduced by the Conservative government after its 2015 General Election victory was a new Migration Bill, which introduced a criminal offence of 'illegal working' (punishment of up to six months' imprisonment and confiscation of wages) and also toughened sanctions against landlords housing irregular migrants requiring them to do background checks. In her speech to the 2015 Conservative Party conference the Home Secretary, Theresa May, disputed the economic benefits of immigration saying that the net economic effects were close to zero and also argued that high levels of immigration threatened social cohesion (BBC, 2015a).

Immigrant policy

We now look at immigrant policy, or, as it has been known in Britain, 'race relations'. There is no overarching integration framework or policy. Only two groups have dedicated integration policies: people awarded refugee status; and permanent residents seeking to become British citizens (who must show linguistic competence and pass a test). Race relations as it developed in the 1960s and 1970s was a response to forms of ethnic diversity that have their origins in immigration, but is not an approach to immigrant integration *per se*. The ideas and practices associated with race relations are deeply embedded in Britain. 'Race' and ethnic origin are frequent points of reference in public debate in ways that they are not in many other European countries. There is extensive monitoring of the composition and effects of ethnic diversity in Britain while a legal framework that has developed since the 1960s prohibits both direct and indirect discrimination.

Even if Britain were to have a formal immigrant integration programme, it would be hard to work out who would be the targets for such a policy. For example, many people who fall into the Black, Asian and Minority Ethnic category (BAME) are British citizens whose origins lie in immigration (sometimes many generations ago). Many people in Britain are also temporary or short-term migrants with around 70 per cent of migrants coming for less than five years (Vargas-Silva, 2011). Meanwhile, the 2.4 million EU citizens living in the UK in 2013 have rights guaranteed by EU laws that affect their residence, employment and access to services as well as guaranteeing non-discrimination on the grounds of nationality. These EU citizens cannot be the subjects of integration measures. As Saggar and Somerville (2012: 3) note this situation 'contrasts significantly with earlier waves of immigration … from the Caribbean, India, Pakistan and Bangladesh, which in part gave rise to the race relations model of addressing integration and inter-group relationships'. Race relations policy was predicated on settlement by ethnically and culturally diverse groups and may well not capture the diversity associated with contemporary immigration and free movement.

While the context for policy is challenging, Saggar and Somerville (2012: 1) identify three areas that have been the focus since 1997:

- national identity both in terms of the meaning of 'Britishness' in a multi-national state and in terms of combating the targeting by populist and extreme right groups of supposed threats to national identity;
- empirical integration indicators such as labour market and educational outcomes for migrants and their families;
- local or neighbourhood integration.

While not amounting to a coherent integration policy, these varying aspects of the response to immigration are seen as contributing to what has been called 'repressive liberalism' (Joppke, 2007) or 'liberal coercion' (Saggar and Somerville, 2012) with increased emphasis on adaptation by migrant newcomers and by settled populations whose origins lie in migration. The reason for this harder and more repressive edge is because of a perception that previous approaches were flawed in design and implementation.

The origins and effects of 'race relations' policy

In the 1960s, Britain looked to North America for a policy model in response to the social effects of post-war immigration. The 1965, 1968 and 1976 Race Relations Acts sought to combat discrimination based on racial and ethnic origin and establish institutions to monitor compliance, particularly in the work place and provision of services such as housing and health care. Further legislation in 2001 extended the scope of race relations legislation to cover the police force in the aftermath of the Macpherson Report's criticisms of the police's investigation of the racially motivated murder of Stephen Lawrence while also imposing tougher equality obligations on employers. In 2007 the Equality and Human Rights Commission (EHRC) had taken on the Commission for Racial Equality's (CRE) responsibilities and the 2010 Equality Act superseded the four Race Relations Acts and brought the previously fragmented anti-discrimination legislation into one broader framework.

The approach upon which race relations policy was based rested on a particular notion of multiculturalism defined in the 1960s by Home Secretary Roy Jenkins as 'not a flattening process of assimilation', but 'equal opportunity accompanied by cultural diversity'. The 1965 Race Relations Act made discrimination on grounds of race, ethnicity, colour and national origin illegal, but was toothless because it only applied to public places such as cinemas and restaurants, and not to areas where discrimination was rife, such as education, employment and housing. The legislation also made such discrimination a criminal rather than civil offence, which meant that the burden of proof was high. In fact, the burden was so high that no prosecutions were brought. The emphasis was placed on conciliation through the newly created Race Relations Board.

The main weakness of the 1965 and 1968 Acts were that they were centred on direct discrimination and that they relied on conciliation rather than legal redress. The institutional architecture of race relations was revealing of a paternalistic approach. Responsibility was devolved to local institutions. The Community Relations Commission set up in 1968 sponsored local Community Relations Councils whose task was the promotion of good race relations. These committees were often composed of the local 'great and good', rather than by immigrants themselves.

The third piece of race relations introduced in 1976 sought to redress the deficiencies of the 1965 and 1968 legislation by introducing the concept of 'indirect discrimination' where treatment is formally equal, but the actual effect is to discriminate against a group defined in racial or ethnic terms. The allocation of public sector housing, for instance, could be formally equal, but the requirement for a certain duration of residence could effectively exclude newly arrived immigrants and thus constitute indirect discrimination. The 1976 Act also allowed for 'positive action', a weak form of US-style affirmative action and established the CRE to monitor compliance and the power to initiate civil proceedings in cases of contravention.

The effect of this legislation was to put in place relatively strong anti-discrimination measures, but also to frame such issues in terms of race and ethnicity in ways that has not occurred in France and Germany (as we see in subsequent chapters). It has been argued that 'racialised' assumptions about immigration have been recycled in the face of large-scale EU free movement and thus that ways of thinking about and responding to immigration in race-related terms have persisted with people from the EU as both victims and perpetrators of racism (Fox, 2013).

Immigrant integration since the 1990s

We now assess approaches to immigrant integration since levels of public concern about immigration began to increase after the mid-1990s. The policy trend has been quite clear and reflects that evident in other European countries: an increased emphasis on adaptation by migrant newcomers. The clearest example of this is the introduction in 2004 of language and citizenship tests that require would-be citizens to demonstrate linguistic abilities and some knowledge of British history, culture and institutions. This also marks a retreat from multiculturalism, although, even though the word has been much used, it would be difficult to identify specific commitments to multiculturalism in policy. Britain is clearly a diverse and multicultural society, but as in other European countries such as the Netherlands there have been attempts since the 2000s by political leaders to distance themselves from what they represent as failed or flawed approaches. The rhetoric accompanying policy emphasised movement away from approaches that support and promote group differences and towards policies that seek to increase the onus on migrant newcomers to adapt to British society and demonstrate commitment to it.

Changes in policy or rhetoric can often be linked to focusing events that trigger a strong public reaction and are seen to require a political response. Between 2001 and 2005 there were three such triggering events: unrest in the northern towns of Burnley, Bradford and Oldham in 2001 (see also textbox 2.2); the 9/11 terrorist attacks on the USA; and the 7 July terrorist bombings in London in 2005. This prompted the three policy strands identified earlier: national identity; focusing on outcomes; and promoting neighbourhood cohesion. These were particularly motivated by the idea that there were some sections of British society such as young Muslim men that were not integrated or that rejected the values of British society. The British-born perpetrators of the 7 July attacks were an example of this concern.

2.2 THE 'MILLTOWN' RIOTS AND THE RISE OF COMMUNITY COHESION DISCOURSE

Immigrant integration is an issue played out predominantly in neighbourhoods, towns and cities with scope for significant local variation (Garbaye, 2005). Success stories often play out at the local level as do tensions. An example of tensions coming to the surface occurred in 2001 when the UK experienced its worst rioting in decades with unrest in areas with relatively large Muslim populations. These Muslim communities were long-established with the rioters being mainly British citizens who were the second or even third generation descendants of immigrants. Beginning in the north west town of Oldham and then spreading to the other northern towns and cities of Leeds, Burnley and Bradford, there were violent protests by predominantly young Muslim men about what they saw as the racist foundations of socio-economic deprivation in ex-industrial towns that had suffered decades of neglect. The then CRE Chair, Trevor Philips, saw these riots as an example of ethnic 'majorities' and 'minorities' leading 'parallel lives'.

These 'Milltown Riots' became the trigger for policy changes. A government-appointed commission led by Ted Cantle advocated a stronger focus on 'community cohesion', to be promoted at the community and local level. The Cantle Commission (Home Office, 2001) proposed well-resourced, locally focused community cohesion plans. Modood (2013) sees these as a strategy to generate 'discursive coherence' that links policy makers with a wide range of 'stakeholders' such as local authorities and academic researchers on questions such as multiculturalism, residential segregation and the (highly contested) meaning of British identity.

It can be very difficult to define Britishness in a multi-national state with Scottish, Irish and Welsh identities, but this has not stopped the valorisation of Britishness. For example, in the wake of the so-called 'Trojan horse' issue in summer 2014, with media accounts of alleged attempts by Muslim school leaders and governors to exert undue influence on the religious content of teaching in state schools, David Cameron announced that not only would schools be required to teach British values (as they already were), but would also be required to promote them (a new requirement). This then re-opened the debate about the meaning of such values with it becoming clear that there were many different views about what these values should be. In an article in the *Mail on Sunday* newspaper on 14 June 2014 Cameron said that these should include freedom, tolerance of others, accepting personal and social responsibility, and respecting and upholding the rule of law.

As already noted, it is not possible to identify a coherent national integration framework or paradigm and the term 'integration' is rarely used. In 2007, a Commission on Integration and Cohesion (CIC, 2007) argued against a 'one size fits all' approach, but rather argued for flexibility in adapting policies to specific local situations (ibid.: 57). This explains why significant differences can be observed in local policies between various UK towns and cities (Scholten, 2014).

There has also been a shift in the language used to describe integration with phrases such as 'community cohesion' more prominent, and less use of the term 'race relations' (Spencer, 2011). A key objective of community cohesion policy is to promote better 'intercultural relations' that can lead to 'bridging' social capital between groups in local communities, prevent 'parallel lives' and promote a shared sense of belonging.

European integration

David Cameron's Conservative government was elected on 2015 with a clear commitment to renegotiate Britain's relationship with the EU and then put this to a referendum in 2016. The Europeanisation of immigration policy and politics in Britain could be seen as ironic given that Britain has long been one of the most Eurosceptic member states. Earlier in this chapter, we saw the extensive impact of EU free movement on flows and politics. In this section, we now look more closely at both the EU's impact on British immigration politics and Britain's impact on EU free movement, migration and asylum policy and politics. We see that British governments have preferred co-operation rather than integration, but that the rapid development of a legal framework at EU level for migration and asylum since 1999 has limited Britain's participation in some of the security and monitoring activities that have developed around the Schengen framework.

An opt-out state

Britain is formally opted out of the migration and asylum provisions of Chapter Four of the EU Treaty, but has opted back in to around one-third of subsequent legislation. Britain is 'out', but also 'in' with a key sticking point being the refusal by British governments to cede power to check passports at borders, leading to a refusal to sign-up to the Schengen passport-free system. This meant that Britain was not covered by the EU relocation scheme for up to 160,000 asylum applicants from Greece, Hungary and Italy and put in place its own scheme to take in 20,000 Syrians over a five-year period.

Earlier, the 1990s were characterised by the EU's movement into areas of 'high politics' that touched more closely upon state sovereignty (see Chapter 7). The Conservative government led by John Major opposed such developments. The Conservatives insisted that co-operation on immigration and asylum provided for by the Maastricht Treaty (1992) should occur in an intergovernmental 'pillar' where member states held sway. Then, when things got more serious in the Amsterdam Treaty of June 1997, the New Labour government (elected only the previous month) secured a British opt-out from the migration and asylum provisions covering free movement, migration and asylum. The British government could choose to opt-out of migration and asylum, but not from long-standing free movement provisions.

What does it mean to be an opt-out state? First, Britain cannot opt-out of free movement provisions, as this is a core EU right guaranteed by law, and limited other forms of free movement (goods, services and capital). The Conservatives after their 2015 election victory sought changes to the EU free movement framework as part of a renegotiation of Britain's EU membership. This entailed a call for a four-year ban on EU migrants accessing non-contributory welfare benefits and social housing. There were significant obstacles to securing concessions in this area. Changes to the EU treaty were very unlikely to occur and would also require arduous ratification processes, including referenda in some member states. Changes to the legislative framework were possible, but the odds seemed stacked against changes to free movement laws. This is an area where the EU's Ordinary Legislative Procedure (OLP) applies. This would require a Commission proposal, a qualified majority in the Council of Ministers and agreement by the European Parliament. The Commission President, Jean-Claude Juncker, stated that he wanted Britain to stay in the EU, but that, for him, free movement was a red line issue on which he would not compromise. Even if the Commission did bring forward proposals they would need to secure approval in the Council. There are potential allies for the British such as the Austrian, Dutch, German and Swedish governments, but other member states opposed any rollback of free movement rights that could negatively impact on their own citizens using these rights. The European Parliament elected in 2014 did contain more Eurosceptic elements, but 70 per cent of MEPs were still aligned to the main centre-right and centre-left groups that would oppose watering-down of free movement. There are significant obstacles to changes to free movement rules. There is a substantial body of case law associated with the free movement framework. Any attempt at roll-back that was seen as imposing blanket rules on, for example, access by EU citizens to services such as benefits, housing and education could be challenged in the EU court. The key point is that free movement is embedded at EU level and has both symbolic and institutional resonance. Its effects on Britain were not fully anticipated at the time of the 2004 enlargement and there is limited room for manoeuvre, and, importantly, there was a willingness to offer Cameron some concessions on welfare benefits and free movement in order to help keep Britain remain in the EU.

Second, a non-negotiable 'red line' for British governments has been the ability to control entry at land, air and seaports and to insist on passport checks. This leaves Britain outside of the Schengen free movement area. Britain does participate in aspects of Schengen such as cross-border police and judicial co-operation, but insists on exercising border controls. The UK did want to participate in the EU's border control agency, FRONTEX, but a 2005 decision by the CJEU ruled that the relevant legislation derived from a part of the external borders element of the Schengen framework from which Britain had opted out. As a result, there are limits on Britain's ability to participate in Schengen-based surveillance, security and monitoring operations.

Third, there are examples of the use of the EU by the British government as an 'external venue' through which it seeks to work with other member states to secure migration and asylum objectives. This has been most evident in the area of asylum policy where the UK did not behave like an opt-out state, but did in fact agree to most EU measures in a bid to, as Tony Blair put it, get 'the best of both worlds' (Geddes, 2005a). The origins of the Common European Asylum System (CEAS) are in intergovernmental co-operation of the 1990s and the establishment of the 'Dublin' principle that provides for asylum seekers making an application in the member state in which they first arrive. Between 2002 and 2003, the CEAS and measures on Temporary Protection were developed. This is described in more detail in Chapter 7, but the key point here is that the British government opted into this framework because it saw co-operation with other EU member states as a way to reduce the chance of asylum seekers getting to the UK.

An issue that crystallises the partial engagement by Britain with the EU framework is relations with France centred on the region around the port of Calais in northern France. This issue was brought home by controversy around the Sangatte camp close to Calais for migrants seeking to enter the UK. The French courts blocked attempts to close this Red Cross run camp while the British and French authorities intensified their co-operation with private actors forced to operate as agents of the immigration control authorities or risk high fines if – wittingly or unwittingly – they brought irregular migrants into the UK. After 2014, more makeshift camps of migrants and refugees were constructed in the Calais area housing predominantly young men hoping to get to the UK. This would involve them in perilous journeys on the back of trucks or holding on to Eurotunnel trains.

The UK and France intensified their co-operation on security – including high security fencing – at the Eurotunnel terminal near Calais.

Fourth, there has been consistent opposition by British governments to EU measures that could be rights enhancing for migrants. The Lisbon Treaty already provides that the numbers of migrants to be admitted is a matter for the member states. British governments have sought to ensure that no EU measures could impinge on the ability to restrict non-EU migration. As we will see in Chapter 7, the UK has opted-out of key EU measures, including the 2003 directive on family reunification and the directive giving long-term (more than five years) residents the same rights as EU citizens, as well as the 2009 'Blue Card' directive on highly qualified migrants and the 2014 seasonal workers directive. In total, UK has been bound by about one third of all the EU measures aimed at harmonising migration and asylum (HM Government, 2014).

Finally, there are examples of ways in which British governments have managed to 'upload' preferred policies to the EU level. This is a rare occurrence for British governments in the areas of free movement, migration and asylum because of the ambiguous, if not hostile, position of British governments on these issues. In the area of anti-discrimination, we can see British influence on the content of two anti-discrimination directives agreed in June and November 2000. The Racial Equality Directive defines and proscribes direct and indirect discrimination and harassment, and provides for positive action to be taken to ensure full equality in practice. It also requires each Member State to set up an organisation to promote equal treatment and assist victims of racial discrimination. Similar in many ways to the Racial Equality Directive, the Employment Equality Directive requires equal treatment in employment and training irrespective of religion or belief, disability, age or sexual orientation. The key point is that both contain measures that reflect British (and Dutch) legislative approaches that tackle direct and indirect discrimination. This is one of the few examples of the British uploading a preferred policy to EU level. The more general story is one of resistance and opt-outs.

Conclusion

It could be tempting to argue that the main concerns of British immigration policy and politics have been to maintain 'fortress Britain' on the edge of 'fortress Europe' probably because of the view that 'fortress Europe' doesn't exist, but that 'fortress Britain' could. Britain could thus be detached from the effects of European integration, while benefiting from restrictive policies, and maintaining its own distinct form of 'race related' immigrant integration policy. Almost immediately, the idea of a European politics of migration convergent in either horizontal or vertical terms is severely dented.

This line of reasoning would be flawed. Migration flows and the politics of migration in Britain have been extensively, even if unwittingly, Europeanised. This has been particularly the case since 2004 when levels of free movement from A8 states occurred that were far in excess of predicted numbers. This proved a pivotal moment in the contemporary history of immigration in Britain. This chapter has shown that British government effectively reasserted controls over Commonwealth immigration in the 1970s and asylum seeking in the 2000s, but that EU free movement provides a much more fundamental challenge because it is an EU right. The British government can and did assert control over asylum, can and did establish quotas for skilled non-EU migrants, but cannot control EU free movement without a fundamental revision of EU treaties and law. The scale of movement has been matched by the high salience of the immigration issue and a sense held by many people that tighter controls are needed. A further distinct element that was added to the mix was the rise to prominence of UKIP, articulating a 'cultural divide' through their opposition to immigration, European integration and to the political class (McLaren, 2012). This chapter has shown how Europe has affected domestic politics in Britain in ways that were unexpected.

It has also considered the issue of immigrant integration. Race relations developed as an approach to ethnic diversity and created particular ways of thinking about and dealing with issues associated with cultural diversity. It is less relevant for the large numbers of migrants that are relatively temporary (staying less than five years) or are EU citizens to whom integration policies don't apply. What has been clearly evident in the UK – and is a trend that is in common with other European countries – is an increased emphasis on adaptation by migrant newcomers measured by linguistic skills and knowledge of/commitment to Britain and its institutions. Citizenship and integration policies are not areas of EU competence, so these are better seen as a form of horizontal convergence rather than EU-driven vertical convergence.

For a country with Eurosceptic tendencies, the politics of migration and immigration in Britain have been extensively Europeanised. This does not mean that a common EU migration and asylum policy has replaced British policy. The effects are evident on movement by people from other EU states and the associated political dynamics that link anti-EU and anti-immigration sentiment. We also see changes to the form taken by British immigration politics. Older certainties about the power of the executive branch of government are questioned by the influence of human rights legislation and EU institutions. Between the 1960s and early 2000s we saw that the British government could act quite forcefully to assert controls and did so over Commonwealth migrants and asylum seekers. European integration poses a different order of challenge and, while Britain is a member and free movement is a core EU provision, requires new ways of thinking about the politics of migration in Britain.

3

France: Still the One and Indivisible Republic?

Introduction

While not the first and last such incident, in October and November 2005 the idea of an 'indivisible' French Republic united by common citizenship and supposedly eschewing divisions of race, culture, ethnicity and religion was confronted by rioting in many French cities. These riots involved mainly young people of Arab and African origin, most of whom were descendants of immigrants. The riots followed an incident where a young boy of immigrant descent died after a police pursuit. These and other riots were seen to show that a French emphasis on assimilation had not addressed serious problems of youth alienation and unemployment and that discrimination was an important concern in the 'indivisible Republic'. For others, the riots fed a growing concern about the corrosive effects of immigration as a threat to national identity and security heightened by the fact that French citizens of North African origin have been involved in terror attacks using Islam to justify their actions, including the terrorist attacks on the offices of satirical magazine Charlie Hebdo and the murderous attacks on Paris by so-called 'Islamic State' terrorists in November 2015.

An interesting thing about the malleable French 'Republican tradition' was that, as this chapter shows, it has been mobilised by both those on the progressive or liberal left concerned about discrimination and those on the right worried about order, security and the terrorist threat. More generally, though, the events were suggestive of a profound unease at the institutional level, including government and the police, when dealing with issues related to ethnicity, culture or religion. The events also revealed a disconnect between the people and their political leaders that has provided fertile ground for the extreme-right FN founded by Jean-Marie Le Pen and inherited by his daughter Marine. The first round of the regional elections in December 2015 saw the FN secure 27 per cent of the vote and emerge as the leading party. The second round a week later saw centre-right and centre-left parties unite against the FN and block their path to assuming power in any French region. This outcome was double-edged for the FN: it showed their capacity to mobilise around a quarter of voters, but also showed the potential strength of an anti-FN voting bloc. This double-edged dilemma is likely to be evident at the 2017 Presidential elections when the FN would hope to get through to the second round.

This chapter demonstrates once again the importance of highlighting the role played by background institutional factors in making migration 'visible' as a social and political issue. To do so requires analysing debates on migration and integration in one of Europe's oldest immigration countries and looking at how the boundaries of French citizenship and the idea of the nation are closely bound to Republican ideas that, while malleable, have played a key role in defining immigration. This also reveals important differences compared to British debates (see previous chapter).

Debates in France about immigration have largely been centred on nationality and citizenship and shaped by:

- responses to movement to France by Muslims from France's former Maghrebi colonies;
- a perceived 'crisis of integration' that had deep roots in French society;
- the effects of social and political developments in the Middle East and North Africa (including the so-called 'Arab Spring' and the 'war' on ISIS declared by President Hollande after the November 2015 terror attacks in Paris) on Muslim communities in France.

It is impossible to understand developments in France without accounting for the sharp politicisation of immigration and, to some extent, of immigrant integration. This has enabled not only the rise since the 1980s of Europe's most prominent extreme right party (the FN) but also a revival of Republican ideas and assimilationist approaches to integration. Yet, as this chapter shows, beneath the thick layer of Republican discourse, there are important elements linking French immigration and immigrant policies to those in other European countries. The French case appears to be caught in the peculiar situation where, despite politicisation and highbrow philosophical debates on French Republicanism at national level, key components of its approach to immigration policy are shaped by the EU while much of its immigrant policy is shaped at local level with variation between cities.

The Republican 'tradition'

The French Republican tradition can be difficult to pin down, but is closely associated with the founding ideas of the French Republic: an emphasis on individual citizenship and a direct 'social contract' between the individual and the state. Brubaker (1992) contrasted this French definition of citizenship related to the state with a German definition of citizenship based on ethnicity, culture and descent (see Chapter 4). The French tradition was summed up as follows: 'French nationhood is constituted by political unity, it is centrally expressed in the striving for cultural unity' (Brubaker, 1992: 1).

Political inclusion within the French nation state has meant the socio-cultural assimilation of both indigenous minorities (Bretons, Basques, Corsicans and the like) and immigrant-origin minorities. Article 1 of the French Constitution stipulates that 'France shall be an indivisible, secular, democratic and social Republic' and that 'it shall ensure the equality of all citizens before the law, without distinction of origin, race or religion' and 'shall respect all beliefs.' Equality and unity in French Republicanism are interpreted as applying irrespective of ethnicity, religion, culture and race. Thus, French institutions are to be 'colour-blind' while these institutions (such as schools) are supposed to secure the successful assimilation of migrants into French society. Often, this French approach is juxtaposed to British and Dutch approaches that recognise ethnic or cultural minorities and collect data about them to measure and monitor their 'integration'. The French approach eschews a focus on 'minorities'. Another central principle is that of *laïcité*, or a specific French interpretation of secularism – the separation of state and religion – which has become a powerful factor in the debate about Islam in French society.

French immigration and immigrant policies develop against the backdrop of this Republican tradition, but can France still be understood as this one and indivisible Republic, or has it changed in the face of immigration and growing diversity? We see continuity in terms of the strength of the Republican tradition as a powerful discourse in French politics, but French Republicanism is challenged from

- 'below' where sub-national governments are becoming increasingly innovative in responding to immigration-related diversity;
- 'within' by the extreme right FN that attacks the French political class and challenges important components of post-war French identity such as its traditional leadership role within the EU;
- 'above' by EU laws that can have a constraining effect on French policies.

Immigration policy

France has a long history of immigration, but, like other European countries has been recently concerned with strictly regulating inflows and being more selective in the migrants that are admitted with a preference for higher skilled economic migrants.

Rather than seeking to 'control' immigration, France has a long history of positively encouraging it because of concerns dating back to the nineteenth century about low levels of population growth (Noiriel, 1996). As Wihtol de Wenden puts it, the attempt was 'to make France with foreigners' (2014: 135). Migrants came from neighbouring or nearby countries such as Italy, Poland, Portugal and Spain. By the 1980s, 25 per cent of people living in France were either immigrants or had at least one immigrant relative.

In the nineteenth century expansive nationality laws allowed France to turn its foreign-born population into French citizens. Article 44 of the 1889 nationality law automatically gave French citizenship at the age of majority to all children born to foreign parents in France without any act of affirmation, such as an oath of loyalty. In 1927, first generation foreigners were given easier access to French nationality via liberalisation of naturalisation laws. In 1945 a reformed nationality law code annulled the racist legislation of the Vichy regime that had removed citizenship rights from Jewish people. After 1945, the nineteenth century nationality law with birth and residence as the basis for the acquisition of French nationality was reaffirmed leading to a relatively open system combining *jus soli* (birth on the territory) and *jus sanguinis* ('blood'/ethnic descent).

Debate about immigration in the 30 or so years after the end of the Second World War between 'economists' who favoured recruiting workers to fill labour market gaps and 'demographers' favouring families coming to France for longer-term settlement with an emphasis on their ability to assimilate was won by the economists, in the sense that French policies remained expansive with no explicit ethnic hierarchy. Weil (1991) has, however, noted a *de facto* ethnic selectivity marked by a decline in North African immigration while immigration from Italy, Portugal and Spain increased. A government ordinance of 2 November 1945 separated work and residence permits, which meant that the right to live in France was not dependent on the possession of a work permit. The 1945 ordinance also created the *Office national d'immigration* (ONI, National Office of Immigration), followed in 1952 by the *Office français de protection des réfugiés et des apatrides* (OFPRA, French Office for the Protection of Refugees and Stateless Persons).

Labour migration to France until the 1970s was organised by the private sector with foreign workers recruited to fill labour market gaps and was thus largely uncontrolled by state authorities (Hollifield, 2014). Many migrant workers entered France during the 1950s and 1960s without the appropriate papers and regularised their status after settling. The French government also signed labour recruitment agreements with 16 European and non-European countries. These reflected rather than created migration flows while extending legal and social rights to these labour migrants as denizens. French nationality law was open and expansive and provided a relatively straightforward route for foreigners to become French.

Decolonisation in the 1950s and 1960s was the backdrop for debates about immigration and nationality in France (as it was in Britain too). Between 1946 and 1990 the proportion of immigrants from other European countries as a share of the foreign population fell from 89 per cent to 41 per cent with strong growth in the numbers of people from the Maghreb. Until 1956, Morocco and Tunisia had been French protectorates. Until independence in 1962, Algeria was regarded as part of France. Under the terms of provisions made in 1947, Algerians had the right to freely enter France. This led to large-scale immigration from Algeria to France (continuing until this day in, for example, the form of family migration). By 2010 there were 471,300 people of Algerian descent in France (see Table 3.1).

The expansionist period came to an end in 1974 when economic recession caused by the oil price crisis led the French government to suspend labour and family migration through two circulars. The Council of State overturned the suspension of family migration in 1978 because it contravened the constitutional

Table 3.1 French immigration, by legal category and immigrant country of origin

	1962	1968	1975	1982	1990	1999	2010	2010 (absolute numbers)
Legal categories (% of population)								
French by acquisition	2.8	2.7	2.6	2.6	3.1	4	4.4	2,904,000
Foreigners (without French nationality)	4.6	5.4	6.5	6.8	6.3	5.6	5.9	3,796,000
Immigrants (French nationality but born outside France)	6.2	6.6	7.4	7.4	7.4	7.4	8.6	5,676,000
Origin countries (% of all immigrants)								Populations for 2008 (SOPEMI, 2012)
Spain	18	21	15.2	11.7	9.5	7.3	4.6	130,100
Italy	31.7	23.8	17.1	14.1	11.6	8.8	5.6	174,300
Portugal	2	8.8	16.9	15.8	14.5	13.3	10	492,500
Poland	9.5	6.7	4.8	3.9	3.4	2.3	1.7	
Algeria	11.6	11.7	14.3	14.8	13.3	13.4	13.5	471,300
Morocco	1.1	3.3	6.6	9.1	11	12.1	12.4	444,800
Tunisia	1.5	3.5	4.7	5	5	4.7	4.5	143,900
Sub-saharan Africa	0.7	1.4	2.4	4.3	6.6	9.1	13	
Asia	2.4	2.5	3.6	8	11.4	12.8	14.5	

Source: INSEE (www.insee.fr/en/themes/theme.asp?theme=2&sous_theme=5&type=1&nivgeo=0&produit=OK)

right to family life. This is a point much emphasised by those who identify the role of courts and rights-based politics in opening 'social and political spaces' for migrants and their descendants in Europe (Hollifield, 1992). The suspension didn't apply to EC nationals moving for purposes of work who could freely enter France, asylum seekers who were covered by separate laws, and high skilled migrants who could still secure access to the French labour market. The circulars had the unintended effect of creating 'illegal immigration' because previous irregular immigrants who had faced little difficulty regularising their status now faced major problems. The suspension also encouraged permanent settlement (Hollifield, 1992). Did continued immigration signify a loss of control? This would be an exaggeration. It makes more sense to argue that French control capacity was constrained in relation to particular types of migration that were linked to the legacy of French colonialism and recruitment agreements, while courts provided some guarantees for migrants' rights.

The 1974 circulars were bureaucratic devices and not widely discussed. The reliance on government circulars and bureaucratic discretion also helped create a tangled web of regulations that gave significant discretion to the state in pursuit of restrictions aimed at non-European immigrants. A 1968 report by the Economic and Social Council had characterised non-European immigrants as an 'inassimilable island' (cited in Schain, 1999: 207). A distinction between 'good' and 'bad' immigrants centred on the question of perceived assimilability. Europeans, particularly Catholics, were seen as more assimilable than non-Europeans, particularly Muslims. In turn, this led to a 'juridical balkanisation' (Miller, 1981) with a tougher regime against non-Europeans. The Badinter Law of June 1983, for instance, gave the police powers to use a person's hair and skin colour when deciding which people to stop for ID checks. This feature was again discussed in 1993, during the debate on the Pasqua law, with an article that stipulated that ID checks should not be based on racial or national origin.

Politicisation and the rise of the Front National

Whereas immigration and nationality had been primarily an administrative issue in the 1970s, they ascended the political agenda during the 1980s. At times this led to intense public debate that divided the main political parties and provided fertile ground for the FN. In this period, the relation between immigration, nationality and citizenship came to the fore in response to a perceived 'crisis of integration' (Wieviorka, 1991). This has largely been seen as a response to movement to France by people from the Maghreb, most of whom were Muslims, but is also linked to deeper economic, social and political changes hitting France in the 1970s and 1980s.

The FN's rise was both a cause and an effect of this politicisation of immigration; it played on existing concern and also helped to fan the flames of hostility to immigration and immigrants. It would be wrong to see the FN as the sole driver of the politicisation of immigration because, not least, that would be to neglect entirely the role of mainstream parties (Carvalho, 2014). The FN issued a familiar rallying call for the populist right, which was to target the failings of the political class that, the FN claimed, had sold-out and betrayed the ordinary man and woman.

The FN rose to prominence when it won control of the town of Dreux near Paris in the 1983 municipal elections (Gaspard, 1995). One result of the FN's prominence and its hard-line anti-immigration and extreme nationalist stance was that its founder, Jean-Marie Le Pen (succeeded in 2011 by his daughter, Marine) was 'at times ... given nearly sole credit for imposing the tone and themes of the political debate, politicising citizenship and generating the rise of racial politics' (Feldblum, 1999: 32). But are other factors at work too? Is the FN a symptom rather than a cause of the politicisation of immigration and nationality? Feldblum (1999) argued that a broader 'new nationalist politics of citizenship' stretched across the political spectrum to include mainstream political opinion and provided a backdrop against which citizenship and membership of the French national community could be re-envisioned. Three factors contributed to this.

First, it was clear by the 1980s that non-European immigrants were permanently settled in France. The ensuing debate about national identity became a reformulation of a longer-standing debate about assimilation within the French national community that dates back to at least the nineteenth century. This debate has been exacerbated by economic problems and increased unemployment.

Second, the stirrings can be detected in the 1960s and 1970s of a debate about pluralism in France encompassing both national and immigrant minorities (Safran, 1985). Mitterrand's Socialist government of the 1980s appeared more receptive to ethno-cultural diversity. For instance, at a 1981 Presidential campaign rally in Brittany, Mitterrand said that 'we proclaim the right to difference'. In the first year of the Socialist government the Ministry of Culture produced a report entitled *Cultural Democracy and the Right to Difference*, applicable to all minority cultures. A denunciation of the left's flirtation with multiculturalism became a key aspect of the right's critique of the Socialist government. The FN took the 'right to difference' and used it in an anti-immigrant 'right to be French' argument (Taguieff, 1991).

Third, the Muslim population in France were represented in ways that directly contributed to the perception of an inassimilable Muslim population and, more extremely, as some kind of subversive fifth column, that has helped to consolidate the idea of a 'crisis of integration' that defied the capacity of French institutions to rectify. Renan's (1882) classic nineteenth-century formulation of French nationhood identified the church, army and schools as key agents of socialisation into the French national community. By the time of the murders at the office of the satirical magazine *Charlie Hebdo* in January 2015, the 'Republican' institutions that many young North African origin youths were most likely to encounter were the housing authorities, criminal justice system and social workers. This represented an on-going and deep-rooted institutional crisis in its broadest terms involving both national identity and core ideas underpinning French institutions (Hussey, 2014).

At stake appeared to be the core institutions of French society in the face of immigration and its effects. This depended on the perception of Muslim immigrants as less assimilable than earlier immigrants. The history of immigration in France – as in other countries – suggests that new immigrant groups have been likely to encounter hostility and that their presence has been accompanied by agonising about what immigration meant for society (Noiriel, 1996). In these terms the response was familiar. What had changed, however, was the diminished confidence in the ability of key social and political institutions to perform an integrating role.

Reforming French nationality, citizenship and immigration laws

The politicisation and presence of immigration has continued to have an effect on French nationality and immigration laws. Under both left and right governments between 1980 and 2010, 12 new laws on entry and stay were introduced (Wihtol de Wenden, 2014: 137). Whereas access to nationality had been largely automatic after five years of residence for those born in France, this automacity became subject to debate. There were three main arguments for more restrictive nationality legislation (Brubaker, 1992). Voluntarist arguments stressed the need for an act of affirmation. Statist arguments focused on the ways that expansive laws allowed some foreigners to evade immigration controls. Nationalist arguments centred on a suspicion that some people were *français des papiers* (French by paper) rather than *français de coeur* (French in the heart).

Articles 23 and 44 were the focus of attention. Article 23 automatically attributes nationality to third generation immigrants. Article 44 extends French nationality automatically to all those born on French soil from foreign parents when reaching the age of majority. Article 23 had already provoked hostility and resentment among some Algerians born before 1962 because even after independence their children were still claimed by France. Furthermore, from a French perspective, Article 23 could mean that migrants could receive French nationality without being committed to it (*Français malgré eux*, or the unwillingly French).

Immigration control and reform of the nationality code re-emerged on the political agenda after the right's victory in the 1993 legislative elections. The Pasqua law of 1994 required foreign workers and students to wait two years rather than one before family members could join them, and prohibited the regularisation of status for undocumented migrants who married French citizens. Mayors were given the power to annul suspected marriages of convenience. Any person expelled from France was denied access to French territory for a year. The Pasqua law also denied welfare benefits to illegal migrants except for obligatory schooling (a duty not a right) and emergency health care.

The Pasqua law also changed Article 44 of the Nationality Code so that children born in France of foreign parents would have to file a formal request for French nationality between the ages of 16 and 21 and have to 'manifest their wish' to be French. The legislation meant a move towards voluntarism rather than automacity. In the immediate aftermath of the law being introduced, the naturalisation rate increased as many migrants wanted to make use of temporary transgression arrangements.

Efforts to restrict immigration continued. The Debré law of March 1997 was a reaction to the issue of immigrants *sans papiers* (without papers), specifying that to renew a residence permit individuals needed to prove that they were not a threat to public order. In effect this required people to prove that they were innocent and for this reason was struck down in April 1997 by the Constitutional Council, as too was allowing police access to fingerprints of asylum seekers. The bill also stipulated that children under the age of 16 would need to prove ten years of residence before they could become French nationals and that foreign spouses would need to be married for two years before they would be eligible for a residence permit. Most controversially, the legislation proposed that French citizens notify the authorities whenever they received a non-EU citizen as a guest. The local mayor would be given powers to ensure that the person had actually left. Nationals of 30 countries were exempted from this measure with immigrants from African countries the main targets. The initial proposals met with strong opposition and were of dubious constitutionality. In the final version of the law the obligation fell on non-EU foreigners to report their movements, but even so was portrayed by opponents as redolent of Vichy restrictions.

As swiftly as the reform of the French nationality code was enacted, it was largely reversed in 1997 when the left won parliamentary elections and a third period of co-habitation began with the executive split between the Gaullist President Chirac and the Socialist Prime Minister Jospin. In June 1997 Prime Minister Jospin's first speech to the National Assembly spoke of a 'new Republican pact', a 'return to the roots of the Republic' and stated that birth right citizenship was inseparable from the French nation and that his government would restore this right (Hollifield, 2000b). The Guigou Law (1998) reversed important elements of the second Pasqua laws. It cancelled the expression of the will to become French at 18 years and restored automatic access to French nationality for the majority of those born in France from foreign partners. It thus rebalanced towards *jus soli* (nationality due to birth on the territory)

(Wihtol de Wenden, 2014: 142). A June 1997 amnesty addressed the *sans papiers* issue by means of a regularisation. By December 1998 143,000 applications had been received and 80,000 residence permits granted. Jospin also announced a review of immigration and nationality legislation (Weil, 1997). The legislation also amended the asylum laws of July 1952 to fall in line with the emerging EU framework by creating the possibility of refusing applicants from countries deemed 'safe' (see Chapter 7). Two new forms of protection were also created: 'constitutional' asylum could be granted to people persecuted because of attempts to promote freedom, and 'territorial' asylum was open to those who could show that their life or freedom was threatened or that they were liable to inhuman or degrading treatment.

Immigration *choisie* and immigration *subie*

In the 2000s, there was a renewed politicisation of immigration. A key role was played by Nicolas Sarkozy, first as interior minister from 2002 to 2007 and then as President of the Republic between 2007 and 2012, during which time he pursued a security-driven approach to immigration and integration (Carvalho and Geddes, 2012; Villard and Sayegh, 2013). A key factor was the FN's continued strong presence. In 2002, the then FN leader, Jean-Marie Le Pen, made it to the second round of the Presidential elections, which were eventually won by Chirac. In 2007, Sarkozy was elected President by explicitly courting FN voters (Carvalho and Geddes, 2012).

As Interior minister Sarkozy sought a more restrictive immigration policy. New laws made family reunification more difficult, lengthened the period for obtaining a permanent residence permit and made more use of short-term visas. Overseeing policy was a new Ministry for Immigration, Integration, National Identity and Co-Development. Sarkozy's main objective was greater selectivity with a preference, as he put it, for immigration *choisie* (chosen immigration) – such as by the highly skilled – rather than immigration *subie* (endured immigration) by which he meant family migration (Simon, 2014: 205). Yet, between 2006 and 2010, economic immigration increased only slightly from six to nine per cent of total immigration.

With Sarkozy in the driving seat, the French government introduced new immigration laws that targeted the relationship between immigrant admissions and immigrant integration. The 2007 law on immigration, integration and asylum introduced a reception and integration contract (*contrat d'accueil et d'intégration*) that committed newcomers to language training and acquiring some basic knowledge of French laws and society. The extension of residence permits was to depend on attainment of these targets.

The 2007 law also introduced a repatriation policy, targeted primarily at undocumented migrants (and migrants whose permit had expired). Targets were set for the number of deportations, rising to nearly 30,000 in 2008 (Simon, 2014: 206). The French government also signed agreements with countries of origin such as Senegal, Ghana and Mali to enable repatriation and stronger border controls in return for development aid (Wihtol de Wenden, 2014: 137).

An issue that was also high on the political agenda at the end of the 2000s was dual nationality. Many French people of migrant origin enjoy dual nationality, combining their French passport with that of their parents' origin countries. The FN continued to emphasise a long-standing theme in debates about nationality about the so-called 'unwilling' or 'paper' French (*français malgré eux* or *français de papier*) who had a French passport but allegedly did not seem to care too much about it. In 2001, this debate was (re-)triggered when, during a France versus Algeria football match in Marseille, the French national anthem was booed, much to the disgust of the French media and public opinion. In 2011 a Parliamentary Information Mission on Nationality Law questioned the extent to which migrants with dual nationality could be loyal to the French state. This contributed to legislation introduced by the Sarkozy government to abolish dual nationality. The bill was rejected, although measures introduced in 2012 further tightened access to naturalisation.

Hollande's approach

Sarkozy's attempts to build an electoral coalition that drew from ex-FN supporters contributed to his 2007 success, but could not help secure his re-election in 2012 in the face of his personal unpopularity compounded by the post-2008 economic and financial crisis. In 2012, the Socialist François Hollande won the Presidential elections. Hollande's policy on immigration did not deviate strongly from the path set since the 2000s, although the discourse softened considerably. Measures were also introduced to once again widen access to citizenship, thus reversing some of the changes adopted under Sarkozy's government. So, while the direction of travel in policy has been towards greater restrictiveness in both immigration and nationality laws, there has been some fluctuation and change in emphasis depending on whether it is the left or right holding the levers of power.

The highly 'politicised' differentiation between wanted and unwanted immigration was also evident in France's response to the refugee crisis in 2014 and 2015. Dramatic media portrayals of migrants trying to reach the EU swung public opinion in August and September 2015 with strong public support favouring letting more refugees into France. In response, Hollande spoke out publicly in favour of an EU-wide relocation system with quotas. He pledged to admit around 24,000 refugees. Together with the German Chancellor Merkel, Hollande made significant efforts to get other EU member states to accept a relocation system. In contrast, the right, including the FN and Sarkozy's new party (renamed Les Républicains in 2015) were fiercely critical of the idea of a European quota system for asylum migrants.

While expressing some support for Europe-wide solidarity, there were concerns about border security, particularly at the French–Italian border. In 2014 and then again in 2015 France temporarily reinstalled controls at the border with Italy to prevent onward movement by refugees and migrants. Hollande blamed Italy for failing to manage the refugee situation and returned large numbers of refugees back to Italy as a clear example of 'burden shifting' between EU member states. After the terrorist attacks in Paris in November 2015, Hollande reinstalled border checks because of security concerns but also due to a view in the immediate aftermath of the attacks that terrorists might have entered Europe amongst the flows of refugees across the Mediterranean. Investigators found that the terrorists were citizens of EU member states, which meant that ease of movement within the Schengen area was more relevant than terrorists infiltrating refugee flows. France, along with other EU countries such as the Netherlands, Germany and Austria, sought a greater emphasis on security and border controls within the Schengen system. This would involve more controls on non-EU citizens, but also much closer checks on EU citizens entering the Schengen area and a better sharing of information about criminals and terror suspects. It became apparent after the November 2015 attacks in Paris that the terrorists holding passports of EU members had been able to travel relatively easily into and out of Europe, including to Syria to fight with ISIS.

The French government also sought to target the 'root causes' of refugee migration to the EU. In 2015 Hollande used the refugee crisis to justify military intervention in Syria. Along with his British counterpart, Prime Minister David Cameron, Hollande also put great emphasis on the need for more aid for refugee camps in Syria's neighbouring countries, both to protect people but also to prevent onwards movement to the EU. French military intervention in Syria against ISIS targets intensified after the November 2015 terrorist attacks on Paris.

Immigrant policy

The French approach to immigrant integration has been labelled as Republican or assimilationist. Integration policy has rested on the idea that as immigrants become 'integrated' then they would disappear as a distinct component of French society so that they would be emancipated from the 'status of minorities as collectivities or communities' (Gallisot, 1989: 27; see also Weil and Crowley, 1994; Favell, 1998). An effect of this is that the concept of minority is absent from French law with policy-makers finding it very difficult to think about the notion of minority groups (Lochak, 1989). French *égalité*, *homogénéité* and *unité* contrast with the opening towards ethnic pluralism and multiculturalism of

British and Dutch approaches (see Chapters 2 and 5). As will be shown, however, there is much more to the French approach than assimilationism because beneath the powerful discourse of Republicanism, there has been significant variation over time and in local level responses.

The right to difference?

The local roots of a *de facto* recognition of ethnic difference can also be traced to the early 1970s, during which time key issues were housing inequalities and discrimination experienced by immigrants and their families. The term integration was first introduced to French official public discourse in 1974 with the aim of embracing expressions of cultural diversity. This included allowing instruction in migrants' own languages at school, although it was unclear whether this was for the purpose of integration or repatriation. In 1979, the Minister of State for Immigrant Workers, Lionel Stoléru, spoke of *le droit à la différence* (the right to difference) in the context of policies that sought to maintain links with countries of origin and was thus 'the antithesis of integration' (Hargreaves, 1995: 194). As Mattelart and Hargreaves observe of diversity in French audio-visual media (2014: 276), the term diversity has been 'endowed with a powerful incantatory power' and 'rosy images', but is also ambiguous and malleable, which means that it has been used to refer both to the integration of immigrants and their descendants, but also as a way to emphasise social cohesion and protect internal security.

Amongst immigrant communities there were signs during the 1970s of mobilisation through housing associations. State institutions began to deal with immigrants in terms of their ethnic collective identities, which signified both a measure of recognition, but also a desire to control and channel these new and potentially challenging forms of political action. Social and economic rights and the fight against discrimination were at the forefront of the agenda of these immigrant groups (Miller, 1981; Wihtol de Wenden, 1988). In the 1980s, the focus broadened to also include political claims-making based on religion with a growing number of organisations established by Muslims. A 1981 law, introduced by the Socialist government, gave associations of foreigners the right to organise on the same basis as French associations via a simple declaration to the interior ministry. This also gave immigrant associations access to the *Fonds d'Action Sociale* (FAS, a social fund that was often used for integration related actions), with immigrants participating in the FAS administrative council from 1983 onwards.

Various organisations composed of or claiming to represent migrants tried to draw attention to diversity issues. Initial attempts to consolidate immigration organisations had a class basis reflected in the aim of the *Conseil des Associations Immigrées en France* (CAIF, Council of Immigrant Associations in France) to create a 'single immigrant worker organisation'. In the mid-1980s other broad-based organisations emerged. *SOS Racisme* was established in 1984 under the leadership of Harlem Désir, who had close connections with the Socialist government. The organisation pursued a rather vague and eclectic multiculturalist agenda that sought to move from the ambiguity of the 'right to difference' and embrace a no less ambiguous 'right to resemblance' (the slogan became the 'right to indifference' – *droit à l'indifférence*) coupled with a commitment to anti-discrimination under the slogan *'ne touche pas à mon pôte'* (don't touch my mate). A rival organisation – France Plus – pursued a more electoralist agenda by seeking to encourage young people of Franco–Maghrebi origin to engage with the political process both as voters and as candidates for elected office.

A revival of Republicanism

It has been argued that immigration and integration became pivotal issues after the 1980s in the context of a broader agenda of a revival of sub-national government (where the FN had most of its support), a decline in national solidarity and increased concern about the centralisation of government powers (Feldblum, 1999). It is in this context that we should understand the FN's rise and its particularly successful efforts to make an issue connection between immigration and concerns about the nation state. The FN effectively managed to make immigration and migrant integration questions of national identity.

The rich but malleable French Republican tradition provides a backdrop to the debate. It has been argued that these ideas underpin expansiveness and inclusion (Hollifield, 1992). Others identify a tension between the commitment to political universalism and egalitarianism, and cultural particularism and intolerance towards 'others' deemed culturally distinct.

3.1 *JUS SOLI* VERSUS *JUS SANGUINIS*

A key difference between the French case and the German case in particular has been its perspective on nationhood. Whereas in Germany nationhood is perceived in terms of descent and ethnicity, or *jus sanguinis* (referring to blood ties), France has historically developed a much more open approach to nationhood, making anyone born on or residing for a sufficient period on French soil a citizen (*jus soli*). The historic reason for the French focus is that there was no clear 'nation' that preceded the French state, as was the case with the German nation that was united only after centuries within a German state. Put differently, the French built a 'nation' by assimilating newcomers and the inhabitants of many different regions into a nation by a conscious effort at nation-building. In this *jus soli* perception of what makes someone a citizen of France also lies the foundation of its assimilationist approach to immigrant policy that still survives.

To use the term 'Republican Model' as an overarching explanatory device causes problems (Bertossi, 2001). French Republicanism is a moveable feast. Left- and right-wing politicians espouse Republican values to justify expansive and restrictive nationality laws. The result is that the term seems to have political rather than analytical usage with the 'model' functioning on a rhetorical level rather than as a practical programme of action (Feldblum, 1993; Schain, 1999).

What is clear is that the politicisation of migration and integration, and the FN's rise since the mid-1980s, provided the context for a reiteration of Republican values and the end to a very brief flirtation with multiculturalism. Both the mainstream left and right united in their support for a revival of Republican ideas that also included a hostility to the 'ethnic minorities' policies pursued by Britain and the Netherlands that were seen as creating divisions and, even worse, ghettos.

An effect of the FN's extreme stance was to create a left–right consensus in favour of Republican values (Favell, 1998; Feldblum, 1999). In the late 1980s, a committee that was established to reform the French nationality code (*Commission des Sages*, the Expert Committee) was also the first to attempt to make sense of Republicanism in relation to immigrant policy.

Based on the commission's recommendations, a High Council for Integration (HCI, Haut Conseil à l'Integration) was established. The HCI advised government on nationality law and integration policies and established policy-relevant research programmes. The HCI's first report in 1991 was entitled *For a French Model of Integration* informed by 'a logic of equality and not a logic of minorities' (HCI, 1991: 19). In 1993 the HCI also provided one of the most influential working definitions of integration *à la francaise*:

> Integration consists in fostering the active participation in society as a whole of all women and men who will be living permanently on our soil, by accepting without ulterior motives the persistence of specificities, particularly of a cultural nature, but emphasising similarities and convergences in the equality of rights and duties, in order to ensure the cohesion of our social fabric. (Simon, 2014: 208–9)

Two other factors helped reproduce Republicanism. First, probably more so than in any other European country, France has a tradition of involvement of intellectuals in public and political life, deriving authority from their academic or philosophical backgrounds, but also from political connections and media profiles (Scholten and Timmermans, 2010). Favell (1998: 58) describes them as:

> a new generation of media-wise, self promoting public intellectuals ... keen to tender for direct political influence via all kinds of government-funded research projects, advisorships and commissions ... as well as their fervent national Republicanism.

A second factor was a series of key incidents that triggered broad national political and media attention and contributed to the strength of the Republicanist discourse. One such incident was the so-called headscarf (*foulard*) affair that first erupted in 1989 when the director of a secondary school decided to expel three girls because they wore headscarves (Simon and Pala, 2010: 101–3). The key issue was the principle of *laïcité*, the separation of state and religion. The school was a public space and the school director argued that wearing a headscarf compromised *laïcité*. France's supreme judicial body, the Council of State, concluded that wearing a headscarf was, in itself, not a contradiction of the principle of *laicité*. However, in 1994 a second stage in the *foulard* affair began, when the Minister of Education himself defined the headscarf as a conspicuous or 'ostentatious' sign and thus a breach of *laicité*. The issue also blurred lines between left and right. For instance, the leading Socialist politician Jean Pierre Chevenement stated in an interview with the *Le Monde* newspaper that the 'right to difference' and what he called the 'American model' were a route to 'a Lebanon very simply' (cited in Feldblum, 1999: 140). The then education minister, Lionel Jospin, asked the Council of State for its advice and then, when a case-by-case approach was recommended, followed it. The issue was particularly difficult for the Socialists because their official policy pronouncements rejected the notion of ethnic politics, or as former Prime Minister Rocard put it to a meeting of the executive committee of the Socialist Party, 'the juxtaposition of communities', the creation of geographic and cultural 'ghettos' and 'soft forms of apartheid' (cited in Feldblum, 1999: 142–3). However, again the Council of State ruled that a general prohibition of the headscarf was unconstitutional.

The issue again came to the fore in 2003 when President Chirac established a Commission chaired by Bernard Stasi to examine the implementation of the principle of *laicité* in the Republic. In the same year, two girls at a secondary school refused to remove their headscarves. The Stasi Commission recommended, amongst many other proposals that involved some recognition of diversity (such as in national holidays), to prohibit the wearing of headscarves in public schools (as well as the kippah and the wearing of crosses of a certain size).

By the mid 2000s, the context of the debate on Islam in France had once again become strongly politicised (Bowen, 2007a). As in other European countries, Islam became a focal point for debate about migrant integration. A 2004 law, implementing part of the Stasi recommendations, prohibited the wearing of signs or clothes displaying religious affiliation in public primary, secondary and high schools. The government did not follow-up any of the more (moderate) multiculturalist recommendations of the Stasi committee, such as embracing certain Islamic and Jewish holidays as national holidays. Once again reflecting the philosophical character of French Republicanist discourse, neither the Stasi Commission nor the government turned their attention to deeper socio-economic problems such as discrimination and poverty (Bowen, 2007b: 19). In 2010 another law was added to this line of legislation, prohibiting the wearing of the niqab in any public space, or in any other way concealing one's face in a public space (Villard and Sayegh, 2013: 244). The debate about the headscarf or veil has been seen as a 'mirror of identity' in that it reflects the tension between liberal and national values in France (and other European countries). The veil may be seen by some as an affront to liberal values, but so too is banning the wearing of a veil (Joppke, 2009).

The continued relevance of Republican ideas in political discourse was reinforced during Sarkozy's Presidency (2007–2012) and demonstrates their malleability as this time they were used by a populist right-wing President. In 2011 Sarkozy publicly condemned multiculturalism as a failure (Carvalho, 2014). Although France had never actually adopted a formal multiculturalist policy approach, Sarkozy used multiculturalism as a 'counter-discourse' to underline his firm commitment to Republican values. The effect was to reinforce the nationally focused immigrant policy that had been initiated by Sarkozy back in 2007. One indicator of this was the creation in 2007 of a Ministry of Immigration, Integration, National Identity and Codevelopment. This experiment was brief and ended in 2010 when immigration and integration were returned to the Interior Ministry, where they remained under Sarkozy's successor as President, the Socialist François Hollande.

The national immigrant policy strategy continued under Hollande. The High Council for Integration was disbanded in 2013. Within the Interior Ministry, a powerful directorate has now developed on Immigration, Asylum and Immigrants. This development seems to be spurred by the continued strong presence of the FN which, led by Marine Le Pen, has sought to 'modernise' itself by creating distance between it and the extreme manifestations of racism and anti-Semitism for which her father's leadership was renowned. Speaking of her father in April 2015, Marine Le Pen said 'Jean-Marie Le Pen is in a spiral between a scorched-earth strategy and political suicide … the National Front doesn't want to be held hostage by his coarse provocations' (Gourevitch, 2015). Marine's stance was seen as part of her effort to reposition the party and bolster her chances of getting through to the second round run-off in the 2017 Presidential elections. While this didn't happen at the 2012 Presidential election, Marine Le Pen achieved the FN's best ever result with 18 per cent of the vote. The 2013 municipal elections showed that support had increased further, and in the 2014 elections for the European Parliament the FN even became the largest party of France with almost 25 per cent of the vote. These elections showed a very similar issue connection between anti-immigrant concerns and growing resentment against perceived EU interference in national policy issues.

Support for the FN by those who see immigration as a threat to national identity and social cohesion were further bolstered by the terrorist attack by Islamic extremists on the French satirical weekly *Charlie Hebdo* in January 2015. *Charlie Hebdo* had published satirical cartoons with the image of the prophet Mohammed. The attack elicited shock and horror around the world and was seen as an assault on French Republican values and on freedom of expression. There were huge protest marches in France and all over the world that while ostensibly bringing people together also showed public unease about diversity and Islam. This occurred at the same time as marches by the anti-Islamic Pegida movement in Germany (see Chapter 4). This was followed by terror attacks in November 2015, again by an ISIS-affiliated group, which led to exceptional security measures across France and in Belgium too (the origin country of some of the attackers). France also led calls for tightening of Schengen controls and intensified its anti-ISIS military actions in Syria.

Beyond Republicanism?

Seemingly apart from the philosophical and at times abstract debate about French Republicanism, the complexities can be seen at local level. Favell (1998: 184) identified a decoupling of highbrow Republican rhetoric and practices at local level. Republican ideas and values can be interpreted very differently, or perhaps even challenged particularly in major French cities.

Much of the actual implementation of French immigrant policies occurs at local level. In this context, a national agency with regional offices, *Fonds d'Action Sociale* (FAS), had played a key role. Formally, the policies that were subsidised through the FAS (and implemented by local government agencies and associations) did not target immigrants and ethnic minorities *per se* but particular neighbourhoods as part of what was called the *politique de la ville*. That said, the contracts signed in the context of FAS between the central state and the local authorities mention the immigrant population and integration issues in the selection of neighbourhoods to receive assistance.

A 'mainstreaming' of immigrant policies as part of French urban policies was reinforced after riots in more than 250 cities in France in October and November 2005 (Simon and Pala, 2010: 100). Formally, President Chirac reinforced the Republican line by framing the riots as an ethnic and religious uprising requiring a firm Republican response. This response was to be in line with the already established *politique de la ville*, converting the FAS (which from 2001–2005 had been known as FASILD, or *Fonds d'action sociale pour l'integration et la lute contre les discriminations*), into the *Agence pour la cohesion sociale et l'egalite des chances* (ACSE, Agency for Social Cohesion and Equality of Opportunities) (Simon and Pala, 2010).

These urban policies have been described as the most concrete manifestation of French immigrant policies on the ground (Wihtol de Wenden, 2014). The first component was targeted territorial action. This included the creation of Priority Educational Zones, first established back in 1981, to provide assistance to schools in specific neighbourhoods to combat social exclusion. Wihtol de Wenden (2014: 143) documents the creation of 911 such zones by 2014, covering about 20 per cent of all pupils in France. Since the 1980s, Priority Urban Zones were also created, although they were re-labelled as *zones urbanes sensibles* (ZUS, sensitive urban zones). The FAS (and now ACSE) involve contracts with selected urban areas to promote social cohesion. Measures can include financial assistance and tax incentives for business start-ups. By 2014, Wihtol de Wenden (2014) identified 50 of these ZUS areas covering 4.5 million inhabitants. Escafre-Dublet (2014: 124) argues that estimates of the number of migrant-origin people living in these areas do play an important role in selection of these ZUS. As of 2015, these ZUS will be replaced by *Quartiers Prioritaires* (Priority Neighbourhoods) comprising low-income neighbourhoods.

A second development is anti-discrimination policy. This development was spurred by EU-level developments, but concerns about racism and discrimination were evident during the Socialist government elected in 1997. A report from the *Commission Nationale Consultative des Droits de l'Homme* (or the National Consultative Commission on Human Rights, 2001) showed the persistence of racist attitudes and some constancy in terms of the groups targeted. An October 1998 circular from the Minister of Employment and Solidarity, Martine Aubry, stated that the fight against racial discrimination was to be regarded as an important government prior-ity. This policy emphasis was reflected in the report produced by the *Haut Conseil à l'Integration* entitled *Lutte contre les discriminations* (The Fight against Discrimination), which proposed creation of an anti-discrimination body. A similar view was expressed in a report by a member of the Council of State, Jean Michel Belorgey. In 2005 a new anti-discrimination law established a fully independent body, the *Haute Autorité de Lutte contre les Discriminations et pour l'Egalité* (the High Authority for the Fight Against Discrimination and for Equality, HALDE). In 2011, HALDE was replaced by *Defenseurs de Droits*, or Protectors of Rights.

Third, there are signs that, in contradiction to the supposed 'colour blindness' of Republican ideas, there is some 'ethnicisation' in France. Schain (1999) explains this apparent opening to ethnic-based difference as the result of a gap between official rhetoric and actual practices. French Republicanism, he argues, has been mediated on the ground by the state's interest in controlling and integrating its immigrant population and that this leads to *de facto* multiculturalism. Schain calls this 'the recognition of ethnicity in practice if not in theory' (1999: 199) and an example of the ways that 'the best Jacobin traditions of French governments are tempered by emerging realities' (1999: 214).

3.2 THE FRENCH TABOO ON ETHNIC STATISTICS

A key element of the French Republican tradition is the taboo on the collection of data on ethnicity, race or religion (Bleich, 2003; Amiraux and Simon, 2006). French official statistics have tended not to systematically analyse the immigrant and immigrant-origin population in the kind of ways that would be familiar in Britain and the Netherlands.

Official data differentiates between French nationals and foreigners without French passports. A 1995 report focused on ethnicity and asked questions about ethnic origin and language that had not previously been asked (Tribalat, 1995). In the context of the EU's two anti-discrimination directives of 2000 (see Chapter 7), there have been calls for collection of ethnic statistics, but as Sabbagh and Peer (2008: 2) note there is some resistance amongst researchers, although others argue that the absence of ethnic statistics makes it difficult to monitor indirect discrimination (Simon, 2014). The enduring strength of French Republican ideas was again revealed when, in spite of plans from the French government in 2007 to allow for the gathering of data on ethnicity, the French Constitutional Council overturned this proposal on the grounds that it would be contrary to the principle of equality (Wihtol de Wenden, 2014: 141). In 2010, a report on inequality and discrimination did finally allow for the collection of data on migrant origin and ethnic discrimination, but only for research purposes (ibid.).

European integration

A powerful national discourse centred on Republican ideas and their interpretation has persisted, but has also been challenged by developments at both local and supranational levels. Within the EU, France has simultaneously shaped EU policies, but has also been affected by EU free movement and its common migration and asylum policy.

Externalising controls

France was a founding EU member state and a founding signatory in 1985 of the Schengen agreement that sought swifter movement towards a frontier-free Europe with compensating internal security measures including immigration and asylum (see Chapter 7). EU-level co-operation has also provided the French state with various opportunities for adopting a restrictive immigration policy. It has already been suggested that the EU can provide new opportunities for its member states to pursue restrictive policies. During the earlier stages of co-operation in the 1980s and 1990s a further advantage of EU co-operation was that it was shielded from national-level legislative or judicial scrutiny.

It has been argued that French support for common European responses to immigration and asylum developed in the early 1980s, when immigration and asylum were not salient political issues, but at a time when the French state had begun to encounter domestic legal and political constraints on its control capacity (Guiraudon, 2000). This accords with Hollifield's (2000b) view that such a preference is an attempt to externalise immigration controls and escape the unwelcome interventions of national courts (Chapter 7 explains why this might not be such an effective strategy in the contemporary EU). From this perspective, the changes made by Pasqua in 1993 to French asylum laws can be seen as an attempt to avoid domestic legal and political constraints.

Could co-operation at European level provide a new venue for the development of restrictive policies where legal and parliamentary constraints would be minimal? James Hollifield (2000b) has argued that French governments have sought to externalise controls via bilateral and multilateral agreements such as the EU and the Schengen arrangements where legal and political constraints are less onerous. Indeed, in response to the second Pasqua Law of 1993, the Council of State warned that measures on family reunification and asylum were likely to be unconstitutional. In August 1993 the highest constitutional authority, the Constitutional Council, deemed the one-year exclusion from French territory for people who had been deported, restrictions on family reunification, marriage restrictions, and EU asylum co-operation to be unconstitutional. Pasqua was not prepared to accept 'government by judges' and pushed the issue to a constitutional amendment passed by a specially convened joint session of the National Assembly and Senate held at Versailles in November 1993.

Participation in EU structures helped the French government to restrict the ability of 'unwanted immigrants', such as asylum seekers, to enter French territory. The Constitutional Council's concerns arose because the French constitution guarantees that people who are persecuted because of their actions in favour of freedom have the right to asylum on the territory of the French Republic. This created a territorial right to asylum independent of the granting of refugee status (Wihtol de Wenden, 1994: 87). The number of asylum requests made in France between the mid-1970s and mid-1980s had risen with more asylum seekers coming from countries such as Vietnam, Turkey and Sri Lanka. The externalisation of controls through European integration was part of the response. The French government also instigated the 2008 EU Pact on Immigration and Asylum that sought to strengthen EU action to regulate entry by Third Country Nationals (TCNs) through reinforced co-operation between members plus joint action with non-member states. The Pact's timing was important because Sarkozy became President in 2007 and identified immigration as a priority. The Pact contained broad regulations regarding labour migration, asylum, irregular migration, return migration and border control. The various measures also legitimated the French approach to constraining so-called immigration *subie* (endured), particularly family migration and the use of integration contracts. The Pact stated that the regulation of family migration could involve reception policies and take into account capacity to integrate.

Carrera and Guild (2008) saw the Pact as an attempt to frustrate the 'Community Method' (meaning more powers for EU institutions), but can also be seen as a good example of how the French government sought to 'upload' their policy preferences to EU level and to legitimate their national approach. Yet, despite these efforts, EU legislation in the field of immigration has also constrained national policy discretion in restricting the 'immigration *subie*' (Chapter 7 shows that decisions of the CJEU have constrained the French state's ability to deport migrants). More generally, Simon (2014: 206) observes a more profound effect of the EU on France's control capacity because he claims that 'only 5 per cent of annual inflows could be controlled at the government's discretion'. For instance, the EU's 2003 directive on family reunification specifies conditions under which family migrants are be admitted while returns and expulsion are similarly bound by the EU's Return directive (2008).

EU citizenship and anti-discrimination policies

Debates about EU citizenship and European identity were very much at the margins of discussion of French nationality already in the late 1980s and early 1990s. The Commission of Experts, convened to consider French nationality law in the wake of the failed 1986 legislation, was asked (in a rather vague way by the Prime Minister) to bear in mind '1992', the year of intended completion of the European single market. The head of the Commission, Marceau Long, called for a form of European citizenship that would disentangle nationality and citizenship although this was long before EU citizenship was created by the Maastricht Treaty, which itself did no such thing. Another member of the Commission, the sociologist Alain Touraine, argued that European integration meant that French national identity was less clear than in the past. The Commission of Experts was understandably unsure about the meaning and extent of a form of European citizenship that had still to be agreed by EU member states.

It is difficult to argue that something that did not exist at the time (EU citizenship) drove debates in France before 1993. Feldblum (1999: 157–8) argues that there was a framing effect in that European citizenship stimulated Republicans of both the left and right to 're-envision' French citizenship as part of a broader defence of national identity. Moreover, the transposition of a derived right of EU citizenship, that is, derived from prior possession of national citizenship onto diverse criteria for allocation of nationality in member states, was bound to create some anomalies. Weil (1994: 184) argued that EU citizenship ran the risk 'of accentuating the marginalisation of non-EU residents that began with the crisis in France's "Republican" institutions and the intensely political nature of the debate over immigration'. Along with the German and British governments, the French government opposed the extension of EU citizenship to legally resident TCNs. In a statement issued after the Tampere summit meeting of EU heads of government in October 1999 the French, German and UK governments noted that TCNs 'residing legally and long term were entitled to be fully integrated' and 'as soon as good integration has been achieved and confirmed, it is natural and desirable that the foreigners defined ... should acquire the nationality of their state of residence' (Statewatch, September–October 1999).

A key effect of EU integration on the French case involves the development of anti-discrimination policies, which had been 'pushed' at the EU level in particular by the UK and Dutch governments that already had extensive anti-discrimination frameworks (and, as noted earlier, counted their 'ethnic minority' populations). The French government has implemented (as it is required to do) the June and November 2000 EU Directives based on Article 13 of the Amsterdam treaty dealing with direct and indirect discrimination on grounds including race, ethnicity and religion. Chapter 7 shows how these EU laws seek to prohibit direct or indirect discrimination on grounds of race, ethnicity and religion in the workplace and in provision of public services such as housing and education. When transposing the legislation into national law the French government added three other motives for discrimination to the list: physical appearance, last name and sexual orientation. The significant point is that France accepted EU legislation that brought British and Dutch practices and ideas concerning 'ethnic minorities' into its national legislation. France did, however, secure a derogation from the EU legislation that meant that when monitoring effectiveness of the legislation it was not required to gather data on ethnic origin. The French authorities would use other methods, although it was not clear what these would involve.

The EU laws agreed in June 2000 provide a more prescriptive model for the evolution of debates about anti-discrimination in France and supplement the vague framing effects of the 1980s and 1990s. European integration could then affect domestic structures in France where the 'fit', in terms of ideas and practices, is not so strong compared to countries like the UK and Netherlands where anti-discrimination laws are well entrenched.

Intra-EU mobility and the Roma

A key issue for France and other EU member states has been migration from new EU member states in Central and Eastern Europe using EU free movement rights. There has been growth in movement from Central and East European countries, including members of the Roma minority. As it was entitled to do, France did impose transitional controls on people from the A8 countries that joined the EU in May 2004 (lifted in 2007) and on A2 countries (Bulgaria and Romania) that joined in 2007 (lifted on 1 January 2014).

Free movement led to a debate that had a particular focus on effects on the labour market and wages. Workers from the new EU member states were prepared to work for lower wages than French workers with the fear that natives would be pushed out of the labour market. The French government has advocated stronger EU level measures to counter what has been called 'social dumping' and has, along with the Dutch and German governments, advocated an EU level minimum-wage.

Related to the issue of intra-EU mobility, there was controversy in France about the presence of Roma. Roma (or Romani, sometimes also called 'gypsies') refer to a roaming people that have been long established in Europe, with a distinct language and culture. Most Roma in Europe reside in (or originate from) Romania, Bulgaria, Slovakia, Serbia or Turkey (see Chapter 9 on Central and Eastern Europe for further discussion). Other European countries, particularly Spain and France (with a concentration in the South of the country) have sizeable Roma populations too. Around 400,000 Roma are estimated to live in France linked more recently to border free travel in the EU. Roma have long encountered discrimination and hostility.

Most Roma in Europe are citizens of an EU member state, and thus EU citizens. Since the late 2000s, the French governments pursued an active policy of repatriation of Roma. In 2008 and 2009 alone around 20,000 Roma people with origins in Bulgaria and Romania were repatriated. Although these Roma held EU citizenship, because of the transitional arrangements (until January 2014) they were not allowed to stay in France for a longer period if they did not have a valid work permit.

The situation escalated in July 2010 when a Roma man who had driven into a police checkpoint was shot and killed by the police, leading to demonstrations and some rioting, including in a suburb of Grenoble. President Sarkozy responded to these events by denouncing the demonstrations, demanding that nationality should be revoked of all those who retaliated against the police (if they had French citizenship), and condemning the situation where over 500 irregular camp sites for Roma had been established in France. Sarkozy announced that more than a third of all Roma camps in France would be gone in three months. Furthermore, he intensified the policy of repatriating Roma with (primarily) Romanian and Bulgarian citizenship.

The situation led to strong international responses led by the EU Justice Commissioner Viviane Reding who described the escalation as a 'disgrace' and even compared the situation to the persecution of minorities during the Second World War. This led to an unprecedented diplomatic controversy between the European Commission and the French government. Whereas the Commission saw the French expulsions as a blatant infringement of EU principles of free movement and anti-discrimination, the French government considered it legitimate under the terms of EU free movement law to expel EU citizens that either did not have a valid permit for either work or study (after a three month period) or were considered a threat to public security. Repatriation to Bulgaria and Romania of Roma people without valid work permits continued until the end of 2013, i.e. after Hollande came to power in 2012. Since the end of the transitional arrangements in 2014 Bulgarian and Romanian people can remain on French territory without a valid work permit.

Conclusion

The questions of convergence, divergence and the development of a European politics of migration have had robust tests in the opening two chapters. Both Britain and France have developed distinct approaches to post-war migration. These distinct approaches are also accompanied by mutual incomprehension and suspicion that widens the conceptual gulf between the two countries. Yet, in both France and the UK there are some similarities at the inter-state or horizontal level; post-war labour migration to fill labour market gaps with post-colonial effects that influenced responses to immigration and its sequels. Even so, strong elements of diversity in the French approach are linked to French history and to specific political–institutional channelling effects. At the same time, both cases also show how organisational contexts in both countries, and changes in these contexts, have important effects on the understanding of international migration and migrants.

Despite the particularities, in both the UK and France the understandings of immigration as a problem were linked to other more deep-seated social, political and economic changes. These changes and feelings of insecurity among some sections of the French electorate provided fertile soil for Jean-Marie and then Marine Le Pen's extreme right FN. Marine Le Pen's strong presence in the French national political arena has propelled immigration, national identity and security to the top of the French political agenda and re-emphasised the familiar extreme right-wing linkage between security/insecurity and immigration.

The social, economic and political changes that have affected France and that contextualised the domestic politics of migration and immigration have a supranational dimension too. This is not to make the extravagant claim that supra- or post-national developments have driven the French approach. At the risk of tautology, debates about immigration in France remain very French. These national and sub-national particularities need to be accounted for because they drive much of the explanation. But when some of the rhetoric is stripped away there are similarities in the response to the objectively similar phenomena associated with international migration that suggest some horizontal convergence associated with political processes in liberal states and some vertical impact from the EU on immigration and immigrant policies that together give us some idea of the parameters of a European politics of migration and immigration rather than a series of distinct national cases.

One trend that has become very manifest in this discussion of the French case – but may in fact apply to many other European countries – is the discrepancy between national policy discourse on the one hand and European and local policy realities on the other. On the national level, the French case stands out with its powerful Republican discourse, often supported by philosophical and historical arguments connecting migration and integration to national identity. Yet, as this chapter has shown, EU developments have limited the scope for national policy action to a much greater extent than is suggested by national debates. At local level too, immigrant policies in France are more flexible in their interpretation of Republican ideas, exhibiting some openness to diversity and extending the gap between policy rhetoric and policy practice that typifies contemporary French immigration politics.

4

Germany: A Country of Immigration After All

Introduction

By the end of 2015, around 15 million of Germany's total population of 80 million had an immigration background either as immigrants themselves or with at least one parent who was an immigrant. By the end of the same year, around 1 million asylum seekers and refugees had entered Germany. Due to its leadership role in the EU and relatively welcoming approach to refugee and asylum migration, Germany found itself both literally and metaphorically at the heart of Europe, but by autumn 2015 was backing away from its open approach to refugees given both the large numbers plus evidence of a political backlash.

Germany was, for many years, resistant to the idea that it actually was a country of immigration (*Deutschland ist kein Einwanderungsland* or 'Germany is not an immigration country' was an official mantra). Until the 1990s, this combined with an ethno-cultural understanding of German nationality and citizenship led to Germany being seen as an exceptional case with denial of its immigration status and a strong ethno-cultural model that made it extremely difficult for non-German immigrants to acquire German citizenship.

Until the early 2000s, Germany clung to the 'counterfactual ideology' of not being a country of immigration (Faist, 1994). Germany's recognition in the 2000s that it was after all a country of immigration via introduction of its first immigration law in 2005 did not mean that it has embraced with enthusiasm immigration and the resultant diversity. True, there are instances of diversity being welcomed and Chancellor Merkel made a point of standing with Germany's Muslim population to denounce the anti-Islamic PEGIDA movement (see below), but Germany can still display ambivalence about integration (Triadafilopoulos, 2012). While Merkel rejected PEGIDA's extremism, in 2010 she had stated that multiculturalism had 'utterly failed' (*Der Spiegel*, 2010). Even in its response to the refugee crisis, there was some ambivalence. Merkel's stance created tensions within her governing coalition as her Bavarian allies in the Christian Social Union criticised her position.

This chapter accounts for important changes in German immigration and migrant policies by doing three things. First, it identifies the drivers of policy and politics and explains why the counterfactual ideology of not being an immigration country became less meaningful in a reunited Germany after 1990. Second, it examines how Germany has managed immigrant integration. Third, the impact of European integration is assessed, in order to demonstrate both the use by German governments of the EU as an institutional venue for pursuing domestic policy objectives while also showing the EU's capacity to feed back into German debates as was the case with the response to the refugee crisis.

Immigration policy

Deutschland ist kein Einwanderungsland was officially adopted as an idea in the 1977 naturalisation regulations, by which time there were already 4 million foreign-born people resident in Germany. For Brubaker (1992: 174) the 'not a country of immigration' statement was neither a social nor demographic fact because patently the reverse was true. Rather it was 'a political–cultural norm' and an element of national self-understanding and, as such, was a normative assertion 'conditional on the context of *de facto* immigration because otherwise there would be no point raising it' (Joppke, 1999: 65). The underlying reasons for this were linked to pre-unification West German history as a provisional state and incomplete nation, geared to the recovery of national unity, which was achieved after reunification with East Germany in 1990.

Table 4.1 provides an overview of net migration to Germany between 1991 and 2014 and captures fluctuations in numbers by showing the peak that occurred in the early 1990s and again in the 2010s. These peaks are linked to a significant degree to large flows of asylum seekers and refugees, which hit high levels in the 1990s and again in the 2010s due to flows from Kosovo, ex-Yugoslavia and the effects of instability in North Africa and the Middle East. Also, other forms of migration have been very important in the German case, such as that by ethnic Germans (*Aussiedler*) in the 1990s and movement by people from other EU member states since the 2000s.

Table 4.1 Immigration to Germany (net immigration foreign citizens, repatriates and asylum seekers), 1991–2014

	Asylum seekers	German repatriates (*Assiedler*)	Net immigration foreign citizens
1991	256,112	221,995	427,805
1992	438,191	230,565	596,394
1993	322,599	217,531	279,188
1994	127,21	218,617	148,241
1995	127,937	211,601	225,26
1996	116,367	172,182	148,89
1997	104,353	128,415	−21,768
1998	98,644	97,331	−33,455
1999	95,113	95,543	118,235
2000	78,564	85,698	86,455
2001	88,287	86,637	188,272
2002	71,127	78,576	152,769
2003	50,563	61,725	102,696
2004	35,607	49,815	55,217
2005	28,914	30,779	95,717
2006	21,029	7,113	74,693
2007	19,164	3,823	99,003
2008	22,085	3,951	10,685
2009	27,649	2,957	27,506
2010	41,332	2,054	153,925
2011	45,741	1,829	302,858
2012	64,539	1,538	387,149
2013	109,58	2,16	450,464
2014	173,072	4,215	576,924

Source: German Statistics Office (www.destatis.de/EN/FactsFigures/SocietyState/Population/ Migration/Tables/MigrationTotal.html)

Immigration to a 'non-immigration country'

Following reunification in 1989, the Federal Republic of Germany reached the end of what Thränhardt (1999) called a provisional period after the creation of East and West Germany in 1949. During this time unique impediments were placed on the capacity of West Germany to regulate international migration. The legacy of migration by guestworkers, relatively liberal asylum provisions and a right to return for ethnic Germans (*Aussiedler*), meant that the newly reunified Germany was the European country that was most open to international migration in the 1990s.

4.1 THE FOUR MAIN SOURCES OF POST-WAR MIGRATION TO GERMANY

Four sources of post-Second World War migration to Germany can be distinguished:

1   *Aussiedler* (ethnic German) migration. Between 1945 and 1955 migration to West Germany by ethnic Germans fleeing persecution in Soviet bloc countries amounted to around 12 million people. Article 116 of the 1949 Basic Law gave automatic German citizenship to people possessing 'German nationality or who, as a refugee, or as an expellee of German descent, or as their spouse or descendant has found residence in the territory of the German Reich in its borders of 31 December 1937'. The *Aussiedler* were seen as part of the German 'community of fate' (*Schicksalsgemeinschaft*) even if they were geographically distant. By 1950, refugees and expellees accounted for 16 per cent of West Germany's population.
2   Guestworkers. Recruitment of guestworker labour migrants was requested first by agriculture and then by industry. Germany signed recruitment agreements with various countries: Italy (1955), Spain and Greece (1960), Turkey (1961). The construction of the Berlin Wall in August 1961 ended movement from East Germany and placed greater reliance on foreign labour to fuel economic growth. Additional recruitment agreements were signed with Portugal (1964), Tunisia (1965) and Morocco (1963 and 1966). The number of guestworkers in Germany peaked at 1.3 million in 1966, but economic recession in 1966–7 appeared to validate the expectation of return migration by the 'guests' because between 1966 and 1967 the number of guestworkers fell from 1.3 million to 0.9 million. Numbers picked up as the economy recovered between 1967 and 1973, but the ethnic composition of the guestworker population changed. There were fewer Italians and Yugoslavs and more Turks. At the beginning of the 1970s, 13 per cent of the foreign population were Turks, which rose to 33 per cent by 1980 (Esser and Korte, 1985: 172).
3   The family members of guestworkers. The so-called *Anwerbestopp* (immigration-stop) of 1973 did not lead to the end of immigration and the foreign population actually increased. As we discuss below, decisions by the courts protected the right to family migration.
4   Asylum seekers, whose rights were protected by the comparatively liberal provisions of Article 16 of the German constitution that recognised the right of asylum applicants to make a claim rather than the obligation of the state to consider a claim. The German government backtracked from this commitment during the 1990s; the symbolic right to asylum in Article 16 remained, but the ability to exercise the right by actually entering German state territory was reduced.

Active recruitment of 'guestworkers' ended with the economic crisis of the early 1970s, but relatively large-scale immigration to West Germany continued after this immigration stop as well. Between 1955 and 1973 economic interests and labour market pressures underpinned the policy of expansiveness. After 1973 economic conditions did not favour the large-scale recruitment of migrant workers.

There was some fluctuation in business attitudes to immigration. In the 2000s, economic interests and labour market pressures underpinned an expansiveness to high skilled migration.

Why was there continued openness to immigration after the *Anwerbestopp*? Perhaps a sense of moral obligation to the guestworkers and their families could be an explanation? In 1982, Interior Minister Gerhard Baum stated that: 'We have brought them to this country since 1955 ... Even if they are without jobs we have obligations towards them'. But how could this vague commitment be given legal or political effect? In answer to this question, Joppke (1999: 69–70) identifies the role of law and the courts utilising two of West Germany's basic constitutional principles: the subordination of state power to the rights of the individual and the granting of the rights enshrined in the Basic Law to all irrespective of their nationality. The effect, Joppke (1999) argues, was that the FRG's sovereignty was 'self-limited'. This argument has more general implications because it runs counter to 'post-national' claims about the power of international legal standards – externally constrained sovereignty – by contending that it was in fact domestic laws that self-limited states. In practical terms, this meant that resident foreigners had equal protection of the law and were able to access social rights. These rights increased with the duration of their residence because of the 'legal fate of dependency': long-term resident foreigners had nowhere else to go and thus should be formally treated in the same way as other Germans.

During the period of socialist rule, East Germany also recruited foreign workers, but also never defined itself as an immigration country. Foreign policy interests determined the East's recruitment of mainly male contract workers aged between 18 and 35 from other socialist states such as Poland, Hungary, Angola, Mozambique, North Korea and Vietnam. By 1989 there were 190,000 foreign workers in East Germany (1.2 per cent of the total population). There were no special integration measures because, according to Marxist–Leninist ideology, nationalism divided the working class while racism and xenophobia did not officially exist (Ireland, 1997). This was convenient because it allowed contract workers to be housed in military style barracks on the edges of towns and cities. The collapse of East Germany in 1989 contributed to fears of large-scale East–West migration, which reinforced restrictive policies. The possibility of large-scale migration affected the reunification debate with the attitude of East Germans summed up by the phrase *Kommt die Deutschmark, bleiben wir; kommt Sie nicht, geh'n wir zu Ihr!* (if the Deutschmark comes we stay; if not, then we leave for it!).

Restricting immigration in a reunified Germany

The end of the Cold War and the reunification of East and West Germany in 1990 transformed the immigration policy context (Green, 2004). Before reunification, the idea of an 'incomplete nation' had triggered a very open immigration regime to German repatriates or *Aussiedler* in particular (in contrast to a more restrictive approach to other migrant categories). Their 'right to return' was exercised by hundreds of thousands of *Aussiedler* in what Thränhardt (1999: 36) called 'the largest single state organised migration flow in the world'. Brubaker (1992: 171) notes that 'what was intended as a transitional legal provision [when the FRG was created in 1949], became something quite different: an open door to immigration and automatic citizenship for ethnic German immigrants from Eastern Europe and the Soviet Union'. Until the late 1980s this movement was uncontroversial because it vindicated West Germany's superiority. The presence of ethnic Germans did, however, become controversial as their numbers increased and the costs of special measures became more apparent.

In the early 1990s, several incremental steps were taken to limit immigration by *Aussiedler*. The first step was to externalise controls. The 1990 Ethnic German Reception Law stipulated that an application to move to Germany had to be made from the country of origin. Further limits were placed in 1992 when quotas were placed on ethnic German immigration by a law that limited the right to claim *Aussiedler* status to people born before 1 September 1993. *Aussiedler* arriving after 1992 were redefined as *Spätaussiedler* (late resettlers). From 1996, local authorities were given the right to disperse *Spätaussiedler* similar to the ways in which asylum seekers were dispersed. These measures gave the state authorities increased powers to monitor, observe and regulate the lives of the *Aussiedler*, which placed them in a similar position to other immigrants (Bommes, 2000). The German government thus used external (application processes in countries of origin) and internal (dispersal and welfare state exclusion) measures to reassert its ability to regulate this form of migration (Bommes, 2000). The number of *Aussiedler* decreased due not only to stronger controls, but also because most of those who wanted to move to Germany had already done so.

The end of the Cold War also led to a big increase in asylum-seeking migration. Between 1990 and 1994 just over 1.2 million people made an application for asylum in Germany. Thomas Faist (1994) argued that asylum actually served as a symbolic concern in German politics that shielded discussion of more fundamental issues such as immigration policy, social rights and nationality law. Article 16 of the 1949 Basic Law enshrined the right of the politically persecuted to enjoy the right to asylum. This recognised the right of the asylum seeker to make an application rather than – as in other European countries – the responsibility of the state to consider a claim. The result was that asylum seekers in Germany were empowered by these provisions while the authority of the state to regulate access to the territory was undermined. In addition, Article 19 of the Basic Law offered the scope for lengthy and exhaustive legal redress. Even if an application was rejected there was scope for a follow-up application that could spin the process out for eight years or more, after which time deportation would probably be ruled out for humanitarian reasons.

The problem, as seen by the German government and as widely discussed in public debate, was that Article 16 constrained the state's capacity to regulate access to its territory; another instance of what Joppke described as 'self-limited sovereignty'. The reasons for this relatively liberal approach lay in West Germany's special obligations after the Second World War. This had resulted in relatively high numbers of asylum migrants when compared to other EU states, reaching a first peak in 1992 of over 438,000 asylum applicants (see Table 4.1). By the 1980s and 1990s West Germany was trying to retreat from the asylum implications of these obligations in debates about immigration, which although tending not to be overtly nationalistic, were certainly more state-centred. As Chapter 7 shows, European co-operation on asylum during the 1990s was intended to strengthen rather than weaken German capacity to regulate access to its territory through measures such as the recognition of 'safe third countries', 'safe countries of origin' and fast-track procedures for 'manifestly unfounded applications'. The construction of a Central and East European 'buffer zone' around the EU and the forging by the German government of a web of bilateral ties with its eastern neighbours was a key element of the reassertion of control by the German government.

In the 1990s German reasserted its ability to control asylum-seeking migration even in the face of ostensibly powerful international human rights standards. Debates about Article 16 of the constitution were the key as was the representation of asylum seekers as 'bogus'. This combined with pressure from the German regions (the Länder) for change because they picked up the costs of accommodating asylum seekers. Finally, there were worrying signs of growth in support for extreme right-wing parties such as the NDP and the Republikaner with racist attacks (such as on a hostel accommodating asylum seekers in Rostock) contributing to pressure for a more restricted right to asylum and for Germany to retreat from its 'special obligations'. The EU provided a route. The amendment made to Article 16 by the so-called 'Asylum Compromise' of 1993 brought German law and practices into line with other EU member states and with the EU's Dublin Convention agreed by those states in 1990 (see also Chapter 7).

4.2 ASSERTING CONTROL OVER ASYLUM-SEEKING MIGRATION IN THE 1990S

In the 1990s Germany retreated from its 'special obligation to asylum seekers' in the face of large increases in the numbers of applicants and public opposition to their presence in Germany. The 1993 'Asylum Compromise' did not supersede the liberal provisions of Article 16 of the German constitution but used co-operation within the EU and bilateral agreements with non-EU member states in Central and Eastern Europe to reassert control.

> The 1993 legislation provided for fast track applications, the definition of 'safe third countries' to which applicants could be returned and fast-track adjudication procedures in extra-territorial space inside airports.
>
> The reassertion of control was also facilitated by stabilisation in the Balkans in the mid-1990s that eased the flow of asylum seekers.

A country of immigration after all

Until the 2000s Germany had neither an official approach to the regulation of immigration nor immigrant integration yet by 2015 had developed a relatively open and liberal approach to skilled migration. The origins of this shift can be traced to the formation of a Social Democrat and Green Coalition government after the 1998 federal elections that sought to modernise German's immigration and citizenship policies (Klusmeyer and Papademetriou, 2009).

In comparative terms, the changes introduced by Germany in the 2000s were not exceptional as other countries also sought to recruit high skilled migration. The issues were, however, highly charged and subject to at times intense political debate. While agreement on recruitment of high skilled migrants has occurred, there are still differences between the mainstream parties of the centre right and centre left on integration. Importantly, however, debate about immigration has been largely confined to mainstream parties as Germany has not experienced the rise of populist or radical right parties as has been seen in France, the Netherlands and the UK. For obvious historical reasons linked to the experience of Nazism there is sensitivity to extremist right-wing parties and a five per cent electoral threshold for representation in elected institutions has effectively excluded smaller and extremist parties.

The debate about immigration has also been shaped by debates about modernisation of the German economy and its international competitiveness as well as other factors such as the effects of demographic change because Germany is projected to have a declining and ageing population. In the early 2000s, the CDU/CSU argued that priority needed to be given to German workers, particularly in times of high unemployment.

In 2000, the SPD/Green coalition launched the so-called 'Green Card' initiative to attract specific forms of high skilled migration, particularly in the IT sector where 75,000 vacancies had been identified (Martin, 2014: 234). The idea was that the German government would issue 'Green Cards' to 20,000 IT specialists giving them five-year work visas. The proposals were portrayed as an attempt to attract IT workers from India to Germany, and were criticised by the CDU/CSU who argued that German children should be trained rather than foreign workers recruited, particularly when unemployment in Germany was high. The CDU/CSU captured this argument in the slogan *'Kinder statt Inder'* (children instead of Indians). The scheme was implemented in 2000 and extended in 2004 (Cerna, 2009), although it experienced difficulty in recruiting Indian migrant workers because of ambivalent signals from Germany about whether Indian IT workers were really welcome, whereas there was less doubt for those moving to countries such as the USA and Canada (Meijering and van Hoven, 2003). The terminology was also confusing. While called a Green Card the German scheme bore little relation to the US Green Card, which offers permanent residence. Instead, the German Green Card scheme 'erected higher hurdles to employers [than its US equivalent the H-1B visa] and did not lay out an easy transition from Green Card to permanent resident status' (Martin, 2014: 235). As Martin (ibid.) goes on to note, perhaps the most significant thing about the German Green Card was that it helped to break the 'not an immigration country' mantra.

Significantly, the SPD/Green government piloted an ambitious liberalisation of the German labour market derived from concerns about inflexibilities and persistent long-term unemployment. The so-called Hartz reforms were controversial because they limited access to welfare benefits for the unemployed to between 6 and 18 months, relaxed job protection laws and reduced taxes on lower paid and part-time jobs (Jacobi and Kluve, 2006). These labour market reforms have also influenced immigrant integration policies with a greater emphasis in the 'framing' of policy on adaptation to the needs of the labour market meaning a focus on education and training coupled with concern about persistent long-term unemployment among some sections of the immigrant origin population, such as people of Turkish origin.

A battle of ideas broke out in the early 2000s about the shape of future immigration policy. In summer 2000, the SPD/Green government established an Independent Commission on Immigration led by a CDU politician and former Bundestag President, Rita Süssmuth. The Süssmuth Commission's report began by stating that Germany needed immigrants and needed to successfully integrate them (Independent Commission on Migration, 2001). It then argued that immigration was key to the German economy's competiveness, especially in terms of high skilled migration and that Germany needed to accept that it was a country of immigration if it were to be able to integrate migrants into Germany society (Green, 2007; Schneider and Scholten, 2015).

As we discuss more fully below, the Süssmuth Commission also looked to the approach developed in the Netherlands in the late 1990s (see Chapter 5) to argue that immigrants should learn German while 'integration contracts' would offer a quicker path to residence or work permits for foreigners who passed a German language test with the other side of the coin being penalties such as delayed family reunification for immigrants that did not learn German. The Commission also proposed that more German language courses be offered to resident foreigners, with funding doubled to DM615 million annually to teach 220,000 people each year.

On 3 August 2001, Interior Minister, Otto Schilly, proposed legislation to give Germany its first ever regulated immigration system. Schilly also made the symbolically important declaration that 'Germany is an immigration country' and linked Germany's labour market needs with 'competition among the industrialised countries for the best minds. That's why we have to direct our immigration law more strongly toward our own economic interests' (*Migration News*, 2001b). Here we see a reiteration of the importance of linking immigration and immigrant policy to the wider setting provided by labour market and welfare state reform. Schilly's proposals on immigration were a substantial re-orientation of policy that necessarily meant recognition that Germany was an immigration country, that immigrant workers would be needed to fill labour market gaps, and that the integration of these immigrants was an issue that governments at federal and sub-national levels needed to address.

Schilly's immigration law was opposed by the CDU/CSU, which offered a very different reading of the costs and benefits of immigration and, at that time, opposed the idea of active immigration policies not least because unemployment stood at 4 million. The CDU/CSU was also more concerned about the impact of immigration on Germany's 'guiding' national culture (*Leitkultur*) (see also the section on immigrant policy, below). This reflected a broader trend of growing public discontent with immigration and multiculturalism that had been evident in the 1990s and was further heightened by events such as the 9/11 attacks on the US. An opinion poll in 2000 found that 66 per cent of respondents thought that 'immigration was too high', while 75 per cent wanted to restrict the maximum stay of refugees to nine months (Martin, 2014: 237).

The new immigration law secured approval in the lower chamber of the German Parliament, but because of a CDU/CSU challenge was nullified in December 2002 by the Constitutional Court as it had not secured a valid majority in the Parliament's upper chamber, the Bundesrat. The dispute was highly technical and related to whether or not votes cast by representatives from Brandenburg were valid. The Constitutional Court ruled that they were not and on this basis the law fell. The law was then re-presented and underwent a gruelling 18 month passage through Parliament with the result being final legislation agreed in 2004 and introduced in 2005 that changed in content and tone from one initially designed to open Germany to new immigration to a law that stated its main purpose as being to control the influx of foreigners into the Federal Republic (Green, 2007).

The new law created a Federal Office for Migration and Refugees (BAMF) that became the co-ordinating agency for all migration (and, increasingly, integration) measures and instigated a more open approach for highly qualified migrant workers, foreign students that had graduated from German universities and those willing to make major investments (at least €250,000). The immigration regime was softened in other areas too, such as recognising persecution by non-state actors and gender specific persecution as grounds for asylum admission and enabling the *Länder* to decide on special rulings based on a hardship clause for individual cases (often irregular migrants) (Klusmeyer and Papademetriou, 2009). In accordance with the 2003 EU directive on the rights of EU citizens that were long-term residents, residency permit requirements for EU citizens were also removed.

The 2005 immigration law with its focus on the highly skilled reflected wider developments in the German economy and welfare state. It did not represent a wider immigration strategy as its focus was on highly skilled migration to which an open approach was adopted. As Martin (2014: 238) notes there were no limits on immigrant visas for people under the age of 45 that would invest at least €250,000 and create five jobs, on scientists and professionals earning at least €66,000 a year and foreign students graduating from German universities who could stay on for a year post-graduation to look for work (Martin, 2014). Green (2013) observes that the new Immigration Law did not appear to have been effective in terms of attracting high levels of high skilled migrants because of high salary or investment thresholds. As a consequence, further measures were adopted to promote high skilled migration shaped also by EU developments such as the so-called Blue Card directive covering highly qualified migrants (see Chapter 7). In 2012, legislation facilitated the recognition of qualifications obtained abroad, which previously had proven an obstacle for labour migrants.

Furthermore, in line with approaches in other European countries, there were attempts to restrict family migration through specific 'integration requirements' as a condition for admission (Michalowski, 2010). The development of these pre- and post-entry integration requirements was inspired by Dutch developments and reflected the broader Europe-wide trend of linking admissions to integration as was also seen in our analysis of Britain and France in Chapters 2 and 3 (see also Scholten et al., 2012). This can be seen as a form of 'horizontal' convergence between European countries that share ideas with each other. These changes were not a direct result of the EU (vertical convergence) but the EU did play a small part in these changes because it created a venue for member states to meet, discuss and share ideas about immigration policy. There were also specific EU measures such as the 2003 directive on family reunification that, in its final form, was strongly influenced by German concern to stress the importance of countries being able to specify integration measures for family members (see Chapter 7).

Pre-entry tests for migrants before they move to Germany are followed by post-entry tests, or so-called 'integration courses' (*Integrationskurse*) after admission that require 900 hours of language training (rising to up to 1,200 hours in specific cases) plus 60 hours of civic education. In addition, since 2007, there has also been a citizenship test for migrants who want to become German citizens. The implementation of these three successive tests (pre-entry, post-entry and citizenship) demonstrates the link between admissions and integration. These measures are not imposed solely to facilitate the integration of migrants once they are in Germany, but also to shape migration to Germany in the first place.

The refugee crisis

By the 2010s, Germany again became a key destination for asylum seekers, and figures were at their highest since the 1990s with estimates of one million asylum seekers and refugees entering Germany during 2015. Germany was, again, Europe's top destination for asylum seekers and refugees.

The German government and Chancellor Angela Merkel took a leading role in the EU in ways that reverberated across the Union but also sent shockwaves through the German political system. Germany effectively overturned the EU's Dublin system by announcing that Syrian asylum applicants could make a claim in Germany irrespective of where they entered the EU. This played a key role in motivating the journeys for hundreds of thousands of men, women and children as they crossed Europe's borders towards Germany. Merkel stated that Germany welcomed refugees and could 'manage the job' even though the task at hand would be bigger than had been the response to refugee flows from former Yugoslavia at the beginning of the 1990s and potentially more expensive than the costs of the financial and economic crisis post-2008. The Slovakian and Hungarian governments criticised Merkel for what they saw as her encouragement of refugee migration across their borders and countries towards Germany. Both the Social Democrats (SPD) and CSU criticised Merkel for having made a huge mistake in being so open and, in their view, inviting large-scale refugee migration. There were also very real and pressing concerns for local authorities that the arrival of large numbers of asylum applicants, who would then be dispersed across the country, would put significant strain on local resources such as housing, education and health care. Merkel had to promise a major multi-year investment to assist local governments. By September 2015, Germany had to some extent retreated from its initial position with border controls re-introduced at its Austrian and Czech borders. This was in response to the concern from local government and political parties about the scale of refugee migration and the extent to which German institutions would be able to cope with the numbers. It could also be seen as a signal to other EU countries that Germany did not want to take sole responsibility for the refugee crisis.

Angela Merkel also adopted a leadership role in advocating an EU-managed relocation scheme. This was a clear effort on Germany's behalf to promote the sharing of responsibility. This quota system, although supported by countries such as France and Sweden, did face opposition from other countries, especially Central and East European countries such as Hungary and Slovakia. The strong political pressure that Germany exerted on the plans for a relocation system also meant that the refugee crisis turned into an EU political and institutional crisis. At an EU Council meeting in September 2015 it was decided that the relocation system would be introduced with up to 160,000 asylum applicants moved from Greece, Hungary and Italy. This decision was, however, made by qualified majority vote in the Council in the face of opposition from governments such as Hungary and Slovakia that were out-voted. Countries that were unwilling to adopt the quota system could now be required to implement it, as this was a binding EU decision. In a sign of the political tensions and her own frustration, Merkel criticised the instrumental use of the word 'solidarity' by Central and East European governments who she said were quick to use the word when seeking regional development funds, but less willing to do so for refugees.

Immigrant policy

This section looks at the two key elements of debates about immigrant integration in Germany. First, movement in the 1990s from an ethno-cultural to a more civic understanding of nationality and citizenship in Germany. Second, the key role played by the German labour market and welfare state in shaping outcomes and concern about the persistently poor integration outcomes (for example, in terms of education and employment) for key sections of the immigrant origin population (such as people of Turkish origin who make up around a quarter of Germany's immigrant origin population).

Even when Germany was not officially an immigration country it developed an immigrant policy that created a 'denizenship' status for permanent residents who possessed legal and social, but not political, rights and encountered an ethno-cultural understanding of what it meant to be German (Hammar, 1985).

Since reunification, German immigrant policies have been shaped by a number of institutional factors and pressures that make it much less exceptional when compared to other European countries. A key role has long been played by the German welfare state as a boundary of inclusion and exclusion with evidence of convergence dynamics, albeit with 'horizontal' lesson-learning from other European countries being more prominent than 'vertical' input into policy from the EU.

Table 4.2 shows that in 2013 by far the largest group in Germany with a migration background were the Turks. There were almost 2.8 million Turks of the first and second generation residing permanently in Germany (see Table 4.2). This Turkish population also has been the main focal point for German debates on multiculturalism and integration. At the same time, the German debates on immigration (but increasingly also immigrant integration) are turning attention to the Polish population that has increased rapidly over the last decade or so (over 1.5 million by 2013) as a very tangible consequence of EU accession of CEE countries (see Table 4.2).

Table 4.2 People living in Germany with a migration background (who have been born outside Germany, of whom at least one of the parents was born outside of Germany), 2013 (x1000)

Greece	381
Italy	783
Croatia	349
Poland	1,535
Romania	568
Ukraine	247
Serbia	280
Turkey	2,793
Russia	1,186
Africa	553
America	390
Asia	2,563
European migrants	11,151
Total	15,913

Source: German Statistics Office (www.destatis.de/DE/Publikationen/Thematisch/
Bevoelkerung/MigrationIntegration/Migrationshintergrund.html)

Ethno-culturalism and *Ausländerpolitik*

The comparative literature on migration studies tended to frequently juxtapose the German and French approaches to nationality and citizenship, although such juxtaposition is now much less relevant given the changes that have occurred. A key reference in this respect has been Brubaker's (1992) highly influential comparison of a French Republican model based on *jus soli* contrasted with the German ethno-cultural model based on *jus sanguinis* and the notion of the German 'community of descent' (*Volksgemeinschaft*) (Brubaker, 1992).

The idea of 'national models' is overly deterministic and neglects scope for change as well as on-the-ground implementation. Instead, these 'models' are better seen as referring to powerful historically developed understandings that have some continued effects on policy-making (Bertossi, 2011; Scholten, 2011b). For instance, Joppke (1999: 62) shows that the German 'narrative' of not being a country of immigration was deeply anchored in Germany's history, culture and nation-building experience, which are all open to various interpretations and re-interpretations.

German nationality and citizenship were based on a clear distinction between nation and state. The German nation was defined as based on ethno-cultural ties, as a *Volksgemeinschaft* or community of descent, characterised by *jus sanguinis*. This conception of the German nation preceded the development of the German state meaning that there were Germans both inside and outside the German state after its foundation in 1871. This idea of a German nation existing prior to the German state was reinforced after the end of the Second World War when Germany was divided between East and West. In turn, this was a key reason behind Germany's reluctance to recognise being an immigration country because doing so would be at odds with the organic conception of the *Volksgemeinschaft* that fed the national longing for reunification. As we saw in Chapter 3, this was in sharp contrast to the French idea of the undivided Republic (Brubaker, 1992: 137).

This ethno-cultural model had both exclusionary and inclusionary implications for German immigrant policies. In terms of exclusion, access to full citizenship was more restricted than in most other European countries. According to Brubaker, naturalisation 'German style' would require 'a social transubstantiation that immigrants have difficulty imagining, let alone desiring' (1992: 78). The 1913 Nationality Law conceptualised the German nation as a community of descent and placed formidable obstacles in the path of non-Germans. Until the 1990s, conditions for naturalisation were covered by Section 8 of the 1913 Nationality Law, which left the matter entirely to the discretion of the authorities. The 1977 Naturalisation Guidelines required spoken and written German, knowledge of West Germany's political system and at least 10 years' residence. Even then nationality would only be granted if it served the public interest because, according to paragraph 2.3 of the regulations: 'The Federal Republic is not a country of immigration, it does not seek to deliberately increase the number of German citizens through naturalisation'. The regulations went on to state that: 'The personal wishes and economic interests of the applicant cannot be decisive'. In addition to socio-economic integration there was also discretion at *Länder* level to require evidence of cultural assimilation.

The consequence of these kinds of restrictive measures was an annual naturalisation rate during the 1980s of less than 0.5 per cent of the foreign population (apart from the *Aussiedler*, for whom naturalisation followed a different trajectory). Dual nationality was not simply ruled out, it was described as 'evil' by a 1976 Constitutional Court ruling. In practice, however, dual nationality became increasingly common.

These exclusionary effects of the German ethno-cultural model were matched by a more inclusive approach at least in terms of rights and access to the labour market and welfare state. Immigrant policy was known as *Ausländerpolitik* (foreigner politics) although policies were not actually targeted at migrant integration, because that would mean admitting that Germany was an immigration country (Bommes, 2010). Foreign workers and their families were given access to social rights on a par with Germans. Article 20(1) of the Basic Law committed West Germany to the social inclusion of all citizens. The Social Security Code 'essentially makes no distinction between Germans and foreigners, but is geared to the residence of the beneficiaries in Germany' (Guiraudon, 2000: 79). Upon arrival, guestworker migrants had similar working conditions to Germans, although they were housed in poor conditions in hostels and then in public housing, which was often of the lowest quality, in high-rise blocks on the edges of major towns and cities.

In 1964 the federal government had introduced measures covering accommodation and social provision for guestworkers, but these were geared entirely towards their temporary presence rather than permanent settlement (Esser and Korte, 1985). The 1973 Federal Government Programme for the Employment of Immigrant Labour was the first attempt to deal with some of the social implications of long-term settlement for foreign workers. The resultant *Integration auf Zeit* (temporary integration) paradigm prompted simultaneous emphasis on measures aimed at integration with others geared towards repatriation.

Bommes (2000) argues that by the 1990s an idea of Germany as a 'community of belonging' had been replaced by a 'community of contributors to the GNP'. This community of GNP contributors included – albeit at a lower level – the foreign population of guestworkers and their descendants, while excluding those deemed 'undeserving' such as asylum seekers, refugees, contract labourers and *Spätaussiedler* ('late' arriving ethnic Germans). The 1994 Asylum Seekers Benefit Law reduced welfare benefits for asylum seekers. Within a six-year period, welfare benefits available to *Aussiedler* became a question of social rather than national integration, which meant the adoption of a policy frame previously used for labour migrants.

4.3 DENIZENSHIP IN A NON-IMMIGRATION COUNTRY

Until the development of an immigrant policy in the early 2000s, Germany held on to the idea of not being a country of immigration. This also meant that no official policy was developed aimed at immigrant integration. Yet, at the same time Germany was relatively open in granting access to social rights. In terms of welfare state inclusion, migrants were relatively well off in Germany. Access to full citizenship, naturalisation and political rights was however restricted. This also reflected the prevailing *jus sanguinis* conception of citizenship on which the German state was founded (see also Box 3.1).

This position characterised by social inclusion and political exclusion has been described by Hammar (1985) in terms of 'denizenship', which means that immigrants became part of German society, but did not fully become German. This is also reflected in the many *ad hoc* efforts aimed at immigrant integration that were taken by churches, labour unions and NGOs in the absence of a formal state approach to immigrant integration.

Towards a German immigrant policy?

Reunification changed the context for immigrant integration policy. As in other European countries, there was evidence of lower levels of educational attainment and employment amongst immigrants, as well as concerns about language acquisition. These concerns were compounded by evidence of racism and discrimination that could take extreme forms such as the murderous attack in Solingen in 1993, when four young men with neo-Nazi ties burned the home of a Turkish family resulting in the deaths of three girls and two women while 14 others were injured, including several children.

Before this terrible attack, in 1990, several changes had been made to the Foreigners Law. The law now permitted naturalisation for foreigners with at least 15 years residence and for those of the second and third generation aged between 16 and 25 with at least eight years residence. This meant provision for as-of-right naturalisation. Foreigners were given greater legal security, but access to German nationality remained difficult. Dietrich Thränhardt (1999) argues that the 1990 Foreigners Law ended the divergence between the French and German models with a move on the German side away from *jus sanguinis* to an element of *jus soli*. Christian Joppke (1999: 200) contends that the changes 'swept away cultural assimilation' with Germany recasting itself as a civic nation. If we compare debates in France with those in Germany we can see that overt displays of nationalism were actually far more evident in 'civic' France (see Chapter 3).

Despite the new legislation, naturalisation figures remained low. In 1995 the naturalisation rate (not including *Aussiedler*) stood at a mere 1 per cent (Joppke, 1997). There was also some relaxation of Turkish laws on property inheritance and changes to nationality laws that allowed former Turkish nationals to reacquire Turkish nationality if they so desired. This helped Turks resident in Germany who had been fearful of the effects on their rights in Turkey if they took German nationality.

The formation in 1998 of the SPD/Green coalition brought to power two parties that were far more amenable to a civic national model. The coalition agreement acknowledged that an irreversible process of immigration had occurred and argued that the aim of policy should be the integration of the resident foreign population. In the face of opposition from the centre-right CDU/CSU, the Red–Green coalition changed nationality law to allow for dual nationality up to the age of 23 for the children of foreigners at which point a choice had to be made. This was opposed by CDU/CSU that saw naturalisation as something more exclusive and led to their more critical approach to dual citizenship. This law also stipulated that each applicant for naturalisation needed to sign a declaration of loyalty to the German Constitution while requiring that a condition for naturalisation would be that applicants had sufficient oral and written German language skills. The changes to the nationality law came into effect on 1 January 2001 with around 200,000 foreigners immediately applying to become Germans (*Migration News*, 2001a).

In the early 2000s, Germany for the first time started to consider development of a national framework for immigrant integration. Approaches were more likely to develop at the local and *Länder* levels rather than at national level, meaning significant variation (Schönwalder, 2010). For example, Alexander (2007) shows that Berlin developed a policy aimed at immigrant integration that embraced the city's diversity. In 1981, Berlin had appointed a Commissioner for Migration and Integration. While Berlin embraced diversity as one of its defining characteristics, other cities and the national government have struggled with these issues and have not always been so willing to positively extol the virtues of diversity.

The absence of a national policy approach did not mean that there were not ideas about the rights and obligations of immigrants. The CDU/CSU instigated discussion of the cultural dimension when they emphasised the importance of a so-called *Leitkultur* or 'guiding national culture'. This was driven by the SPD/ Green coalition's 1999 law easing access to citizenship. The CDU/CSU stressed the importance of preserving a *Leitkultur*, within which they emphasised knowledge of the German language, loyalty to the German nation and acceptance of German social and political institutions (Klusmeyer and Papademetriou, 2009). The CDU also launched its own Immigration Commission to counteract the Independent Commission on Immigration established by the SPD/Green government. This move was controversial because the government's Independent Commission was actually chaired by a prominent CDU member, Rita Süssmuth. The government Commission came up with very different recommendations – such as easing access to citizenship – compared to the more conservative approach proposed by the CDU commission that argued for a more restrictive approach towards dual citizenship (Klusmeyer and Papademetriou, 2009: 247).

A second strand of debate was linked to the relationship between immigration, integration, the labour market and the welfare state. It was becoming clear – as was also the case in other European countries – that some immigrant-origin groups such as Turks were experiencing poor educational outcomes, lower employment levels with tendencies towards lower skilled work as well as higher unemployment levels. The Hartz reforms of the labour market and welfare state were controversial but signalled a significant reorientation of the broader politics of integration as it related to all German citizens and to immigrants. For immigrants, this meant a dual focus on attempts to recruit the highly skilled while at the same time trying to deal with issues associated with failed integration as evident in education and employment outcomes for some sections of the immigrant-origin population.

The 2005 immigration law brought with it increased federal government concern about immigrant integration (Klusmeyer and Papademetriou, 2009). Angela Merkel's grand coalition, comprising the CDU/CSU and SPD, launched a Federal

Integration Programme to be co-ordinated by the BAMF (Bendel, 2014: 147). A first 'National Integration Summit' was held in 2006 bringing together local and state authorities with national government. This led to the first National Integration Plan (2006) that developed into a National Action Plan on Integration (2007) containing more than 400 concrete measures and commitments to be taken and implemented by the federal government, *Länder*, cities and NGOs.

A particularly important component of this approach has been language training for new migrants via the provision of integration courses, introduced by the 2005 immigration law. These are part of a broader set of integration requirements that are a condition for access to permanent residence and naturalisation. In 2007, a citizenship test was introduced in which migrants have to prove basic knowledge of German society while a pre-entry integration test (inspired by a similar Dutch test) was aimed primarily at family migrants and had a focus on language skills. As in the Netherlands, migrants have to find and finance their preparation for these tests in the country of origin (Michalowski, 2010: 193).

Klusmeyer and Papademetriou (2009) note that aside from these integration courses and language training, German immigrant policies remain relatively modest. Most measures that were relevant to migrant integration were not actually specific to it, which means that policies have been developed in areas such as education, employment and housing that affected migrant integration without framing them explicitly as part of an immigrant policy. In this sense, German policies reveal continuity rather than radical change and affirm Bommes' (2010) point that German approaches still retain a strong welfare state context and will thus be framed by wider debates.

The CDU/CSU victory at the 2013 federal election and Merkel's reappointment as Chancellor led to further reform of the Nationality Law with the elimination of the *Optionspflicht* that required dual nationals born in Germany to choose at the age of 23 one citizenship or the other, with the vast majority opting for German citizenship.

There were also only limited developments on the socio-cultural dimension. Musch (2011) shows that the German authorities have been making efforts to work with migrant organisations, but not to the same extent as in countries such as the Netherlands where there have long been extensive consultation structures. That said, Germany has developed a number of dialogues on integration issues, including perhaps most importantly the Islam Conferences, held in 2006 and annually since 2010, bringing together government representatives with representatives from religious and Islamic organisations to discuss various issues related to Islam and German society. This led to the establishment of a Co-ordinating Council for Muslims that, in spite of internal disagreements, has promoted measures in the field of education and training of imams.

While populist and extremist parties have not had the same prominence in Germany as in other European countries, there is evidence after 2010 of anti-immigration sentiment and opposition to the presence of Islam in Germany. One instance of this was the debate provoked by a book authored by a former Bundesbank board member, Theo Sarrazin (2010), entitled *Deutschland schafft sich ab* (*Germany Abolishes Itself*) that criticised both the economic effects and composition of immigration flows to Germany. Sarrazin portrayed Turkish people as welfare dependents with high crime rates and as the source of a potential demographic disaster for German society because their high birth rates would cause the percentage of Turks amongst the German population to further increase.

This kind of publication and the wider debate related to it both reflected and reinvigorated the *Leitkultur* debate that had begun a decade earlier. Both the SPD and CDU leaderships denounced Sarrazin's book, but the debate did help to demonstrate that beneath the surface there were concerns about the effects of immigration (Wasmer, 2013). This moved Chancellor Merkel in 2010 to publicly state that attempts to build a multicultural society in Germany had 'utterly failed' (ibid.: 163).

Wasmer (2013) argues that attitudes in Germany to diversity remain ambiguous, as there is evidence of both an increase of support for diversity as an enrichment of society combined with an increase in the numbers of people who see immigrants as a threat to national identity and social cohesion. The debate about immigration-related diversity in Germany continues to be framed by various events that provide a focus for public debate, such as the Sarrazin book and the controversy that erupted in 2011 when the German police uncovered a series of murders of Turkish and Greek immigrants by a neo-Nazi terrorist group. The then Turkish Prime Minister Recap Erdoğan caused further controversy when he said, referring to Turks in Germany, that 'Our children must learn German, but first they must learn Turkish' (Wasmer, 2013: 175).

Although the concern itself was not new, the anti-Islamic PEGIDA (Patriotic Europeans Against the Islamisation of the West) movement burst to prominence in 2014 when tens of thousands of people joined its marches protesting against, what they claimed was, the Islamisation of Germany. PEGIDA began in the eastern city of Dresden in 2014 and saw the locations of demonstrations spread across Germany and involve over 25,000 participants in a January 2015 rally, spurred by reaction to the murders at the offices of the *Charlie Hebdo* magazine in Paris. In various German cities, and in other European cities such as Vienna, PEGIDA spin-offs emerged. Despite some of its claims to the contrary, PEGIDA had a clear far-right origin amongst its instigators and, as well as focusing on what it calls Islamisation, it seeks restrictions on immigration to Germany. Social and political tensions around the refugee and migration issue were heightened after the events at the 2015–16 New Year celebrations in Cologne where large numbers of women were physically and sexually assaulted with reports that the attackers were young men of Arab and North African origin. While saying that the attacks should not be used to stigmatise all refugees and migrants, Chancellor Merkel was aware of a less welcoming public mood in Germany and, on top of border controls that had already been introduced, pledged to step up efforts to ensure that foreign criminals would be deported (*Financial Times*, 2016).

PEGIDA put an undercurrent of resentment felt by some in German society against Islam on the public agenda and showed to the world that in Germany, as in many other European countries, there were relatively large numbers of people that were concerned about, or hostile to, Islam. A December 2014 poll in Germany by YouGov found that 49 per cent of respondents agreed with the demonstrations by PEGIDA with 30 per cent fully agreeing with the protests and 19 per cent partly agreeing with PEGIDA's claims. In contrast, 23 per cent rejected the rationale for the protests.

PEGIDA's activities provoked large-scale counter-demonstrations. In January 2015, Chancellor Merkel was strongly critical of PEGIDA when speaking at a Muslim-led rally in Berlin where she said that 'hatred, racism and extremism have no place in this country'. PEGIDA's fortunes also faded when the extreme right associations of its leaders became more widely known, while PR disasters (such as the photograph of PEGIDA leader, Lutz Bachmann, dressed as Adolf Hitler) alienated many who might have had some sympathy to its claims about supposed Islamisation. The refugee crisis provided a boost to PEGIDA's flagging fortunes with an estimated 15,000–20,000 people marching to commemorate its first anniversary in October 2015 facing a similarly sized counter-demonstration arguing that refugees should be made welcome. There were also attacks on pro-posed refugee accommodation, including arson attacks on five proposed accommodation centres in Thuringia (*The Guardian*, 8 October 2015).

As in immigration policy, the stylised representation of Germany as an exceptional case now no longer holds in the area of immigrant policy. We see reforms of nationality and citizenship that accord with practices in other European countries as well as a reorientation of background welfare and labour market conditions that have fed through into expectations about immigrant integration. As in other European countries, there is concern about social and economic exclusion of immigrants and their children, with a much stronger focus on socio-economic integration and linguistic adaptation to tackle problems of low educational attainment and welfare dependency among some immigrant groups, such as people of Turkish origin. There are significant local variations, which are not surprising within the German federal system, but there is also now a much greater reliance on the market to deliver 'solutions' as a result of the liberalisation of the German labour market and welfare state.

European integration

A long-standing and deeply embedded ideological commitment to European integration is a hallmark of German politics, policy and state identity. A choice for Europe is combined with a more practical view that European integration can be a way to resolve key policy problems. In Germany, the post-2008 financial crisis, the refugee crisis and the shock waves they sent across the EU have tested this idea and led to some growth in German Euroscepticism.

This section looks at how Germany has pursued its policy preferences at EU level and also examines the extent to which immigration and immigrant policies have been Europeanised. The conclusion is that there is more evidence of 'horizontal' convergence – lesson learning and policy transfer between European countries – with significant difficulty establishing common EU policies or standards, such as an EU wide relocation system for asylum seekers.

Uploading German policy preferences to EU level

In spite of, or perhaps even thanks to, the peculiarities of the German case and reluctance to recognise that it had become a country of immigration, the EU has played a very significant role in the shaping and making of German immigration and immigrant policies. Or perhaps the other way around, as Germany has been a key actor at various stages, including the recent European refugee crisis, in framing EU immigration policies.

The constraints on not developing an immigration policy until the 1990s are key factors that help to explain why Germany was actively engaged in the development of EU migration policies, partly compensating for the absence of national policies. In the 1990s, for example, the EU's Dublin system for asylum applications enabled Germany's 1993 'Asylum Compromise' that helped to significantly reduce the numbers of asylum seekers entering Germany and defuse the asylum crisis. During the 1990s, there were also efforts to use the EU as a way to 'externalise' immigration policies by drawing non-member states into the web of EU controls. Germany was also a founder member of the Schengen agreement on free movement within the EU and its 'compensating' internal security measures. During the 1990s Germany actually advocated much more far-reaching forms of European co-operation and supranationalisation than were eventually agreed upon by EU member states in the Maastricht (1993) and Amsterdam (1999) treaties. The German government has also been a supporter of the sharing of responsibility for the reception of asylum seekers.

The German case seems to reflect what we have described in the introduction and Chapter 7 as the 'escape to Europe' thesis, where the EU offers a chance for ministers and officials to dodge domestic legal and political constraints in the pursuit of restrictive immigration and asylum policies formulated in executive-friendly Euro forums. However, as Chapter 7 also shows the EU is now far more developed as a political and institutional setting in its own right and cannot be understood as simply derivative of member states' policies. Empowerment of the CJEU by the Lisbon Treaty has led to decisions that constrain the executive branch of national governments in the areas of expulsion, family migration and integration.

As Chapter 7 shows, an intergovernmental versus supranational dichotomy might not be the best way to understand the EU. Rather, it is better to see the EU as a hybrid structure containing both these elements. The result is that patterns of relatively intense interaction between national government officials and EU actors can develop within which the sharing of ideas and information occurs on a regular basis. This is precisely the kind of setting within which ideas about 'integration contracts' can be exchanged. Other examples are the EU's 2003 directives on the rights of long-term residents and on family reunification. The German government (along with the Austrians and Dutch) insisted that scope for respect of national 'integration measures' was included in EU laws. Germany, with its allies in the Council of Ministers, played a key role in changing the initial Commission proposals for these directives in a direction that allowed more discretion for member states to require the migrants to accord with national integration measures. This shows how the EU 'venue' allowed for the uploading of policy preferences that were consistent with the domestic approach and its emphasis on pre- and post-entry integration programmes for TCNs.

The 2015 refugee crisis saw the German government once again as a key actor shaping a European response. The Dublin agreement, which had also been strongly influenced by German preferences in the 1990s, could no longer offer an adequate response to asylum flows. Subsequently, Angela Merkel's government defined the EU response through its initial welcoming approach that saw around 1 million refuges and migrants move to Germany. The German government also put great political pressure on other EU member states to accept a relocation system for the distribution of asylum seekers and refugees across Europe. By re-installing controls at its border with Austria in September 2015, Germany also made a clear statement that if Europe was not able to resolve the crisis, it could also adopt measures on its own.

Migration from Central and Eastern Europe

Besides the refugee crisis in the 2010s, a key issue in the German–EU relationship since 2004 has been movement by EU citizens from new member states in Central and East European countries, especially from Poland. Following accession by the A8 countries in 2004 and the A2 countries in 2007, Germany imposed the maximum seven-year restriction on free movement of workers (until 2011 and 2014 respectively). This explains why movement from new EU member states to Germany has been lower than to Britain, which as seen in Chapter 2 did not impose transitional controls. For instance, even for Polish–German migration, which has traditionally been significant, the scale of movement has been smaller than Polish to UK movement. A clear example of the path dependency of past decisions, the scale of Polish–UK migration has continued to exceed that of Polish–German migration since then (for instance an overall total of 642,000 Polish nationals in the UK compared to around 560,000 in Germany in 2013 [CSO, 2013]). As in the UK, Germany has sought to recruit highly skilled non-EU migrants while those from other EU member states are often employed in low-skilled work.

That said, since 2004, the number of Polish people in Germany has grown to be the second largest as the Turkish population decreased due to the effects of naturalisation and emigration. There has always been a relatively sizeable Polish population in Germany for historical reasons and as a result of labour recruitment agreements. As Table 4.3 (below) shows, after the end of the transition period for free movement of workers (which was 2011 for the 'A8' countries, including Poland) the number of people moving from Poland to Germany increased steeply. Similar trends can be found for other Central and East European (CEE) countries plus for Bulgaria and Romania even before the end of their own transition period in 2014.

Movement by nationals from new EU member states in Central and Eastern Europe has stirred public debate in Germany. One of the focal points of this debate was the effect of workers from Poland on Germany's economy. As in the UK and the Netherlands, some saw Polish workers as a threat to German low-skilled workers. Particular controversy was triggered by competition of Polish workers in the transport and construction sectors, where they enjoyed different labour conditions and could thus compete at lower prices than German workers.

In response, the German government, together with the Austrian, British and Dutch governments, have sought action to limit the welfare state entitlements of people benefiting from EU free movement rules. This does, of course, assume that the main reason for their movement is to access welfare benefits even though evidence suggests that employment is the main motive (Kahanec, 2012). For domestic political reasons rather than because of any compelling evidence of 'welfare tourism' the Austrian, British, Dutch and German governments have raised concerns about the effects of EU free movement and are looking at ways to restrict access to benefits (for example, by restricting the ability of people from other EU member states to send child benefits back to their origin county). German efforts were aided to some extent by a CJEU ruling in November 2014 that denied access to welfare benefits to a woman from Romania resident in Germany on the grounds that she was not seeking employment, although evidence shows that EU citizens in Germany have predominantly moved for employment and make a positive contribution to the German economy.

These efforts to limit access to welfare benefits in particular cases where an individual is not seeking employment do not indicate any lessened support for the general principle of free movement. This contrasts with the approach of the Conservative Party within the British Coalition government between 2010 and

Table 4.3 Numbers of EU citizens from A8 and A2 member states living in Germany (by citizenship, 2006–2012, absolute figures)

	2006	2007	2008	2009	2010	2011	2012	2013
Bulgaria	39,053	46,818	53,984	61,854	74,869	93,889	118,759	146,828
Baltic states	32,775	33,704	34,268	37,181	42,173	50,854	59,537	67,585
Poland	361,696	384,808	393,848	398,513	419,435	468,481	532,375	609,855
Romania	73,353	84,584	94,326	104,980	126,536	159,222	205,026	267,398
Slovakia	23,835	24,458	24,477	24,930	26,296	30,241	35,372	41,436
Czech Rep.	33,316	34,266	34,386	34,337	35,480	38,060	41,865	46,484
Hungary	52,347	56,165	60,024	61,417	68,892	82,760	107,398	135,614
Turkey	1,738,831	1,713,551	1,688,370	1,658,083	1,629,480	1,607,161	1,575,717	1,549,808

Source: Federal Office of Statistics (www.destatis.de/EN/FactsFigures/SocietyState/Population/MigrationIntegration/ForeignPopulation/Tables/CitizenshipTimeSerie.html)

2015 and in single-party government after 2015 that entangled efforts to restrict EU migration with a more general debate about whether Britain should even be an EU member state. In Germany, EU membership is a powerful and defining feature of state identity, which means that debate possesses nowhere near the resonance that it does in Britain.

Conclusion

This chapter began by setting out to explore the scope, extent and significance of change in German immigration and immigrant policies since the 1990s. The analysis has been framed by the movement of refugees and asylum seekers at the beginning of the 1990s as a result of conflict in ex-Yugoslavia and in the mid-2010s by the refugee crisis. A lot has changed between these two events, but much of this change has been incremental and there remains ambivalence about Germany's status as an immigration country. In a sense this is a change in itself. Germany has gone from seeing itself as 'not an immigration country' to considering its identity and future as an immigration country. Germany's central role in the refugee crisis of 2014 and 2015 only confirmed its status as one of the top destination countries for refugees and migrants, and positioned Germany as a country open to immigration.

As was shown, the reasons why Germany did not see itself as an immigration country were deeply rooted in the very specific history of Germany as a divided nation for a long period after the Second World War. By definition, the idea of *Kein Einwanderungsland* inhibited the development of German immigration and immigrant policies until after reunification. Even though millions of ethnic Germans, labour migrants, family migrants and asylum seekers moved to Germany, there was no systematic policy framework for the management of these flows until 2005. That said, the absence of a formal framework did not mean that new migrants were not included within German society. In this respect, the roles played by the German welfare state and labour markets were crucial.

Although the emergent contours of a nascent immigration policy became evident in the 1990s, it wasn't until 2005 that an immigration law was agreed and, even then, in a watered down form compared to the original proposals. Nevertheless, this was an important turning point. As in other European countries, Germany's approach involved a combination of restrictive policies regarding those forms of migration defined as 'unwanted' (such as family migration) and a more positive approach to high skilled labour migration with active recruitment for the first time since the 1970s. It is plausible to argue that by 2015 and for higher skilled migration Germany operated one of the most liberal migration regimes in Europe, combining routes for labour migrants with a relatively open approach to asylum-seeking migration.

While there remains significant scope for local variation within the German federal system, the parameters of a national approach to immigrant integration have also become clearer, although a key point here is the broader context of labour market and welfare reform which places more emphasis on the market to generate integration. That said, when compared to Britain, the Netherlands and Sweden, Germany's framework is modest and highly decentralised. Developments do reflect a deeper change in how the relationship between migrants and the state is perceived in Germany. In the 1990s, changes were made in the Nationality Law, involving a move towards a civic model with a combination of *jus soli* and *jus sanguinis*. This was a clear move away from Germany's traditional *jus sanguinis* model where blood ties defined access to citizenship in the context of the German *Volksstaat*, which had made the German case so 'exceptional' in the twentieth century. In immigrant policies too, there is a strong ambivalence between focusing on integration on the one hand and growing public and political resentment towards immigration-related diversity, multiculturalism and Islam on the other. In a way very similar to many other European countries, Germany is experiencing a revival of national culture, values and norms in relation to migrant integration, particularly in the context of debate on the German *Leitkultur*.

The end result is that we should probably not overstate the scope, extent and nature of change in Germany since the 1990s. Even by the 1970s, Germany was combining the surface mantra of *Kein Einwanderungsland* with welfare state mediated inclusion of labour migrants (who came as 'guests' but stayed). This reflects the importance of legal and social rights short of full citizenship, or denizenship as it was known. Yet, welfare state inclusion can be a double-edged sword. It is ideas about welfare state abuse (for example in the case of asylum seekers in the 1990s) and 'welfare tourism' (by migrants from other EU member states) that is a key driver of public resentment towards immigration. In this concern – sometimes turning to outright or overt hostility – Germany fits with a more general European trend, albeit with strong domestic norms that militate against success for extremist right-wing parties. In addition, the EU as a process, a structure and a set of ideas has long played a central role in the development of German approaches to immigration and its effects. Precisely because of the absence of a national policy framework, the German government frequently acted in accordance with what we have described as the 'escape to Europe' thesis. By this is meant EU co-operation was seen as a way to attain domestic objectives with less constraint from domestic legislative and judicial interests. As we see in Chapter 7, changes at EU level have weakened this 'escape to Europe' thesis while Germany has clearly become one of the EU's leading destinations for people fleeing conflicts in the Middle East and Africa.

5

The Netherlands: Beyond Multiculturalism?

Introduction

Rhimou Chakroun moved to the Netherlands from Morocco in 1970. Similar to many supposedly temporary labour migrants, Mr Chakroun ended up staying permanently. He experienced the multicultural era of the 1980s and its distinct approach to integration as well as the effects on policy since the 2000s of populist and anti-immigration political parties. In 2006, Mr Chakroun applied for a residence permit for his wife of 34 years. The Dutch authorities refused to grant this permit as Mr Chakroun had been unemployed in 2005 and fell foul of a new rule that meant that his welfare benefits did not amount to the 120 per cent of the national minimum wage threshold that was necessary for him to be joined by his wife. This policy was a product of the restrictive approach to family migration from the government formed with support from the populist anti-immigration party founded by the late Pim Fortuyn. In 2010, the CJEU annulled this decision on the grounds that the income requirement was contrary to the provisions of the EU's 2003 directive on the right to family reunification (see Chapter 7). The Chakroun case highlights four things that are central to this chapter's analysis of the politics of immigration in the Netherlands:

- movement towards stringent entry criteria;
- effective abandonment of a multicultural approach to integration;

- influence of populist, anti-immigration political parties on government policy;
- the CJEU's role in national immigration politics since the Lisbon Treaty came into force in 2009.

From a relatively open and tolerant approach to immigration the Netherlands has experienced an anti-immigration backlash and has gone from being a pro-EU country to one with prominent Eurosceptic political parties. The Netherlands was once renowned for a multicultural approach to immigrant integration that developed in the 1980s. Since the early 2000s the Netherlands has gone through a sharp 'assimilationist turn' and, in the 2010s, has also pursued so-called 'policy mainstreaming' that seeks to embed immigrant integration within more general policies targeted at the whole society. This chapter explains why a country once known for its multicultural approach changed course and what this tells us about changing immigration and immigrant policies in a comparative European perspective.

Immigration policy

The Netherlands is a fascinating case for three reasons. First, it has been a labora-tory for policies including so-called 'civic integration' that places more onus on immigrants to demonstrate their capacity and willingness to adapt via, for exam-ple, citizenship tests (Goodman, 2014). This idea has also 'travelled' to other European countries, as was seen in the previous chapter on Germany. Second, the Netherlands shows that policy can change swiftly and dramatically because of, for example, changes in underlying institutional factors such as the welfare state and the rise of populist, anti-immigration political parties. As with other countries, we do not ascribe the politicisation of immigration solely to these populist or extreme right parties as they can capitalise on concerns as much as they generate them. Finally, the Dutch have played a key role in the Europeanisation of immigration and immigrant policies and now find them-selves constrained by the EU policies they helped to create.

This section explains why and with what effects the Netherlands accepted its status as an immigration country and then sought to regulate flows. We see clear points of comparison with other European countries as well two key aspects that relate to the distinct Dutch setting.

1. The Netherlands has a long tradition of consensual and coalitional forms of politics known as consociational democracy (Lijphart, 1975). Political structures were designed to promote accommodation between different religious groups in Dutch society. The resultant 'pillars' provided cradle to grave inclusion for their members, with overarching elite-level accommodation within Coalition governments to bring these pillars together. Since the late 1960s, social changes have resulted in these

pillars losing their meaning and relevance with the consequence being major changes in the Dutch party political system.

2. Since the 2000s there has been increased support for anti-immigration political parties who tap into specific resentment about immigration among some sections of the Dutch population, as well as a broader decline in trust and confidence in political institutions and political leaders. As McLaren (2012) shows, there is a correlation between those who have lost trust in their political leaders and hostility to immigration that she calls a 'cultural divide'. The Netherlands conforms with this broader European trend.

There are also clear historical commonalities because, as did Britain, France and Germany, the Netherlands experienced labour migration in the 1950s, only reluctantly recognised that it was a country of immigration in the early 1980s and has sought to regulate those forms of migration it defines as 'unwanted'. Despite restrictive measures, levels of immigration continued to increase in the second half of the 2000s. Figure 5.1 shows that this is linked in particular to EU free movement, which was a key source of new (mostly labour) migrants to the Netherlands albeit, of course, a right to move guaranteed by EU law. The impacts of immigration are significant. In 2014, around 21 per cent of the Dutch population was either foreign-born or had at least one parent that was foreign born. In the two largest cities, Amsterdam and Rotterdam, this proportion of foreign-born rises to around 50 per cent.

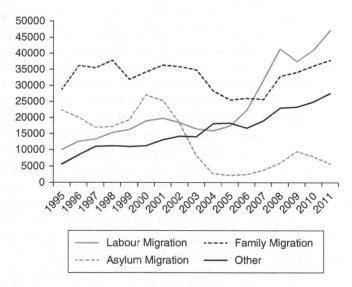

Figure 5.1 Immigration to the Netherlands, according to migration motive (labour, family, asylum, other such as return migration and student migration)

Source: http://statline.cbs.nl/Statweb/selection/?DM=SLNL&PA=70693NED&VW=T

A country shaped by immigration

Immigration and emigration have had important effects on Dutch society (Lucassen and Penninx, 1997). Emigrants went to former Dutch colonies such as Surinam, the Antilles, South Africa and the former Dutch East Indies (nowadays Indonesia). From before the Second World War until the 1950s, large numbers of Dutch migrants also moved to the United States, Canada, Brazil, Australia and New Zealand. Immigration has also been extensive. Between the sixteenth and early eighteenth centuries, the Netherlands attracted large numbers of migrants for religious reasons as it provided a safe haven for groups including Huguenots fleeing France. It is from these early waves of immigration that cities such as Delft, Leiden and Amsterdam inherit their tradition of diversity.

Following decolonisation, large numbers of Dutch settlers as well as natives who had worked with the Dutch were 'repatriated' to the Netherlands (around 300,000 between 1946 and 1962) (Van Amersfoort and Van Niekerk, 2006). They were dispersed throughout the country and re-assimilated into society, often with little respect for the cultural heritage that they brought from the former colonies (Schuster, 1992). Many of the 43,000 Moluccans (from what is now part of Indonesia) who moved to the Netherlands were employed in the Dutch Army (as 'ethnic soldiers'). They initially moved to the Netherlands with the intention of returning to an independent Moluccan Republic that was never established. People from Surinam arrived throughout colonial history, but in particular in the years before its independence in 1975 and again in 1980 when the right to move to the Netherlands ended. By 2015, there were around 350,000 people in the Netherlands of Surinamese origin, which makes this one of the largest migrant groups. A final group of colonial migrants are people from the former Dutch Antilles. Inhabitants from Bonaire and the upper islands (Saba, St. Maarten and St. Eustatius) are still able to move freely as these islands still form part of the Netherlands. Special arrangements apply to the islands of Curacao and Aruba, from where large numbers of migrants have also settled in the Netherlands.

A second category is labour migrants. In the 1960s and early 1970s, the Netherlands actively recruited 'guest labourers' from mainly Mediterranean countries. Recruitment agreements were signed with Italy (1960), Spain (1961), Portugal (1963), Turkey (1964), Greece (1966), Morocco (1969), Yugoslavia and Tunisia (1970). These migrants were supposed to provide a temporary 'reservoir of labour' for the post-war reconstruction of the Dutch economy; revealingly the term 'international commuters' was often used. This ostensibly temporary form of migration would, however, eventually lead to the formation of some of the largest migrant-origin groups in the Netherlands today including people of Turkish origin (over 395,000 in 2013) and people of Moroccan origin (around 369,000 in 2013). Recently, numbers of people moving to the Netherlands for work has increased, but primarily in the form of EU free movement.

A third category is refugees and asylum migrants. In the second half of the 1990s and early 2000s, the Netherlands received asylum migrants from conflict zones such as former Yugoslavia, Iraq, Afghanistan, Iran, Somalia and Ghana. In the mid 2000s, asylum migration to the Netherlands decreased significantly (see Figure 5.1). Asylum applicants increased again in the 2010s in the context of the European refugee crisis. From fewer than 10,000 applications in 2013 numbers rose to almost 24,000 in 2014 and an estimated 35,000 in 2015. This put asylum and humanitarian protection back on the political agenda in the Netherlands.

A fourth category of immigrants to the Netherlands are family migrants. To a large extent this involves migration as a consequence of earlier movement by 'guest' labourers, colonial migrants and asylum migrants re-uniting with their families, and thus bringing over their spouses and children, as well as Dutch-born people marrying someone from abroad. From the 1990s to the mid 2000s, family migration was the largest migration flow to the Netherlands (see Figure 5.1). Although since the mid 2000s labour migration has once again become the largest immigration category (even though the level of movement by family members has been increasing), mostly linked to EU free movement rights for people from Central and Eastern Europe (Bonjour and Scholten, 2014).

The piecemeal development of Dutch immigration policy

Even though Dutch society has been profoundly shaped by immigration throughout its history, there was, as in other European countries, reluctance to recognise that it had become – or had always been – a country of immigration. A key turning point in Dutch immigration policies was the 1973 oil crisis that hit labour intensive industries particularly hard. This led to an end to the active labour recruitment policies of the 1960s and early 1970s and saw large-scale labour migration come to a halt. The ending of labour recruitment was also an explicit objective of the Dutch Labour Party (PvdA) and other parties on the left that saw labour migration as weakening the position of the working class. In contrast, the Liberal Party (VVD) supported labour migration for economic reasons.

In the wake of the economic recession of the mid 1970s and structural changes in the Dutch economy that saw increased investment in less labour intensive technologies, it was expected that many labour migrants would return to their origin countries. This, however, did not happen; the supposed 'guests' had come to stay.

As rules governing labour migration became stricter there was increased family migration. Bonjour (2009) shows that the debate on family migration in the 1970s and 1980s in the Dutch parliament had a strong 'moral' character. The Christian Democrat Party (CDA), then by far the largest party, stressed protection of 'the united family'. Centre-left parties, including the PvdA, also defended the right of workers to be united with their families. The liberal VVD, however, became more negative towards immigration because its economic utilitarianism was offset by what it saw as the potential costs of family migration for the welfare state. At this time, the views of the PvdA and CDA prevailed, but, since the end of the 1990s, family migrants have been increasingly defined as an 'unwanted' form of immigration in the Netherlands (Bonjour, 2009). Systematically, across Europe, family migration has been downgraded as a supposed drain on welfare resources rather than as a positive factor that could contribute to social stability and cohesion (Honohan, 2009). Strictly regulating family migration became one of the primary objectives of 'civic integration' policies, discussed more fully below. Dutch governments also sought to restrict family migration by raising the minimum age level to 21 and raising the required income level to 120 per cent of minimum wage level, although this fell foul of EU law, as we saw in the Chakroun case referred to earlier. The Dutch had actually been major proponents of the development of the EU's Family Reunification Directive, although it was this directive and the CJEU ruling in the Chakroun case that forced the Dutch government to lower the income threshold to 100 per cent.

Populist influence on the Dutch government has also become much stronger and reflects both anti-immigration sentiment as well as deeper underlying changes in the Dutch political system. This applied to the Fortuyn Party that became the second largest party after the 2002 parliamentary elections, and even for a brief period was included in a government coalition. The Fortuyn Party was a populist party that acquired support from mainly native working class voters, claiming to represent 'the voice from the street' and aiming to open up the 'back room politics' of national government. A direct inheritor of the Fortuyn Party's vote was the Freedom Party (PVV) led by Geert Wilders who was known for his anti-immigrant, anti-immigration and anti-Islamic views. In 2010 a centre-right minority government formed by the VVD and CDA was dependent on the support of the Freedom Party. This coalition promised in its coalition agreement that it would do all it could to change the EU Family Reunification Directive. Although this coalition fell in 2012 due to difficulties in finding co-operation with the PVV, the political pressure to have restrictive immigration policies has continued under a new coalition led by the VVD, together with the PvdA, in the face of strong political opposition from Wilders' PVV.

The first policies aimed at the regulation of refugee and asylum migration were not developed until 1987. Until then, refugee migration was managed by use of annual quotas. With the increase in largely spontaneous asylum migration in the late 1980s, a more systematic policy was required. A Regulation on the Reception of Asylum Seekers (ROA) was introduced that offered reception centres to house asylum seekers. This relieved many of the immediate housing concerns in the major cities. In response to increased asylum migration in the early 1990s, these facilities were expanded.

The Netherlands was also one of the most vigorous supporters of the development of a common EU migration and asylum policy, including 'burden sharing' between member states (Bonjour, 2009). Measures introduced in the 1990s sought to discourage asylum migration, including 'fast-track' procedures lasting between four to eight days from application to decision and the tightening of visa regulations. The 2000 Aliens Act introduced a single status for all asylum seekers, which involved an initial temporary status for five years that could then be changed to a permanent status under specific conditions. In 2010 the asylum procedure was tightened substantially. After a reception period lasting six days, the asylum procedure should take no longer than eight days. Only in exceptionally difficult circumstances could the procedure be extended to six months. In 2011, 56 per cent of all cases were processed within the eight-day period (Bonjour and Scholten, 2014).

A key issue has been return policies for migrants whose residency application had been rejected, mainly refused asylum applicants. Since 2000, the Dutch government has actively facilitated the return of such migrants to their countries of origin. In practice, however, many rejected asylum applicants simply stayed and became so-called 'irregular' or 'illegal' migrants. The minority government led by the VVD Prime Minister Rutte that came to power in 2010 (with support from Wilders' Freedom Party) sought to increase repatriation efforts and introduce legislation to prohibit any form of assistance to irregular migrants. This coalition fell in 2012 with a new VVD/PvdA coalition formed after 2012 elections. This second coalition led by Rutte was not dependent on the support from Wilders and there were tensions between the VVD and the PvdA about provisions that made providing assistance to irregular migrants a criminal offence, which led to the plans being abandoned.

Whereas immigration policies have remained fragmented for different migrant categories to a large degree, efforts have been made to develop a more integrated approach to immigration policy through the so-called 'Linkage Act' (introduced in 1998). This sought to make it possible to directly connect the legal status of a person to rights and entitlements such as social security, housing, health and education and sought to build an 'internal border' against irregular migration while enforcing the differences in legal status of different migrants.

Civic integration

'Civic integration' programmes developed in the Netherlands and spread to other European countries (Goodman, 2014). The idea emerged in the early 1990s when there was official recognition that the Netherlands was an immigration country. Until then, immigration had been seen as a historically unique event with policies aimed at specific groups rather than at the on-going arrival of newcomers. Recognition of the permanent character of immigration led to a shift in focus from the groups that had immigrated in the past to the arrival of newcomers (Entzinger, 2003).

Deeper, underlying changes were relevant too. Of particular importance was welfare state retrenchment that began in the second half of the 1980s under the Christen Democrats-led governments of Prime Minister Ruud Lubbers (Scholten, 2011b). Initially, the economic downturn and welfare retrenchment did not lead to reform of the 'Minorities Policies' (discussed below) because of the view that the relatively weak position of immigrant minorities deserved measures that offered special protections. By 1989 Lubbers was stating that he was 'losing his patience' with ethnic minorities, and that he wanted to stress their social rights and duties (Scholten, 2011a). This took legislative form after 1994 when a civic integration policy was introduced aimed at promoting the socio-economic participation of newcomers.

Whereas civic integration programmes were initially voluntary, after 1998 a coalition comprising the PvdA/VVD with the smaller D66 party made participation mandatory. In 2007, the coalition, led by Prime Minister Balkenende, introduced new legislation that further increased the threshold needed to pass a civic integration test, particularly the language requirements. The obligation applied, in principle, to all non-EU citizens with permanent residence being made dependent on passing the test. Since 2010, passing the test is also a condition for naturalisation. The test involves a component oriented at different forms of participation in Dutch society (such as work, business and care) plus a component that tests language skills and basic knowledge of Dutch society, including gender equality, acceptation of sexual orientation and basic details of schooling and health care (Roggeband and Verloo, 2007). Initially, local authorities provided (via the private sector) courses in preparation for the test, but since 2012 migrants have to finance the courses and the test themselves (which can cost around €3,000).

Civic integration acquired a new dimension after 2006 with the introduction of 'civic integration abroad' that involves a pre-entry test that has to be passed before a migrant receives a temporary residence permit allowing him or her to move to the Netherlands and continue towards permanent residency (asylum seekers, temporary migrants and EU citizens are exempt from the test). The government does not itself provide pre-admission courses in the countries of origin. Migrants can choose how they prepare for the pre-admission tests with the government offering an information and training package for purchase. The language is of inclusion, but an underlying purpose of civic integration is to reinforce efforts to control and regulate immigration (Goodman, 2010).

'Civic integration' and 'civic integration abroad' strongly reflect the politicisation of immigration since the 1990s that accelerated with populist and extreme right influence since the 2000s. It would be wrong to attribute these policies entirely to the influence of Pim Fortuyn and Geert Wilders. Connecting immigration with integration preceded the success of Fortuyn, but his influence and that of Wilders' PVV can be seen on the way in which these ideas were taken forward, as well as on the stances and actions of mainstream parties. The Fortuyn Party effectively came from nowhere to be the second largest party after the 2002 parliamentary elections and entered coalition with the CDA and VVD. The murder of its leader Pim Fortuyn by an animal rights fanatic and internal tensions led to the Party's disintegration in 2003, but it clearly tapped into a strand of anti-immigration sentiment in the Dutch electorate while the momentum that had been created was capitalised upon by Wilders' Freedom Party.

Mainstream parties also adopted a much tougher line on immigration. For example, the VVD immigration and integration minister, Rita Verdonk, connected her political reputation to the success of civic integration laws. Verdonk was clear that these measures were not only to promote integration, but also to discourage immigration, particularly family migration from countries such as Morocco and Turkey. There was strong public support for these measures and significant parliamentary majorities for their introduction. One of the explanations was that besides the urge to restrict immigration and promote assimilation, these civic integration programmes could also garner support from political parties on the left (such as the PvdA) because the laws sought to equip migrants to participate in society, while also promoting other values such as respect for family life and gender equality.

A further important political impact of these civic integration laws and their development was the growing emphasis on individual responsibility. Migrants were already responsible for financing and preparing for the pre-entry test and, since 2012, the post-entry test as well. This reflected a broader political strategy, strengthened under the cabinets led by the VVD Prime Minister Rutte, which was to emphasise migrants' individual responsibility to become self-sufficient and manage their own 'civic integration' (see Chapter 6 on Sweden for parallels). There are generous loan schemes for migrants that cannot afford to pay for their preparatory courses themselves, but these appear to be little used. More generally, self-sufficiency reflects a broader government strategy to the labour market and welfare discussed in more detail below.

5.1 HOW IDEAS TRAVEL: THE CASE OF CIVIC INTEGRATION

The Netherlands has been a pioneer in Europe in terms of the development of civic integration programmes for newcomers. It was the first country in Europe to develop civic integration programmes in 1994, the first to make participation in these programmes mandatory in 1998, the first to introduce mandatory civic

(Continued)

(Continued)

integration programmes abroad in 2006 and the first to introduce mandatory (post-entry) civic integration tests in 2007.

Although many of these developments have at times triggered significant controversy they have been an important source of inspiration for the development of similar programmes in other European countries. This signals the 'horizontal' travel of policy ideas between European countries, facilitated by the many venues for horizontal lesson sharing and policy learning that the EU offers. Germany, Austria, France and the UK have developed civic integration programmes that are similar to the Dutch approach. They all monitored the Dutch initiatives and exchanged knowledge and experiences with policy-makers involved in the Dutch approach.

At the same time, the development of these programmes has seen an ongoing conversation with developing EU legal principles as well as the European Convention on Human Rights. In particular, the Dutch case has in many cases been a test case as to whether the suggested measures would be feasible under EU law. This applies in particular to the Right to Family Life that is granted under the European Convention on Human Rights that could be disproportionately hampered by civic integration programmes. Similar provisions in the EU's long-term residency and family reunification directives could have similar effects and have left the Dutch government open to EU level legal action (see below and Chapter 7).

Migration from Central and Eastern Europe

The Dutch government imposed transitional controls on migration from new EU member states after 2004, which lasted until 2007. The key point (see Chapter 7) is that EU free movement is guaranteed by the Union's supranational legal framework. Along with the Austrian, British and German governments, the Dutch authored a letter in summer 2013 to the President of the EU Council claiming negative welfare state effects of EU free movement.

Most EU citizens moving to the Netherlands using EU free movement rights do so for work. Even before the 2004 enlargement there was a growing presence of people from new EU member states in sectors such as agriculture, horticulture, construction and transport, supplemented by increased numbers of people from Romania and Bulgaria after they joined in 2007 (see Figure 5.2). There is evidence that workers from other EU member states have been joined by family members while the post-2008 crisis saw increased movement to the Netherlands from badly hit countries such as Greece, Italy and particularly from Spain (see Figure 5.2).

While EU mobility was framed as temporary and circular, there is evidence that some are settling more permanently in the Netherlands (Engbersen et al., 2013) plus some evidence of shorter term, circular or 'commuting' migration in seasonal sectors such as agriculture.

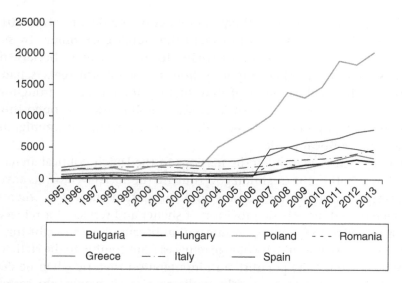

Figure 5.2 Presence of nationalities from selected Central, Eastern and South European countries in the Netherlands (annual volumes of immigration)

Source: http://statline.cbs.nl/Statweb/selection/?DM=SLNL&PA=37946NED&VW=T

Settlement has opened a (renewed) debate about integration. While levels are not on the same level as the UK (see Chapter 2) there has been evidence of growing concern. In 2013, polls showed that around 5 per cent of respondents saw immigration and integration as the most important issue facing the Netherlands, rising to 10 per cent in 2014. This was seen as primarily linked to movement from new member states (COB, 2014). As we have seen, EU citizens protected by EU laws cannot be compelled to undertake the kind of training and testing that non-EU migrants are compelled to undertake, because doing so would infringe EU rules prohibiting discrimination on the grounds of nationality.

There have been attempts to fan the flames of public concern about EU free movement. In 2012, Wilders' PVV set-up a telephone 'hotline' for people to complain about alleged anti-social behaviour by people from other EU member states. Concern was particularly focused on cities such as Amsterdam, The Hague and Rotterdam that have experienced the largest inflows and subsequent pressures on housing, language training plus concerns about labour exploitation. An attempt to appease anti-EU free movement sentiment occurred in 2014 when the government announced that EU citizens could voluntarily participate in civic integration schemes.

The Dutch struggle with the refugee crisis

The attention paid to intra-EU mobility faded in 2015 in the context of the refugee crisis. The Netherlands attracts nowhere near the same number of refugees as Germany, but an estimated number of 60,000 arrivals in 2015 was seen as a challenge. These arrivals caught the Dutch government by surprise and it was ill-prepared for providing shelter to the newcomers because during the 2000s facilities for the temporary housing of asylum seekers had been abandoned. The establishment of new shelters for refugees throughout the country caused controversy, with large-scale mobilisation in opposition not only by those living near to these shelters but also from anti-immigrant and extreme-right political parties.

The refugee crisis aggravated the tensions in the Dutch political arena, mentioned above. Within the Coalition government, the Social Democrats advocated more investments in better housing and integration measures, whereas the Liberals advocated more basic provision of shelter and services for refugees and were less receptive to spending on integration because they thought that a less welcoming approach would discourage refugees from coming to the Netherlands. Geert Wilders upped the populist, anti-immigration rhetoric when he declared the Dutch Parliament to be a 'fake parliament' as it would not sufficiently respond to concerns and fears about refugees.

As well as national political controversy, the Dutch government made controlling and limiting refugee flows to Europe a key item of its EU and international policies. Alongside Germany, the Dutch supported the EU wide relocation system agreed in September 2015 and advocated more stringent border controls in the Schengen area.

Immigrant policy

Once renowned for a multicultural approach that was seen as an exemplar for other countries, the Netherlands has gone through a sharp 'assimilationist turn' that, interestingly, is also now used as an exemplar by other countries. In the 1990s a widely shared view emerged that the multicultural approach of the 1980s had not led to good relations between minorities and the wider society because there was insufficient social, economic and cultural integration by immigrants and their families. This concern predated the rise of populist anti-immigration parties, but has been capitalised upon by them since the 2000s.

This perceived failure by the state to integrate migrants was also at the core of the critique of the political class and political system developed by Pim Fortuyn, which powerfully challenged the Dutch political status quo, as did Wilders subsequently. Yet, even in the wake of high levels of politicisation, 'everyday' migrant integration has developed over the years despite – or perhaps because of – these political controversies (Entzinger, 2013). To understand this requires tracing the history of Dutch integration policy.

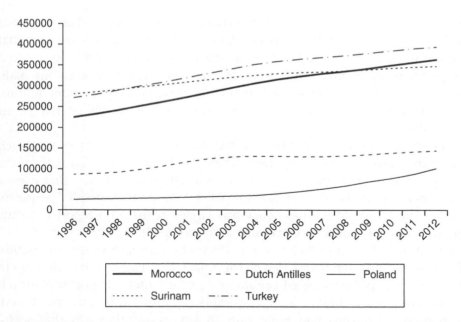

Figure 5.3 Development of largest immigrant groups (1st and 2nd generation) in the Netherlands

Source: http://statline.cbs.nl/Statweb/selection/?DM=SLNL&PA=37946NED&VW=T

The rise and fall of multiculturalism

Until the early 1980s, there were only *ad hoc* policies aimed at migrant groups. Except for repatriates from the former Dutch East Indies, most groups were initially seen as temporary. Until the 1970s, there was a consensus that the Netherlands was not and should not be a country of immigration (Scholten, 2011b) both for economic reasons and because of the view that the Netherlands was already too densely populated to become a country of immigration. The resultant integration policies were highly fragmented with big differences between immigrant groups. In the 1980s, policies promoted socio-economic participation, but integration understood in more socio-cultural terms was not promoted and in some respects even discouraged. For instance, migrant children experienced 'Education in the Own Language and Culture' with the intention of facilitating return. Some groups, particularly the Moluccans, were housed separately.

The development of immigrant policy, although the term integration itself was not used until the 1990s, occurred in the late 1970s. While not the only driver of policy, terrorist acts committed by people of Moluccan origin heightened awareness of the need for some kind of integration policy for a group that had been 'temporary' in the Netherlands for over 25 years. The result was an Ethnic Minorities Policy that developed in the 1980s. The key idea that helps us understand this approach is 'depoliticisation', by which is meant that the policy reflected not only a wide degree of consensus between the main political parties and other key actors such as business and the trade unions, but also a desire to make integration a non-partisan issue. Policy had the air of a 'gentleman's agreement'.

One striking aspect of the Dutch context was the role played by experts, such as academics, in policy development, which can be seen as a sign both of the attempt to depoliticise the issue and also as a reflection of a view that science and evidence could be a better base for policy than partisan politics (Scholten, 2011a). The Ethnic Minorities Policy was largely based on a report from the Dutch Scientific Council for Government Policy (WRR) of 1979.

The Ethnic Minorities Policy was a systematic approach to the integration of migrant groups that formalised the approach that had begun to develop in the 1970s. The policy targeted certain groups for which the government felt an 'historic responsibility': foreign workers (mainly Moroccans and Turks), Surinamese, Antilleans and Moluccans. A key assumption was that socio-cultural 'emancipation' of these groups was required in order to enable them to participate in Dutch society. For instance, Education in Minority Languages and Cultures that developed in the 1970s was continued, but now with the aim of cultural emancipation rather than return migration. The Ethnic Minorities policy defined Dutch society as a 'multicultural' or 'multi-ethnic' society and attempted to encourage wider awareness of this reality. For example, 'intercultural education' (involving lessons about minority cultures in primary education) was adopted for the whole society while an elaborate consultation structure was established to give migrant organisations a voice and involve them in the policy-making process. These measures gave rise to the characterisation of policy as multicultural while some analysts saw this as representing a distinct Dutch model of integration (Sniderman and Hagendoorn, 2007).

In addition to a social and cultural orientation, the Ethnic Minorities Policy concentrated perhaps even more on socio-economic participation and on legal and political rights. In terms of actual policy measures, an impressive array of developments occurred in the 1980s, including anti-discrimination policies (which would later help to inform EU anti-discrimination policies) as well as laws related to housing, education and labour. Forms of 'positive action' were introduced to promote equal labour market participation and improve housing conditions. Additional school funding was made available for children of immigrant origin as well as more resources to support Dutch language teaching.

5.2 PILLARISATION AND MINORITIES IN THE NETHERLANDS

Some of the peculiarities of the Dutch case cannot be understood without reference to a very specific aspect of Dutch history: pillarisation. Dutch society has always been very fragmented culturally, religiously and socially. In the late nineteenth century, this fragmentation was institutionalised in the form of four pillars in society: the Protestants, the Catholics, the Socialists and the Liberals.

These pillars divided society with each having its own schools, sport organisations, broadcasting agencies and political party. Dutch politics since then evolved around the creation of a balance of power and trust between these four pillars.

Although 'depillarisation' had been occurring since the 1960s, the arrival of immigrants in the 1960s and 1970s was framed by the legacies of pillarisation. Dutch society had already been accustomed to 'national minorities', making it just a small step to recognise 'ethnic minorities' as well. The balance between pillars could only be maintained by a high degree of 'tolerance', which was now also extended to ethnic minorities. And the recognition of culture and religious institutions for every pillar was now also extended to the new minorities, leading for instance to the establishment of Islamic schools with state funding.

This connects the debate on immigrant policy that would evolve since the 1980s directly to the depillarisation of Dutch society. It shows how institutions may have powerful 'feed-forward' effects, which mean they affect future politics and policies long beyond the survival of these institutions themselves (Vink, 2007).

Did this Ethnic Minorities Policy actually amount to a multicultural model? Here it is important to note that the policy clearly draws from the 'pillarisation' of Dutch society and politics as a form of conflict resolution and consensus-building. Dutch immigrant integration policy could thus be understood as an attempt to create a 'pillar' for immigrants to provide them with resources but also to include them within overarching social and political structures to build consensus and political stability. A problem was that this attempt was made at just the point in the 1970s and 1980s when the social basis that sustained the pillars – such as religious observance – began to crumble.

The result was a Dutch multicultural model that sought to create institutional structures to accommodate migrant groups, but immigrant groups never obtained a position similar to that of 'national' minorities that would be necessary for a balance of power in a pillarised system (Rath, 1996; Maussen, 2012). In addition, the 'depillarisation' that occurred from the end of the 1960s undermined the wider social and political basis and rationale. While there was a 'pillarisation reflex' (Vink, 2007) in the framing of ethnic minorities and associated policies, the group-based multicultural elements have been exaggerated by, for example, politicians seeking to blame this past response for current policy failures. Many of the measures labelled as part of this multicultural approach were part of wider policies in areas such as education and housing that were not targeted at immigrants *per se.*

Socio-economic integration

While we could be fixated by radical and populist parties and by personalities such as Geert Wilders, it is important to bear in mind that by the late 1980s and early 1990s, the Ethnic Minorities Policy had already started to change. A key reason for this was that the economic crisis of the mid-1980s encouraged the CDA-led governments of Prime Minister Lubbers to pursue retrenchment and welfare state reform to create an 'activating welfare state' with an emphasis both on rights and duties for all citizens. Entitlements became more dependent on efforts of citizens in the spheres of education and employment. By the end of the 1980s, a more critical discourse emerged both among politicians but also amongst the experts whose views informed policy, such as the Scientific Council for Government Policy (WRR), which saw the necessity for this 'rights-and-duties' approach to welfare state solidarity to be extended to immigrants (Scientific Council for Government Policy, 1989). Lubbers advocated the inclusion of Ethnic Minorities policies within the reform process. In the early 1990s, the VVD leader, Frits Bolkestein, targeted multiculturalism arguing that it was too strongly relativist, neglected core liberal principles such as gender equality, and turned a blind eye to the relevance of Dutch language and knowledge of national history and culture to integration.

Simply put, in the early 1990s, two sets of ideas coalesced to inform the critique of Ethnic Minorities policy. One was based on the need for welfare state reform and the other on cultural concerns.

In response to this politicisation, and reflecting calls for welfare state reform, an Integration Policy was developed in 1994 with a stronger socio-economic focus, stressing education, housing and employment as key sectors for integration. The 'activating' welfare state approach that had emerged in the 1980s was now also directly applied to immigrant policy. The previous group orientation was abandoned for a more individual-oriented approach targeted at 'good citizenship', which meant individual self-reliance as well as participating in and contributing to Dutch society. This was reflected in civic integration linking admission to integration. Under the so-called 'purple' coalitions (VVD, PvdA and D66 between 1994 to 2002) cultural identity was seen as a largely private matter in which government should not interfere. There was also a growing involvement for local authorities, particularly the larger cities, with many parts of immigrant integration policy incorporated within a more holistic approach to urban governance.

The assimilationist turn

What explains this assimilationist turn? Evidence of poorer employment outcomes, higher unemployment and worse educational outcomes for immigrants and their descendants helped to shape wider public debate. Also influential was an opinion piece by a PvdA associated academic, Paul Scheffer, that called for a stricter approach to socio-cultural integration, blaming excessive tolerance of cultural differences and a lack of attention to Dutch language, history and culture for what he called the 'multicultural tragedy' (Scheffer, 2000). This debate was further impelled by the aftermath of the 9/11 attacks in the USA and the rise of the populist Pim Fortuyn. Following his victory in local elections in Rotterdam, Fortuyn competed in the national elections in 2002 and, on the very day that polls indicated that he would win, was murdered by an animal rights activist. Fortuyn's populist agenda accused the political elite of ignoring ordinary people. He also called for zero immigration and for a 'cold war against Islam'. After his death, his party joined a CDA coalition led by Prime Minister Balkenende.

The debate about immigrant integration was never far from the headlines with coverage of stories, for example, of an imam refusing to shake hands with the female Minister of Immigration and Integration, Rita Verdonk, in 2006. There were also violent events that led to a focus on immigration and crime. Most notoriously, a famous filmmaker and well-known critic of Islam, Theo Van Gogh, was murdered by a radical Muslim in Amsterdam in 2004. Public perceptions were strongly influenced by the idea that immigrant policies had failed, that multiculturalism was the problem and that the cosy political consensus was to blame. The mainstream parties did adjust their rhetoric and policies to reflect the challenge posed by Fortuyn. There was also a parliamentary investigation in 2002 that was charged with the task of looking closely at integration policy. The committee's report actually concluded that the integration process had been 'relatively successful', but this only led to the committee being attacked for its naivety. The media and general public seemed unwilling to accept such findings, which demonstrated the power that events such as the rhetoric of Fortuyn and the murder of Van Gogh had on public perceptions of the issues. The response to the parliamentary report was interesting because it also showed a lack of confidence in and distrust of experts. In the past, expertise had always been an important source for policy-making; now it was rejected and politics took primacy, with the foundations of the previous consensus kicked away.

Politicisation and the challenge of populism triggered a change in policy towards what has been described as 'Integration Policy New Style' (Scholten, 2013) that saw the 'cultivation of differences' as a problem and emphasised the importance of Dutch history, values and norms. The content of these values and norms remained rather abstract, in spite of a national debate triggered by the Christian Democrat Prime Minister Balkenende. In terms of concrete policy measures, the pre- and post-entry civic integration measures, formulated under the leadership of Rita Verdonk, were a clear example of the renewed emphasis on socio-cultural integration or assimilation. This applies in particular to the basic knowledge of Dutch society that is part of these tests, including questions about Dutch history and how to behave and interact in Dutch society. A ceremony is held to celebrate the naturalisation of migrants and to signify the importance of citizenship.

An effort that clearly reflected the more assimilationist policy discourse in this period, but in the end could not be put into practice, involved the wish of the three centre-right governments in the 2000s (under the leadership of the Christian Democrat Balkenende) to make civic integration mandatory for so-called 'oldcomers'. 'Oldcomers' are migrants who had already been in the Netherlands for a considerable period, who had perhaps even naturalised as Dutch citizens. Minister Verdonk wanted to introduce a civic integration obligation on any migrant receiving welfare state benefits in order to make a direct connection between linguistic competence, cultural integration and the ability of these 'oldcomers' to participate in society. The problem was that this obligation could not be implemented because it discriminated against citizens. The desire to make civic integration obligatory by law was to some extent symbolic, as the welfare state system already allowed government to withdraw benefits if someone refused to take Dutch language classes or if unemployment was due to the wearing of a Burqa (though this was rarely applied in practice).

Another much debated issue in the 2000s was dual nationality. Since 1997, it was not formally permitted to have dual nationality; the original nationality citizenship had to be renounced before Dutch citizenship was granted. In practice there were exceptions, for example, for countries that did not allow migrants to renounce citizenship, such as Morocco and Turkey. Since 2003, obtaining citizenship was clearly defined as the successful end-result of integration rather than as a condition for integration, and a naturalisation test was to be passed before citizenship could be granted. Since 2009, migrants are required to declare allegiance to the Dutch Kingdom and its constitution. In 2013, the Dutch government also announced plans to facilitate the withdrawal of Dutch citizenship for persons with dual citizenship that commit serious crimes or are involved in terrorist activities.

5.3 POPULISM, MIGRATION AND INSTABILITY IN DUTCH POLITICS

Immigration and immigrant integration were key issues in the transformation of Dutch party politics. The Netherlands has traditionally been characterised by a consensual political culture as governments were based on coalitions of various parties, leading to an emphasis on consensus building amongst political elites and tendencies to depoliticisation of controversial issues.

This changed in the early 2000s with the rise of populism and later also anti-immigrant parties. These introduced more polarisation and politicisation, and contributed to significant instability. This began with Pim Fortuyn, a former Communist and, later, Labour Party member who won the city council elections in Rotterdam for the Liveable Rotterdam Party in 2002. He did so with a clear agenda of restricting immigration, being tough on assimilation and in particular with controversial statements against the growing influence of Islam in Dutch society.

Fortuyn's assassination in 2002 shook the previously peaceful and consensual Dutch political arena to its foundations. The Fortuyn Party still finished second in the 2002 elections, and was in a new government coalition under the leadership of the Christian Democrat Prime Minister Balkenende. However, in subsequent years, the LPF disintegrated due to internal disputes. 'Fortuynism' has, however, remained a force in Dutch politics ever since.

Fortuyn used immigration and integration as central issues for his broader populist agenda, as in these areas he claimed the discrepancy between the Dutch political elite and the 'voice from the street' had been the largest. This also affected mainstream parties, and the Liberal Party (VVD) in particular. Liberal Verdonk had served as Minister of Immigration and Integration from 2003 to 2006, acquiring fame for her tough approach to immigration and civic integration. Subsequently, she made a bid for the party leadership, which she only lost to the later Prime Minister Rutte by a tiny margin. She subsequently began her own party, *Trots op Nederland* (Proud of the Netherlands), although this never made it into parliament.

Geert Wilders left the VVD because of his opposition to Turkey's EU membership to form the Freedom Party (PVV). The PVV was much more narrowly an anti-immigrant and anti-Islamic party than the LPF had been. The PVV entered parliament with nine seats in 2006, growing to 24 seats in 2010 making it the third largest party. After 2010, a minority coalition was established by the Liberals and the Christian Democrats that was dependent on PVV support in parliament, giving the party significant influence on governmental policies. In 2012 the PVV withdrew its support for the government. In that year's general election PVV representation in Parliament fell to 15 seats with the party winning 10 per cent of the vote.

Beyond assimilation?

In the second half of the 2000s, migrant integration policies in the Netherlands again appeared to be taking a different direction. Three factors contributed to this new policy turning point. First, the post-2008 economic crisis hit the very open and trade-oriented Dutch economy particularly hard. The government was forced to slash spending. A victim of the cuts was immigrant integration policy, especially after the election in 2010 of VVD Prime Minister Rutte. Immigrant integration gradually disappeared as a separate policy domain at national level in contrast to the continued strong focus on immigration control. After 2012, there was no longer a minister with special responsibility for immigrant policy and the responsibility was absorbed within the role of the Minister of Social Affairs and Employment.

Second, most of what was left of Dutch immigrant policies had been decentralised to local governments. This trend had already been established during the 1990s only to be briefly supplanted in the early 2000s by a more centralist approach. The most substantial part of immigrant policies, the civic integration programmes, were strongly local, while cities such as Rotterdam, Amsterdam and The Hague developed their own approaches that differed not only from each other but sometimes also from national policies. Differences between Rotterdam's policy orientation on employment and gentrification and Amsterdam's policies on 'interculturalisation' and diversity are remarkable for two cities that face relatively similar issues (Scholten, 2013).

Third, political dynamics within the governing coalitions, led by VVD Prime Minister Rutte, led to further emphasis on the importance of migrants' individual responsibility for their own integration. Partly responsible for this was the influence of Wilders' Freedom Party, which entered parliament at the 2006 elections (with 9 out of 150 seats), but became particularly important after the 2010 elections where it was the third largest party (with 24 seats and almost 16 per cent of the vote). Its support was essential for Rutte's first cabinet between 2010 and 2012. The Freedom Party focused on prohibiting dual nationality, adopting a more Eurosceptic approach and enforcing strict immigration controls, including on EU free movement from new member states, and, perhaps most importantly, on Muslims who were seen by Wilders as un-assimilable (in a way very similar to their allies in the European Parliament, the French FN). VVD and Freedom Party perspectives converged on shutting down government subsidies for integration and strengthening individual responsibility.

Withdrawing specific integration policies and embedding integration measures into generic policies aimed at the entire population have been described as 'mainstreaming'. This is precisely what happened in the 2010s in the Netherlands with the eradication of immigrant policy as a policy domain at the national level and the embedding of measures into generic policies that are primarily situated at the local level (such as education, housing and employment). National budgets for immigrant policies were slashed and the national-level central policy co-ordination structure that had evolved over decades was dismantled, including support for consultation with migrant organisations dating back to the 1980s.

Similarly to Britain, the Dutch authorities collect large amounts of data on the ethnic minority population in order to monitor policy effectiveness (Guiraudon et al., 2005; De Zwart, 2012). Unlike the UK, the Netherlands does not have a census, but does collect ethnic statistics. Without the need for central policy co-ordination, ethnic statistics help to evaluate the effects of generic policies for specific groups. Consequently, they help identify those areas where policies would need to be intensified in order to cope with specific problems, without the need for group-specific policies. In particular, the annual reports from the authoritative Social and Cultural Planning Office (SCP) and the Central Bureau of Statistics play a key role in targeting the effects on immigrants and their descendants of more generic policies in this way.

This 'mainstreamed' approach to migrant integration has, however, revealed clear weaknesses (Scholten et al., 2016). By 2014 and 2015, public and political debate emerged about the need for a renewed integration policy. Local governments in particular, such as the cities of Rotterdam and The Hague, argued that many intra-EU migrants appeared to be settling permanently and that new integration efforts were required, especially for housing and education. It became clear that generic policies were insufficient for addressing the issues faced by people from other EU states. In response, the government announced new investments in civic integration, language education, housing and labour market integration, signalling yet another turn in the development of Dutch migrant integration policies.

In sum, the Dutch case has been one of the most versatile in Europe. Since the 1970s, fundamentally different approaches to migrant integration have come and gone. Once internationally famed for its multicultural approach, since the 2000s it has become one of the clearest examples of assimilationism and policy mainstreaming. Our discussion in this chapter shows that the politicisation of immigration was a key factor in these changes leading to the strong presence of anti-immigrant and populist parties, although the role of mainstream political parties should not be neglected. The Dutch case also shows that it is important to be aware that underneath the sometimes very sharp changes in political discourse, actual consequences in terms of policies on the ground may be much more modest.

European integration

The Netherlands was a founder member state of the EU and has played a key role in European integration. Until the early 2000s, the Netherlands was an important and active proponent of common EU migration and asylum policies. The Dutch were also frontrunners in more informal co-operation. For example, in the early 1990s in the midst of concern about growing numbers of asylum seekers, the Dutch government helped to create:

- the EU-level Centre for Information, Reflection and Exchange on Asylum (CIREA) for information exchange on asylum between EU member states;
- the Eurodac scheme for storing data such as fingerprints of asylum seekers;
- the High Level Working Group on Migration, which linked the internal security with foreign policy and development concerns and thus, in EU jargon, linked the 'two' pillars created by the Maastricht Treaty (1992) on Justice and Home Affairs and Common Foreign and Security Policy.

The Dutch government also advocated EU laws covering anti-discrimination (2000), family reunification (2003) and the rights of long-term residents (2003). These can be seen as examples of the 'uploading' to EU level of Dutch policy ideas.

There are various reasons for this strong role of Dutch government in the development of common EU migration and asylum policies until the early 2000s. First, the Netherlands is a relatively small country with an open economy and openness to immigration flows that cannot attain its objectives without 'pooling' sovereignty. The Dutch have enjoyed a free movement arrangement with Belgium and Luxembourg dating back to 1948 and were also keen advocates of the Schengen zone (and were one of the five original members). Second, as one of the relatively large recipients of immigration, the Netherlands sought benefits from 'burden sharing' for asylum-seeking and family migration, the latter of which was by far the largest migrant category in the Netherlands in the 1990s. Third, Dutch governments have assumed a 'guiding role' at EU level. Consequently, the Dutch pro-European stance in the 1990s can be explained by a mix of the 'escape to Europe' thesis with attempts to gain greater control of immigration and share the burden with other countries but this would also necessarily mean some ceding of sovereign authority to EU institutions.

A lot has changed since the 1990s. Paradoxically, Dutch governments in the late 2000s were confronted by the unanticipated consequences of EU laws and policies that it had once advocated. For example, the Dutch government argued for EU measures on family reunification, but then found that it was forced as a direct result of the EU's 2003 directive to reduce the income requirement for family migration from 120 per cent to 100 per cent precisely because of CJEU's interpretation of the provisions of the Family Reunification Directive. Civic integration also came under scrutiny and was permitted only insofar as it would not constitute a disproportionate obstacle to immigration (this was linked to a case brought to the CJEU by Ms Mohammed Imran: see Acosta and Geddes, 2013). Importantly, especially in terms of the number of migrants involved, the Dutch were obliged to exempt migrants from Turkey from the civic integration obligation because of the EU association agreement with Turkey.

Since the 2000s, the attitude of Dutch governments towards EU policy has become more critical. At domestic level, immigration became linked to increasingly negative attitudes to the EU. Mainstream parties like the VVD as well as the anti-system Freedom Party explicitly connected immigration policy to a desire to limit the influence of 'Brussels' on national policies. The first cabinet formed by the VVD Prime Minister Rutte in 2010, with Freedom Party support, explicitly promised in its coalition agreement to renegotiate EU Directives, such as that on family reunification. Interestingly, the method it uses to advocate a more restrictive directive in this area is similar to the informal modes of co-operation associated with 'transgovernmentalism' and an attempt to dodge the limits imposed by EU laws and institutions (see Chapter 7).

The attempt to benefit from the governmental networks that have developed at EU level has also been clearly evident in Dutch involvement in the immigrant integration agenda. It was under the Dutch Presidency of the EU Council in 2003 that the Common Basic Principles on Immigrant Integration were first formulated. The Principles are quite bland and general, but contain recognition that integration is a 'two way process', and the importance of adaptation at national level by migrant newcomers. It was necessarily the case that the Principles were non-binding as the EU possesses no formal competence in this area, but can try to stimulate national agendas as well as trying to bring the member states together to discuss common problems. The CBPs would later form the basis for the EU's Common Integration Agenda.

It is also highly relevant to note that the hallmark of Dutch policy since the 2000s – the civic integration programmes – inspired similar policy developments in various other European countries. This can be seen as a form of horizontal, state-to-state convergence that can be enabled by co-operation and discussions at EU level, but primarily reflects the valorisation of the national frame of reference in integration policies.

Since the 'big bang' enlargement of May 2004, the issue of EU free movement has become salient in the Netherlands. As we saw in Britain, the debate about immigration has been strongly dominated by EU free movement and the entanglement of anti-immigration and anti-EU sentiment. Free movement is a right guaranteed by EU law and EU citizens that avail themselves of this right cannot be required to undertake integration programmes. Instead, their rights are protected in relation to accessing employment and key services while discrimination is prohibited. Cities such as The Hague and Rotterdam have been actively lobbying in Brussels for more attention to the inclusion of EU free movers. In 2013, together with a number of EU countries (Germany, UK, Austria), the Netherlands appealed to the EU for explicit policies regarding the inclusion of EU citizens exercising their free movement rights. There is a broad political consensus in the Netherlands that such policies would be required, and the VVD/PvdA coalition in power after 2012 announced efforts in this regard with the Social Affairs Minister Lodewijk Asscher co-authoring a newspaper article, 'Code orange regarding free movement of workers in the EU' (Asscher and Goodhart, 2013), that sounded the alarm regarding the lack of inclusion of EU migrants. Furthermore, this government has been lobbying at the EU level for more uniformity in labour regulations throughout the EU. Because of current discrepancies in labour conditions, businesses and workers from CEE countries sometimes have a structural advantage over those in other EU countries, which (because of the free movement of services) can have a corrupting effect on competitiveness.

In sum, the Dutch position and role in EU policy developments in the sphere of immigration and integration has changed dramatically. From being a very active proponent of stronger EU legislation regarding migration and asylum and from being the founding father of the EU Common Basic Principles of Integration, the Dutch stance toward the EU's involvement in these areas in particular (and to the EU in general) have become more critical. In fact, the Dutch are now actively trying to limit the constraint imposed by EU regulations, which has become particularly clear in the area of free movement of EU workers. Paradoxically, the Dutch government are faced with the effects of EU policy constraints that they helped to create.

Conclusion

This chapter has shown significant change in Dutch immigration and immigrant policies. Until well into the 1990s, the Netherlands was known for its multiculturalism while also playing a key role in the Europeanisation of asylum and migration policies by providing a model for EU anti-discrimination policies and a 'civic integration' template. Rapid change occurred in a short time frame. Since the 2000s, immigration and migrant integration have been highly politicised and prominent within a populist challenge to the political status quo, instigated by Pim Fortuyn in 2002 and continued by Wilders' Freedom Party. This led to important changes in the position of mainstream political parties. The result is that the Dutch government is now struggling with the effects of EU regulations that it advocated, including the Family Reunification Directive. The Netherlands is also struggling with the consequences of freedom of movement within the EU after the accession of a number of CEE countries, most notably from Poland.

Behind the façade of politicisation of immigration and immigrant integration in the national political arena, the competencies of national government in these areas have actually decreased dramatically. Alongside the Europeanisation of asylum and migration policies, immigrant policies in the Netherlands are largely decentralised. For example, Rotterdam and Amsterdam have developed immigrant policy philosophies of their own, which on various points are distinctly at odds with national policies. This means that immigrant and immigration policies in the Netherlands have, over the past decades, become characterised by growing complexity. The result is that, as well as the rather dramatic changes in policy discourses and goals over the past decades on the national level, immigration and immigrant policies have also become increasingly fragmented between approaches at different levels at government.

6

Sweden: Immigration Politics in an Advanced Welfare State

Introduction

The regular 'Transatlantic Trends' survey of public opinion on immigration in Europe and North America consistently shows Sweden to be one of Europe's most pro-immigration countries. The country has been traditionally open to labour migration, asylum seekers and refugees. In 2014, 60 per cent of Swedish respondents approved of their government's handling of immigration while 77 per cent, 75 per cent and 73 per cent in Spain, Greece and the UK respectively, disapproved. When respondents were asked whether there were too many immigrants in their country 17 per cent of Swedish respondents agreed (when given the actual number this increased to 19 per cent). In the UK, 54 per cent of respondents unprompted by the actual number said that there were too many, falling to 31 per cent when told the actual number. Sweden has been a key destination for asylum seekers and refugees fleeing conflict in the Middle East and North Africa. These attitudes were challenged by the refugee crisis. In October 2015, the Swedish Migration Board doubled its estimate of arrivals in 2015 to 190,000, including 33,000 unaccompanied children, and estimated the cost of the inflow as £5.4 billion (BBC, 2015b). By the end of 2015, growing concern about refugee arrivals led the Swedish government to impose controls at its border with Denmark on the iconic Øresund Bridge.

This chapter explains why Sweden has Europe's most open approach to labour migration and has long been seen as a safe haven for refugees and asylum seekers. All the political parties in the Swedish Parliament (the *Riksdag*) – aside from the extreme-right Sweden Democrats (SD) – supported the maintenance of Sweden's relatively welcoming approach to migrants, refugees and asylum seekers. This was put under severe strain in October 2015 when an agreement between mainstream parties to exclude the Sweden Democrats came under pressure. Rather than accommodating the SD or even forming governments that either included them or relied on their support, Sweden's mainstream parties reached an agreement in December 2014 to effectively shun the SD and not include them in governments. The result was that the SD were able to exploit the European refugee crisis to their own political advantage leaving two alternatives for the main parties: a grand coalition of centre-right and centre-left to formally exclude the SD, or right-wing parties accommodating the SD as happened in the Netherlands with Wilders' Freedom Party (see Chapter 5) (*Financial Times*, 2015a).

Since the 2000s, there have been important changes both to labour migration and integration policies. Understanding these developments requires knowledge of the origins and effects of this Swedish approach to immigration politics, which is inextricably linked to the organisation, structure and future of the welfare state, as well as to party politics and competition between Sweden's political parties.

This chapter shows that:

1. contemporary debates about immigration in Sweden have their origins in links between nation-building, the welfare state and social democracy in post-war Sweden;
2. all three of these have been challenged; and
3. these challenges have important implications for immigration and immigrant policy.

This book's Introduction looked at how immigration is made visible as a social and political issue by the borders of states, which are not only territorial (land, air and sea ports of entry) but also include 'internal' organisational boundaries, such as those regulating access to the labour market and welfare state, plus conceptual boundaries of identity and belonging. The organisation of the Swedish welfare state plays a key 'internal' role in structuring immigration politics because it forms the backdrop against which the causes and consequences of immigration are debated. As we see, welfare state pressures can also translate into party political debate.

Immigration politics Swedish-style

Debates about immigration in Sweden have both domestic and international dimensions, not least because Sweden sees itself as a 'humanitarian superpower' offering rights and protection for its residents and a haven for those fleeing conflict and persecution (Borevi, 2012). Since Sweden joined in 1995, the EU has added another international dimension to Swedish immigration policy, for example, in May 2004 Sweden was one of the three EU member states (Britain and Ireland being the others) that allowed immediate access to its labour market for nationals of the A8 Central and East European countries.

The welfare state is central to Sweden's identity as a state and nation. Three key characteristics of the Scandinavian welfare state type have been identified (Brochmann, 2014: 283): *comprehensiveness* in relation to needs; *institutionalisation* of social rights giving all legal residents (whether citizens or not) a decent standard of living; and *universalism* with social rights granted to all residents and not just to those identified as being in need. More accurately, this is, to use Benhabib's (2002) phrase, a form of 'bounded universalism' because access to the welfare state and its benefits are combined with restrictions on access to the state territory.

Swedish social democracy and immigration

In the late 1960s, the Social Democratic Party (SAP) and its trade union allies were using arguments about protecting the welfare state to justify restrictions on immigration. Hinnfors et al. (2012) link this long-standing focus on restriction by the Swedish centre-left to the enduring legacy of social democratic ideology:

> regardless of voter opinion or the level of party threat (be that in the form of electoral competition from populist parties or from non-socialist parties with varying degrees of support for a more liberal immigration policy), the SAP's entry policies have remained restrictive. (2012: 599)

This applied in the 1960s and in the early 2000s in seeking to impose restrictions on EU free movement.

A key motive for the SAP and trade union position is that extending rights to immigrant newcomers can be costly, but not extending them can be costly too. Ruhs (2013) argues that states seek to strike a balance between the openness of their policies and the level of rights that they offer to migrants. For decades, Sweden pursued restrictions on immigration (external exclusion) combined with generous welfare state policies (internal inclusion). As we see, the post-2008 reforms to labour migration policy introduced by a centre-right government mean that Sweden is relatively open to new labour migration with emphasis placed on the market and market forces rather than the state. The corollary of this is an immigrant integration policy that emphasises individual self-reliance.

In contrast to the SAP, the Conservative *Moderaterna* party has, at times, flirted with populist rhetoric on immigrant integration. Although, as Green-Pedersen and Odmalm (2008) point out, since 2004 the *Moderaterna* has also argued for an open approach to both EU and non-EU labour migration. In government, as part of the centre-right Alliance for Sweden between 2006 and 2014, the *Moderaterna* played a key role in major changes to immigration and immigrant policies that emphasised labour market integration and individual self-reliance. This challenge from the centre-right to prevailing SAP ideas about immigration and immigrant policy also influenced Sweden's relatively open approach to EU free movement after 2004. This was followed in 2008 by an employer-driven approach to non-EU labour migration and (introduced between 2008 and 2010) a changed approach to integration, away from what the then Integration Minister Erik Ullenhag called a 'hand-holding mentality' with immigrants considered 'weak individuals', to a strong focus on rapidly finding a job (cited in Fredlund-Blomst, 2014: 8).

Given the centrality of work and welfare to the politics of immigration in Sweden, it is hardly surprising that economic recession in the 1990s and the effects of the post-2008 economic crisis had powerful effects on immigration politics. In the 2000s, Sweden was seen as a shining light by international organisations such as the OECD because of its ability to recover from the recession in the 1990s by implementing labour market and welfare reforms that led to high growth rates. Sweden's response to the economic crisis of 2008 was swift: tax increases, cuts in public sector employment and cuts to welfare benefits and social services. A *Washington Post* columnist referred to Sweden as 'the rock star of the recovery' (cited in Fredlund-Blomst, 2014: 4). Increased unemployment and a steep growth in inequality have, however, put pressure on the foundations of an approach to immigration and immigrant politics that have been rights-based and inclusive. Immigrants and their descendants are far more likely to be unemployed than native Swedes (Fredlund-Blomst, 2014). In 2009–10 Sweden had the highest gap between native and immigrant employment rates of any OECD country. This reflects the findings of the MIPEX survey and its ranking of European and international efforts at immigrant integration, which show Sweden to be good at legislating for equality but less good at turning law into outcomes.

Immigration policy

Sweden is a country with an open trading economy, a strong international outlook and a history of immigration. In 2012, the foreign born population accounted for 15.4 per cent of the total population while around 20 per cent of the population were either born abroad or had two immigrant parents (Fredlund-Blomst, 2014: 2).

The close links in Sweden between nation building, social democracy, the welfare state and immigration become evident through the idea of the *Folkhem* (Peoples' Home) with 'very clear limits to the ability of the *Folkhem* to make room for those from outside' (Hinnfors et al., 2012: 601). The *Folkhem* was central to the SAP's philosophy. The SAP belief in the *Folkhem* was concomitant with the understanding that there were limits to the country's ability to absorb new immigrants. This meant that the SAP could advocate strict controls on immigration on the basis of '"welfare state protection", preservation of "union strength", "public sector financial stability", "consensus building" and allusions to "Swedishness"' (Hinnfors et al., 2012: 590).

These precepts of the social democratic foundations of the Swedish welfare state, and to the SAP as the pre-dominant governing party in the post-war period, explain a dual focus on regulating access to the state territory combined with a swift recognition of permanent immigration for those immigrants that were 'in'. Between 1948 and 2002 the SAP averaged over 42 per cent in parliamentary elections (Aylott and Bolin, 2015). SAP pre-dominance was challenged for a brief period between 1991 and 1994 and then for a longer period by four centre-right parties gathered within the Alliance for Sweden between 2006 and 2014 that oversaw changes to labour migration laws and integration policies between 2008 and 2010.

Clearly, as elsewhere in Europe, control and integration are not separate debates, but two sides of the same coin; debates about control are shaped by ideas about integration and vice versa. Contemporary European policy jargon refers to this as the admissions/integration nexus, but this relationship has long been the core dilemma in Swedish immigration policy. As Brochmann (2014: 285) puts it: 'controlling inflow has been seen as a prerequisite for maintaining the welfare system, which can be undermined by excessive burdens'. This also translates into a preference for higher skilled labour migration rather than family members or asylum seekers, although migration to Sweden since the 1970s has been predominantly by family members and asylum seekers/refugees. Figure 6.1 provides a breakdown of migration flows to Sweden between 2005 and 2014 and shows the dominance of the family (reunification and formation) and asylum/refugees routes. It also shows the steep spike in asylum applicants reflecting both the effects of conflict in the Middle East and North Africa, and Sweden's status as an EU member state with a relatively strong commitment to international protection, and also thus an EU member with an interest in seeing a stronger EU commitment to the sharing of responsibility. The sharp acceleration in refugee and asylum inflows in 2015 put strain on the reception system, led to political tensions and to the reimposition of border controls with Denmark in a bid to stem refugee arrivals.

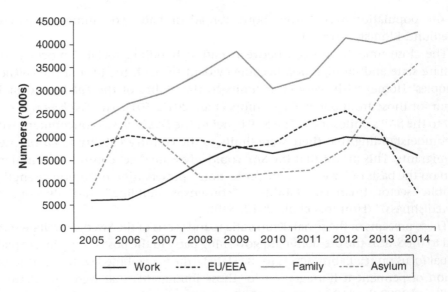

Figure 6.1   Breakdown of migration flows to Sweden 2005–14

Source: Swedish Migration Board (www.migrationsverket.se/English/About-the-Migration-Agency/Facts-and-statistics-/Statistics.html)

A Scandinavian migration regime

Sweden's control capacity has been aided by its geographical position. Its only land border is to the north with Finland. Sweden is closely linked to its Scandinavian neighbours through the Nordic Council (including Denmark, Greenland, Åland Islands, Faroe Islands, Finland, Iceland and Norway). Until the 1970s, the main migration flows into Sweden came from other Nordic countries, particularly Finland. Since 1954 there has been free movement within the Nordic labour market for citizens of member states and the right to reside and work in other member states. These provisions are similar to those applying to EU citizens since Sweden joined in 1995.

Sweden was not a large-scale recruiter of migrant workers until the 1960s when the main source countries for migrants were Greece, Turkey and Yugoslavia. In 1965, the unexpected arrival of workers from Yugoslavia prompted an Aliens Decree, which was issued without reference to the *Riksdag*, the Swedish Parliament. This specified that in order to enter Sweden, migrants needed to apply for a work permit in their country of origin. In 1968, guidelines to regulate migration were issued and the Swedish Migration Board was established with responsibility both for regulating migration and the integration of immigrants. Sweden has since elaborated a system of controls that combines external controls (visas) with internal controls (residence and work permits).

Labour migration reached a peak in 1969–70. The Swedish trade unions accepted immigration so long as migrant workers were entitled to the same conditions as other workers. Immigrants also received the same social benefits as Swedes, including unemployment benefit. This welfare state reception was in line with the rapid acceptance of permanent immigration and was accompanied by liberal nationality laws. In contrast to other 'older' European immigration countries such as Germany and the Netherlands, Sweden explicitly pursued an immigration policy rather than a guestworker paradigm predicated on the flawed assumption of temporariness. After one or two years in Sweden, migrants could establish permanent resident status with the rights of denizenship and after five could become Swedish citizens. Even by the late 1960s there were concerns, particularly from the trade unions, about the effects of labour migration on the Swedish welfare state (Hinnfors et al., 2012).

Expansive recruitment policies ended during a short economic recession in 1972. At this time, a major decision on immigration was made without reference to the *Riksdag*. As Hammar (1999: 174) puts it: 'the political system was not involved, and the general public was not informed'. This echoes the points made in earlier chapters about the importance of identifying the venues within which decisions are made about immigration policy. In Sweden, we see a corporatist style of policy-making that was relatively shielded from wider public debate. Hammar calls this an 'apolitical tradition', although the corporatist origins of this particular form of 'apolitical politics' are revealed when it is noted that the Swedish trade unions' national federation, the *Landsorganisation* vetoed continued labour migration. Rather than being apolitical, what were evident were corporatist politics with 'insider' interest groups such as trade unions playing a key role in shaping policy. The trade unions were worried about labour migration's impact on the salaries and working conditions of their members. In 1973, the closing of the immigration door was made abundantly clear when a new law forced all employers of any foreign worker to foot the bill for 400 hours at their employees' full salary cost to allow immigrant workers to take Swedish language classes.

Labour migration was to be tightly regulated based on judgements about Sweden's capacity to provide employment, housing and social support for migrants on the same terms as Swedes. As we saw with other European countries, closing the door to labour migration did not mean the end of migration with family migration continuing plus a growth in the number of those seeking protection as asylum seekers or refugees.

A humanitarian superpower?

Refugee migration has been a key in-flow and is central to an important component of Sweden's identity as a 'humanitarian superpower' (Borevi, 2012). Migration by people seeking protection has been a recurring political issue since the 1990s. By 2014, with 2,900 applicants per 1 million population, Sweden had the highest proportion of asylum seekers in the EU (followed by Denmark on 1,300 and Malta on 1,000 per million, respectively) (Eurostat, 2014).

There are two main asylum routes into Sweden.

- 'Quota refugees' agreed with the UNHCR and managed by the Swedish Migration Board. The *Riksdag* decides an annual refugee quota and then allocates funding for the resettlement of between 1,700 and 1,900 persons each year. As Fredlund-Blomst (2014: 3) points out, by 2014, the town of Södertälje about 30 km South west of Stockholm with a population of just 80,000 had taken more Syrian refugees than the whole of Canada and the USA.
- 'Spontaneous' asylum seekers who claim recognition under the terms of the Geneva Convention (on the basis of a well-founded fear of persecution).

We can look back over the last 35 years or so to see that, in the early 1980s, the number of spontaneous asylum seekers was low, at around 5,000 each year. This increased to around 12,000 to 15,000 between 1985 and 1988 and to around 30,000 a year between 1988 and 1991. In 1992, the number reached 84,000, mainly from ex-Yugoslavia. During the 1990s, asylum-seeking migration increased the range and diversity of migrant-origin groups in Sweden. The numbers of migrants from other Nordic countries fell to around 30 per cent of the total (from nearer 70 per cent) while the number of people from outside Europe grew to around 50 per cent of the total with increased numbers of Kurds, Iranians, Iraqis and Lebanese.

Sweden developed a dispersal policy for the reception of asylum seekers, which meant that the politics of asylum had a strong local component. The early successes of the anti-immigration New Democracy Party in the late 1980s were at municipal level, as later were those of the SD in the 2000s as they sought to exploit hostility to migrants and asylum seekers (Bolin et al., 2014).

Prior to 1985, the Swedish Labour Market Board managed dispersal, which was beneficial in that it maintained strong links to the labour market. In 1985 responsibilities were transferred to the Swedish Migration Board. Initially, asylum seekers were accommodated in 60 of Sweden's 284 municipalities deemed to have suitable characteristics for reception. By 1989 and in the face of increased numbers, 277 of the 284 were involved. Previously housing, education and future employment had all been considered as relevant factors.

By the late 1980s the concern was mainly with the availability of accommodation. Tapping into some local resentment about asylum-seeking migration, the extreme right New Democracy party polled 8 per cent of the vote in the 1991 national elections, although its representation lasted only until 1994 and there were no populist, anti-immigration parties in the *Riksdag* until the Sweden Democrats crossed the 4 per cent electoral threshold securing 5.1 per cent of the vote at the 2010 general election (Green-Pedersen and Odmalm, 2008: 372).

It is important to note that advocacy of restrictions on immigration is not solely an extreme right position. While certainly not sharing New Democracy's radical right orientation, the SAP also had a restrictive approach to asylum and refugee migration that can be linked to its traditional concerns about implications for the welfare state. In the area of refugee and asylum policy, this meant a preference for temporary protection and then repatriation. The SAP saw repatriation as a better solution when compared to long-term integration into the welfare state. On this basis the SAP opposed the centre-right government issuing residence permits to Bosnian refugees in the early 1990s, making the argument that people from Bosnia could make an important contribution to the post-war rebuilding of that country if they returned.

If we look at the case of the Bosnians we can see how the ability of asylum seekers to enter Sweden was reduced with visa policy playing a key role. In 1993, the centre-right Coalition government, in the face of SAP opposition, granted permanent residence status to Bosnian refugees already in Sweden. Ostensibly this was an inclusive step, but, at the same time, a visa requirement was introduced for all new arrivals from that country, which would make it much more difficult for people from Bosnia to get to Sweden. Evidence for this was that the flow of people from Bosnia stopped almost completely because the journey became near impossible. In 1997, legislation abolished the categories of *de facto* refugees, war refusers and the granting of residence permits on humanitarian grounds. At the same time, the 1997 legislation also introduced four new protection categories (capital/corporal punishment, non-state persecution, gender and sexual orientation).

As in many other European countries, enforcement has been problematic because, for example, many asylum seekers arrived without documentation that would allow their country of origin to be easily ascertained. The number of rejected asylum seekers hovered at between 8–10,000 a year through the 1990s. A sanctuary movement developed to protect asylum seekers in response to what was seen as draconian encroachment by the state on migrants' rights and a breach with Swedish traditions of international solidarity.

Figure 6.1 above showed a spike in asylum numbers provoked mainly by people fleeing conflict in the Middle East and North Africa. In 2012, Sweden, along with Germany, declared that people fleeing Syria and making a claim for asylum would automatically be granted protection on the basis that return to Syria would create a serious risk of the person being tortured. Predictions from the Swedish Migration Board of an inflow in 2015 of 190,000 led Prime Minister Fredrik Reinfeldt to argue that such a scale of arrivals could 'cause tensions' but that Swedish people needed to 'open their hearts for those vulnerable people' (Aylott and Bolin, 2015: 733). Even though it was strikingly open to asylum when compared to other EU governments, Reinfeldt's speech attracted some criticism from the left because of its reference to the costs and burdens of such numbers. By the end of 2015, concern about numbers led the government to impose controls at the Swedish border with Denmark.

The presence, after 2010, of the strongly anti-immigration SD (with 49 of the 349 seats) in the *Riksdag* (up from 20 at the 2005 general election) had destabilising effects on the Swedish political system and contributed to high political drama in December 2014 when the SAP Prime Minister, Stefan Löfven, elected only 3 months previously, dissolved parliament and called a snap election scheduled for March 2015. This happened when the SD broke with parliamentary convention to vote with the four parties of the opposition centre-right 'Alliance' grouping against the government's budget. In response, just before Christmas 2014, the main centre-left and centre-right parties agreed to a package of mutual support whereby, for two parliamentary terms, the smaller of the two 'political constellations', whether it be centre-right or centre-left, would allow the other one to govern. As Aylott (2015: 3) notes: 'this limited aggression pact is designed to largely deprive the SD of parliamentary influence'.

The wider significance of this development was that the mainstream parties resolved to isolate the SD, which can be compared with developments in neighbouring Denmark where the extreme-right, anti-immigration Danish Peoples' Party offered support to centre-right governments in return for concessions that saw significant tightening of immigration laws. The SD might seem marginalised, but, playing on concerns about increased asylum seeking and immigration, it has had effects on political debate and enforces discussion of 'the sustainability of the current "volume" of immigration' (Aylott, 2015). Also, while pushed to the margins in Parliament, the SD was presented with a potentially golden opportunity to present itself as the only true opposition.

Liberalising labour migration

Figure 6.1 (above) showed protection and family reasons to have dominated as motives for movement to Sweden since the 1970s. The diagram also shows a near threefold increase in non-EU labour migration from just under 6,000 in 2005 to just under 16,000 in 2014. A new openness to both EU and non-EU labour migration began in the 2000s and following a controversial parliamentary vote and strong opposition from the SAP, the Swedish government also decided not to impose restrictions on A8 citizens after accession on 1 May 2004.

The 2008 immigration law introduced by the centre-right 'Alliance for Sweden' Coalition government (of four centre-right parties with support from the Green Party) established a demand-led system to allow employers to meet their requirements for both high and lower skilled labour without labour market tests. The Immigration Minister of the time, Tobias Billström, was eager to proclaim the merits of an approach that meant, as he put it in 2012, Sweden had 'one of the most flexible and efficient systems for labour migration in the world' (cited in Emilsson, 2014: 6)

The 2008 law reflected deeper changes in Swedish politics with greater emphasis placed on business interests, the views of employers and a 'market forces' rationale. In turn this reflected the view that Sweden needed to attract labour migrants to sustain its knowledge-based economy and counter the effects of an ageing population on its labour market and welfare state. The SAP opposed these changes because of the threat of new labour migration to the welfare state, the need to ensure that any new immigration occurred on the same employment terms and also because the law was passed without reference to the views of trade unions, thus challenging corporatist style decision-making (Hinnfors et al., 2012).

Swedish immigration policy can be understood as arising from a wider political debate about the past, present and future of the welfare state. A logic of external closure and internal inclusion is strongly associated with the social democratic ideology of the SAP. Changes in immigration policy in the 2000s reflect a weakening of the social democratic welfare state consensus and movement towards market forces and individualisation.

As in our other chapters, the focus on the structure of the welfare state and the dynamics of party competition and party ideology demonstrates that it would be a mistake to ascribe too much causal significance to immigration as a driver of policy change without first thinking about how the politics of immigration are shaped by broader social, political and economic factors. We see that this is also the case when we shift attention to the linked issue of immigrant policy.

Immigrant policy

Between 2008 and 2010 a reorientation of Swedish immigrant policy occurred, led by a centre-right government that saw a market-driven approach focused on getting immigrants and their descendants into employment. In these terms, Sweden can be seen to conform to a trend towards 'transitive' assimilation in the terms identified by Brubaker (2001), meaning trying to secure similar outcomes in key areas such as employment levels between immigrants and the native population.

Equality and utilisation of welfare state rights has been central to the Swedish approach to both immigration and immigrant integration. The new approach heralded by the 2008 reforms could be seen as a move away from 'multiculturalism', although, as we will see, multiculturalism Swedish-style has been debated since the 1980s. This cautions against overstating the influence of extreme and populist anti-immigration parties such as New Democracy in the early 1990s, or the SD after

2010, at the expense of other, more structural aspects of the debate, as well as the role played by mainstream parties.

To understand the scale, extent and effect of change requires some grasp of what happened before and, of course, the meaning of multiculturalism. Like most terms in debates about immigration, multiculturalism is contested and brings with it considerable ideological baggage. An important part of the context in Sweden is that multicultural policies were set against the backdrop of a highly developed welfare state.

The idea of multiculturalism refers to interactions in culturally diverse societies with its particular form depending on the types of diversity (Guttmann, 1994; Kymlicka, 1995). Charles Taylor (1992) links the idea to 'the politics of recognition' and argues that withholding recognition of cultural differences can be a form of oppression. This leads towards the politics of difference and identity politics. Parekh (2000: 3), however, cautions that

> multiculturalism is not about identity per se but about those embedded in and sustained by a culture; that is a body of beliefs and practices in terms of which a group of people understand themselves and the world and organise their individual and collective lives.

As such, these culturally derived differences have a 'measure of authority' (ibid.). Multicultural policies thus go beyond a plea for tolerance and involve the public affirmation of difference as socially desirable. This suggests that cultural rights can be added to the familiar Marshallian panoply of legal, political and social rights as the hallmarks of modern citizenship.

In the Swedish context, it would mean group rights for migrants defined in cultural terms with the aim being to facilitate their integration into the Swedish welfare state. Multicultural integration in Sweden rested on four pillars: the swift recognition of permanent immigration; the social democratic welfare state with 'cradle to grave' protection; a corporatist policy style with an emphasis on consultation and dialogue; and, fourth, ideas about international solidarity and the responsibilities of richer countries to less economically developed countries that informed refugee and asylum policy. Formally, however, multiculturalism wasn't the official policy approach until the mid-1970s and by the mid-1980s was already being questioned.

The development of Swedish multiculturalism

Before 1945 there was little non-Nordic migration to Sweden and no integration policy. There was, however, a rather sinister aspect of this period. Ideas about the superiority of the Swedish people were prevalent in both social democratic and right-wing thought in the inter-war period. In 1921, the *Riksdag* created a special institute for Racial Hygiene. A policy of sterilising people seen as unsuitable parents persisted into the 1970s with some esti-mates of around 60,000 people being subjected to this scheme (*The Economist*, 1997). Between 1945 and 1964, Swedish responses to immigration rested on an expectation of assimilation.

Between 1964 and 1975 as labour migration increased there was a shift towards 'mutual adaptation' with the provision of language training, home lan-guage instruction and the creation of local immigrants' councils. Foreign workers were quickly given the status of denizens as a way of ensuring their welfare state integration. Hammar (1999: 178) describes the measures between 1968 and 1975 as 'social engineering' with attempts to extend the principle of equality to all legal residents with the social and political participation of new-comers as an objective coupled with 'vague ideas' about ethnic minority rights in a multicultural Sweden (ibid.). These measures were remarkably inclusive, particularly when it's remembered that other European countries were still strug-gling to recognise that the 'guests' had stayed. Another element of mutual adaptation was that immigration and immigrant policies were dealt with in corporatist structures.

Concerns about numbers of migrants necessarily fed into debates about inte-gration, with housing a key concern. In 1974 the government embarked on the 'Million Programme' of house building. In terms of numbers built the pro-gramme was relatively successful, but they were often the lowest quality housing stock with a bad physical environment and poor access to services and employ-ment. The high concentration of immigrants in this new housing stock also led to residential segregation. By 2008, 60 per cent of Swedes were living in areas where the population was also predominantly Swedish, 20 per cent lived in areas that were virtually 100 per cent Swedish, while 20 per cent of Sweden's immi-grant population lived in areas where more than 40 per cent of the other residents were also immigrants (Fredlund-Blomst, 2014). An unintended effect of the Million Programme was the creation of *betongförorter* (concrete suburbs) with large immigrant populations. The footballer Zlatan Ibrahimović (the son of Croatian and Bosnian parents) tells the story in his best-selling book of his upbringing in the Malmö 'concrete suburb' of Rosengård and how this distanced him from mainstream Swedish society (Ibrahimović, 2014).

Sweden also made it easy for immigrants to become Swedish. Referring to the 1970s and 1980s, Miller (1989: 131) notes that: 'Naturalisation in Sweden is relatively quick and easy, and naturalisation rates are high'. Brubaker (1989: 10) links this to a faith in welfare state institutions to level out social inequalities in the same way that French institutions were supposed to level out cultural differences. In both Sweden and France there has been a dimin-ished confidence in core institutions' ability to perform these roles, which was at the heart of the politicisation of immigration, but is more than simply an immigration issue.

6.1 MULTICULTURAL INTEGRATION SWEDISH-STYLE

A landmark event in the history of multicultural integration Swedish-style occurred in 1974 when a parliamentary commission on immigration mapped out a multicultural Sweden with 'equality', 'freedom of choice' and 'partnership'.

- Equality meant living conditions comparable with Swedes.
- Freedom of choice meant a genuine choice about retaining cultural identity.
- Partnership meant co-operation and solidarity between Swedes and newcomers.

Ålund and Schierup (1993: 99) described the policy as an

> ambitious attempt to create social equality among ethnic groups [with] its respect for immigrant culture and its emphasis on providing immigrants with resources with which to exercise political influence.

It also demonstrated a confidence in the ability of the Swedish state to act as the guarantor of inclusion.

From 1975 onwards attempts were made to put these ideas into effect. As well as full welfare state membership, local voting rights to immigrants were extended after 36 months legal residence. Immigrant associations were subsidised. From 1976, Swedish nationality could be obtained after five years of residence. From 1977, the children of immigrants had the right to be taught their native language.

A 1984 parliamentary report linked future migration to Sweden's ability to integrate newcomers. The report also argued that the multicultural approach was too broad in terms of its recognition of group rights. Instead, it was proposed that more effort at adaptation was required from immigrants. This meant that immigrants' languages and cultures could be protected, but in a more limited sense that did not conflict with core Swedish values. On the issue of assimilation the Swedish state declared itself to be neutral; it would neither promote nor oppose it.

By the mid-1980s there was already a move away from some aspects of the multicultural policy towards an approach that placed more emphasis on Swedish language and adaptation by immigrants. Sweden was a trendsetter in immigrant policies both in the formulation of a multicultural approach and then in the movement towards increased emphasis on socio-economic and linguistic adaptation by newcomers. This coincided with evidence that the employment and income levels of immigrant-origin people were lagging behind those of other Swedes, which only became more pronounced in the 1990s and 2000s.

The economic recession of the 1990s led to increased unemployment amongst the immigrant and immigrant-origin population, as well as concern about 'ethnic segregation' in the 'concrete suburbs' referred to earlier. This coincided with diminished confidence in central planning with some state enterprises sold off to the private sector and a more neoliberal, market-oriented policy approach (Rothstein, 1998).

Economic recession and pressures on the welfare state were conditions affecting all people in Sweden. They were not caused by immigration but Soininen (1999: 691) observes that the Swedish government's stance on immigrants in the 1990s can be traced to pressures on the Swedish model. In 1996 a designated minister with responsibility for integration policy was established. Greater emphasis was placed on individual rights while terms such as self-sufficiency and self-support were adopted in order to encourage immigrant participation in Swedish society. While Sweden was recognised as 'an unavoidably multicultural society', this was seen as an argument for the maintenance of 'Swedish cultural heritage' and the basic principles of Swedish law and democracy (cited in Soininen, 1999: 692).

Identifying the emergence of a debate about the effects of multicultural policy in the 1980s helps to avoid the mistake of ascribing change solely to the effects of extreme right or populist political parties. New Democracy in the early 1990s and the SD since the 2000s have influenced debate about immigration, but they were capitalising on issues raised by mainstream parties well before they rose to prominence. From a very different position on the political spectrum, the centre-left SAP has long advocated restrictions on immigration coupled with a rights-based and inclusive approach to integration. It did not, however, want to find itself bracketed with the SD. Similarly, the centre-right *Moderaterna* flirted with populist rhetoric on immigration, but, in the 2000s, moved towards an open approach to labour migration and openness to EU migration, and in 2014 entered into agreement with the centre-left parties to marginalise the SD in the *Riksdag*.

This movement away from multicultural policy was confirmed by the 1998 law on immigrant integration that created the Swedish Integration Board (NIO). The NIO had specific responsibilities to develop programmes to monitor the integration of immigrants, particularly in socio-economic terms. The NIO's role was outlined in a 1997 government report entitled 'Sweden, the Future and the Plural Society – From Immigration Policy to Integration Policy'. The report called for the mainstreaming of immigrant integration measures across social and labour market policies based on the principles of non-discrimination, equality, diversity and mutual respect. The policy placed far more emphasis on individual self-reliance (Green-Pedersen and Odmalm, 2008).

6.2 THE DISCURSIVE SHIFT IN SWEDISH INTEGRATION POLICY

To get a sense of policy change in the area of immigrant integration consider these two statements below.

Writing in the 1990s, the academic Yasemin Soysal (1994: 80) wrote that Sweden's multicultural approach defined 'migrant groups as ethnic minority communities, and … aims at equality between ethnic groups while emphasising separate existences … and collective identities'.

By 2008, the integration minister Erik Ullenhag from the centre-right 'Alliance for Sweden' Coalition government was calling for the end of 'hand holding' that led to 'weak individuals' unable to take their place in Swedish society.

Movement away from identity-affirming, multicultural policies actually can be traced to the 1980s, acquiring more momentum in the face of economic recession in the 1990s, and can be compared with similar developments in other European countries. Soininen (1999: 691) observes similarities between Sweden and the Netherlands (see also Koopmans, 2010):

Even the arguments for this orientation raise the same points. Namely that the accentuation of values deemed deviant by majority cultural standards risks making integration more difficult and that certain values are in conflict with the fundamental principles of the Dutch and Swedish societies.

The 2008–10 reforms to Swedish immigrant policy with their strong labour market focus also brought a greater centralisation to policy as responsibility was taken from local authorities and given to the Swedish Public Employment Service. As with the 2008 law on labour migration, changes were designed to activate market forces with the idea that the labour market would determine settlement patterns rather than the allocation of funding to local authorities to host immigrants (Fredlund-Blomst, 2014). New immigrants would be offered counselling, coursework and training for up to two years. Employers would also receive subsidies if they offered apprenticeships or internships to immigrants. This would include language instruction through a Swedish for Immigrants programme as well as a more general civic orientation to the history, norms and values of Swedish society. Elements of conditionality were introduced that made welfare benefits contingent on participation in the 'Swedish for Immigrants' programme, with possible sanctions for those that didn't.

While conforming to the more general Europe-wide trend towards socio-economic and linguistic adaptation by newcomers, it is also important to consider specific features of the Swedish case. In 'older' immigration countries, increased immigration after the 1970s by refugees and asylum seekers, as well as by family members, coincided with economic difficulties, welfare state pressures, the weakening of corporatist structures, individualisation and Europeanisation. In Sweden, these pressures dented the ability of the Swedish state to act as the sovereign arbiter of inclusion and exclusion. Linked to this has been some decline in trust in Swedish political institutions and politicians (Holmberg, 1999). This is not to say that the Swedish model has been cast asunder; rather, previous assumptions have been questioned or abandoned with powerful implications for ideas about immigrant integration. A lack of orientation to Swedish society by immigrants became seen as a problem, but, behind this, Swedish identity and values were themselves under examination. A renewed emphasis on newcomers acquiring these values has occurred at a time when these values are themselves in flux.

European integration

By this point in the chapter it probably won't come as a surprise to discover that the Swedish approach to EU free movement, migration and asylum has been strongly influenced by debate about links between immigration and the welfare state. The key point is that a right to free movement in the EU meets the territorial borders of the Swedish welfare state. Something would have to give. There were two options: either transitional controls would be imposed on migrants from new member states or Sweden would open its labour market to newcomers.

As Chapter 7 shows, much EU action has been concerned with stemming unwanted migration flows at the EU's eastern and southern borders. Sweden is fully incorporated within the free movement, migration and asylum provisions of Chapter 4 of the EU Treaty and is a Schengen member state. Sweden has also been a key destination for asylum seekers and refugees with a high point reached in 2015 with just under 200,000 asylum applicants arriving in Sweden. This led the Swedish government to be an advocate of greater sharing of responsibility within the EU through schemes such as mandatory relocation.

For free movement, as already noted, the EU has no power to regulate member state approaches to the numbers of non-EU migrants to be admitted, but free movement rights have been granted to citizens of all EU member states, upwards of 500 million people. As already noted in previous chapters, this became an issue across the EU when eight Central and East European countries, the A8, joined in May 2004. Of the 15 member states, 12 imposed transitional restrictions lasting up to seven years, while Sweden along with Britain and Ireland allowed immediate access. In the case of Sweden, the reasons for this demonstrate changes in some of the basic precepts of the 'social democratic' approach to immigration. At stake in the debate about opening up to EU migration was liberalisation of the Swedish welfare state, which was why passions ran high.

EU free movement and the welfare state

The centre-left government at the time of EU enlargement in 2004 was opposed to immediate opening up of the Swedish labour market. A report was commissioned from the former Director of the Swedish Migration Board, Bertil Rollén, which highlighted the potential risk without transitional controls to the Swedish welfare state because of the relatively low entry threshold of just 10 hours work a week would allow entitlement. During a transitional period it was argued that one-year work permits could be issued to citizens of new EU member states once they had a job offer (Bucken-Knapp et al., 2014).

As the May 2004 accession date drew closer, the SAP proposed a further restriction by requiring those seeking a one-year work permit to apply from outside Sweden, but once 'in', citizens from new member states would have the same entitlements as other EU citizens resident in Sweden. Thus we see once again the SAP focus on restrictions at the external frontier but internal inclusion as a way to protect the welfare state from cheap foreign labour.

The alignment of the parties in Parliament would be key to whether or not Sweden would open its labour market to nationals of the A8 states. Both the Left Party and the Green party broke from the SAP approach to announce that they would oppose transitional measures. The four-party centre-right Alliance for Sweden was also opposed to transitional rules, although, within the coalition, the Liberal Party agonised about the issue and offered support for immediate opening only if EU citizens were required to provide documentation to demonstrate that they had the resources to support themselves. The parliamentary numbers were against the SAP with the Riksdag voting to allow immediate access to the Swedish labour market for nationals from the A8 countries. The Prime Minister, Göran Persson, described the vote as 'extremely irresponsible' (Bucken-Knapp et al., 2014: 561).

The difference between the 2004 vote on whether or not to apply transitional restrictions and the subsequent 2008 vote on liberalising non-EU labour migration was that the latter was a much simpler left–right affair. The 2004 vote cut across the left–right divide with the Left and Green parties both aligning with the centre right. This didn't mean that the Left and Green parties shared the ideological stance of the centre-right. In fact, the Greens opposed transitional restrictions because they feared they might stir up anti-immigration sentiment while the Left Party wanted to see tougher labour market rules.

Subsequent migration flows to Sweden were not on the scale of those to Britain. Baltruks (2015) ascribes this to the difference between the liberalised UK economy with a strong demand for, and dependence upon, temporary and flexible migrant labour compared to the co-ordinated Swedish economy with an emphasis on longer-term employment relationships and a more tightly regulated labour market.

Conclusion

A social democratic consensus associated with the SAP and its predominant position in the Swedish party system translated from the 1960s until 2008 into a focus on external controls to regulate access to the welfare state, coupled with rapid inclusion for new migrants to avoid any risk that the welfare state would be eroded by cheap immigrant labour. Associated with this was a form of multicultural politics that developed in the 1970s but that was already the focus of debate by the 1980s.

The 1990s saw some elements of the social democratic consensus begin to unravel with a move towards a stronger focus on integration to the labour market and acquisition of language skills by immigrant newcomers. Economic difficulties exacerbated the position of immigrants and their descendants in the Swedish labour market and prompted both mainstream parties on the centre- and radical-right to question the social democratic consensus. The centre-right Coalition government (between 2006 and 2014) oversaw major changes in Swedish immigration policy with a greater emphasis on individualisation and self-reliance and less on the collective remedies associated with multicultural integration in the Swedish welfare state. Coupled with this was an opening of the Swedish labour market to new migration. This occurred both through the granting of immediate access to the Swedish labour market for citizens of the A8 states and, after 2008, an employer-led approach to immigration by skilled migrant workers.

As in other European countries, there has been a challenge to mainstream parties from the anti-immigration radical right. The roots of the current debate about immigration and immigrant policy in Sweden can be traced to the 1970s, which means that it would be a mistake to focus only on debate since the 2000s and to ascribe causal significance to the SD. Changes in policy direction have been driven by mainstream centre-left and centre-right parties while, in December 2014, agreement was reached between the two main political constellations in the Swedish parliament to marginalise the SD. This does not mean that the SD has been irrelevant and will be powerless. Its exclusion allowed it to portray itself as the only real opposition while its stance on immigration and associated rhetoric strikes a chord with a section of the Swedish population (typically male, lower educated and in lower status employment).

This chapter has affirmed a point that is central to this book's analysis, which is that the welfare state as both an organisational structure and a complex set of social practices provides a backdrop for debates about immigration in many European countries. It is through the prism of social rights and welfare that both control and integration have been politicised, as became very clear in Sweden.

7

Towards Common EU Migration and Asylum Policies?

Introduction

Between January and December 2015, the arrival of more than 1 million people in the EU via Mediterranean routes, plus the scale of the loss of life in the Mediterranean – around 3,771 reported deaths during 2015, on top of 3,279 in 2014 – raised important questions about EU migration policy, or, perhaps more accurately, its absence (see Table 1.1). This chapter analyses the development and limits of the common EU response including policies on migration and asylum that mainly focus on border controls, the development of the Schengen system, plus the free movement framework for EU citizens that effectively creates open borders for nationals of 28 European countries. It is also important to understand how the EU has played a part in creating the migration and refugee crisis on its borders and not simply assume that this is external pressure, completely detached from the effects of member state and EU migration policies and their foreign, security, trade and development policies.

The obvious drawback with a focus only on people smuggling and irregular crossings is that it gives the impression that migration is some kind of natural or personal disaster conducted *in extremis*. In fact, most migration to the EU occurs perfectly normally and without risk and forms part of the circulation of people that is a daily reality for well-functioning societies. The EU's focus in its migration and asylum policies has tended to be on border controls, restricting immigration and working with non-EU member states (known as 'externalisation' of migration policy). The EU has also provided a policy template for new member states and introduced some laws and approaches that have strongly shaped immigration policies and politics within all member states, with knock-on effects for some non-member states. It may well be that the dreadful events in the Mediterranean show the relevance of the EU, as well as its limitations. This chapter will seek to explain how the EU's role has developed and what this means for its member states as well as for non-member states.

The essential dilemma addressed by this chapter is that: while the EU and its institutions play important roles in immigration policy, it is also the case that the EU is a creature of its member states and reflects their interests. To explore this tension the chapter first asks why and with what effects European countries have established an area with free movement of people for EU citizens and pursued aspects of a common policy on migration and asylum related to TCNs. It also looks at other forms of co-operation that have been agreed and that also draw in neighbouring non-EU countries through its Global Approach to Migration and Mobility (GAMM) (CEC, 2011).

The chapter follows in key respects the structure of other chapters by looking at immigration and immigrant policies but with some important differences that need to be noted immediately. The term 'immigration' is broken down to reflect a distinction between free movement and policies for non-EU migrants. It is crucial to note that the EU Treaty creates a legally guaranteed right to move for EU citizens but specifically excludes EU involvement in the numbers of non-EU migrants to be admitted, which is a national prerogative. The chapter's focus then shifts to immigrant policies where we see that EU citizens cannot be subject to integration policies and we also see significant limits on the EU's role because here too the EU Treaty recognises integration is a matter for the member states, albeit with some evidence in integration policies of new dynamics that link at least in part to the EU.

Why European integration?

Fundamental to this chapter's analysis is a distinction between EU citizens who, with only limited restrictions, have the right to move freely within the EU and with migrants from outside the EU (TCNs) that have national laws as a key point of reference, not least because national governments retain control over the numbers of migrants to be admitted. Put simply, the EU has an open borders framework internally, but a lot of its effort externally is dedicated to stemming or restricting migration. The result is that EU member states cannot control intra-EU free movement but can regulate admission by TCNs. This distinction is crucial. Some entirely reject the idea that intra-EU free movers can be understood as 'migrants' because they are EU citizens availing themselves of a right that is guaranteed by EU law. For others, EU free movement is analogous to migration because it still involves crossing state borders and becomes 'visible' in social and political debate in the member states as an immigration issue.

Since the Treaty of Amsterdam came into force in 1999 there has been an increased pace of activity at EU level with migration and asylum becoming key issues. While none of the various EU laws determine the basic issue of admissions, there are EU laws covering asylum, the return/expulsion of TCNs, family migration, the rights of TCNs who are long-term residents, highly qualified migrant workers, seasonal migrant workers, and a single permit directive linking work and residence. In addition, there are a plethora of other activities, including EU-wide databases that store information on migrants and asylum seekers such as the Second Generation Schengen Information System (SIS II), Visa Information System (VIS) and the Eurodac biometric database holding fingerprint data of failed asylum seekers. A European Asylum Support Office (EASO) based in Malta provides support and assistance to member states while extensive co-operation on border security is co-ordinated by an EU agency, FRONTEX. In December 2015, the Commission proposed creation of a European Border and Coast Guard to deal with some of the inadequacies exposed by the refugee crisis. Added to this is the external dimension of policy in the form of the 'Global Approach to Migration and Mobility' (CEC, 2011) and a budget settlement for the period 2014–2020 that committed €3.1 billion to an Asylum, Migration and Integration Fund (AMIF) and €2.8 billion to an Internal Security Fund to include co-operation on border controls. This €5.9 billion allocation was a significant increase from the €4 billion allocated by the EU budget between 2007 and 2012 to what was known as the General Programme 'Solidarity and Management of Migration Flows'. At the very least this suggests that there is something going on at EU level that requires assessment and that the EU cannot be dismissed as an irrelevance.

A further reason why we need to think about the EU's role is the growth in support for populist parties that can oppose EU free movers, non-EU migrants and the EU itself. At the May 2014 elections to the European Parliament, a variety of parties professing various combinations of opposition to the EU and to migration/free movement secured around 30 per cent of the seats in the EU's directly elected institution that has, since 1999, seen its role in decision-making enhanced, including (after the Lisbon Treaty came into effect) in the areas of migration and asylum. These Eurosceptic parties are not a cohesive bloc and range from the far left to the far right. The point is that they represent a disillusion felt by some citizens with the EU and also with national politics. It has been shown that those who feel a lack of trust in their political leaders and political institutions are more likely to oppose immigration (McLaren, 2012).

A question that stands out is why would European countries do all this? The rationale for free movement of people has been economic and is associated with the core founding principles of the European project, bolstered by the symbolic resonance of 'the European project'. When free movement levels were low it scarcely registered as an issue. When levels increased there was more opposition from those who did not see the distinction between EU free movers and immigrants.

The rationale for co-operation on migration and asylum is more difficult to assess. It could be that it is a spillover effect of free movement because creating border free travel within the EU then requires action on external border controls. There is some truth to this, but there is no over-riding logic of spillover, as member states have been very cautious about ceding sovereignty to the EU for non-EU migration, as demonstrated by the reaction from some member state governments to plans for relocation of 160,000 asylum seekers in the Commission's 2015 Agenda for Migration. Some member states do favour common EU policies on migration and asylum, while some are sceptical or opposed. For all member states there is an acute awareness of the political sensitivity of the migration issue. In some senses, the EU is caught between a rock and a hard place: it is expected to be able to respond to events such as the loss of more than 6,600 lives in the Mediterranean in 2014 and 2015, but the member states have at times been reluctant to cede the necessary powers to EU institutions and struggled to reach agreement on taking joint responsibility for people fleeing conflict and oppression in countries such as Syria.

Supranational governance

A key feature of the EU system is that it is supranational, which means that the treaties between member states agreed in public international law have the potential to be turned by EU political and legal processes into laws that bind those states. The EU's supranational processes – which are its unique and distinguishing feature as an international organisation – can lead to 'constitutionalisation' with laws established above the member states that over-ride national laws (Stone Sweet and Sandholtz, 1997). European politics becomes more hierarchical and rule-bound while the EU is a political system in its own right (Hix and Høyland, 2011).

One explanation for the development of laws and policies on aspects of migration and asylum could be that this is involuntary and related to the effects of globalisation, rather than meaning that European states are 'losing control'. From this perspective, economic interdependence and globalisation have driven European integration and eroded the territorial and functional foundations of the nation state (Sassen, 1998, 1999). European integration represents a further erosion of core nation state functions with regards to border control, membership and belonging. Sassen (1999: xx) argues that

much as states have resisted and found it incompatible with their sovereign power, they have had to relinquish some forms of border control and have had to accept court rulings which support the human rights of immigrants and the civil rights of their citizens to sue their own government.

She goes on to argue that the EU is becoming 'a testing ground for the relationship between the national state and supranational or transnational actors' (Sassen, 1999: xx). This view is linked to analyses of supranational governance that identify self-reinforcing processes associated with the development of transnational society, the pro-integration activities of supranational institutions and the density of supranational rules which 'gradually, but inevitably, reduce the capacity of the member states to control outcomes' (Stone Sweet and Sandholtz, 1997: 299). This elite-level perspective on the formation of supranational institutions from 'above' needs to be considered alongside the effect that migrant transnationalism can have in creating overlapping membership between political systems because migrants can, of course, have affinities in more than one place. This can change the meaning of citizenship in the places they leave and the places to which they move (Bauböck, 2003).

An alternative can be called the 'escape to Europe' hypothesis that sees the ceding of power as a voluntary, interest-driven act on the part of states aimed at attaining their material and security objectives and at reinforcing their capacity to exert controls on immigration. In such terms, EU action has been deliberately sought by member states as a way to pursue control and also to avoid domestic legal and political constraints. Thus, member states in the 1980s and 1990s established new institutional venues at European level where they could meet but also where oversight was relatively weak, which meant avoiding some of the legal and political constraints encountered at national level (Joppke, 1997; Freeman, 1998; Guiraudon, 1998, 2000). In such terms, a common EU migration and asylum policy is a reassertion – not a loss – of control capacity and strengthens rather than weakens states.

These two hypotheses – 'losing control' and the 'escape to Europe' – distinguish between the role played by global and domestic factors in an attempt to explain European integration. They see different motive forces, highlight the role of different actors, and identify different EU-level 'political opportunities' arising as a result of economic and political integration. The two approaches offer distinct explanations for the timing of the shift to Europe, the content of policy, institutional roles, and the actors who have tended to predominate.

While both accounts offer important insight, both are incomplete. The 'losing control' hypothesis highlights the importance of social, economic and political power 'beyond' the state, but neglects the key role that member states still play in EU migration and asylum policy while also exaggerating the extent to which member states are losing the ability to control outcomes. Rather, it is more likely the case that the context within which member states seek to attain these outcomes has changed and that this has important implications for their role as states. This does not necessarily mean a loss of control.

The 'escape to Europe' argument correctly identifies the key role that member states have played and continue to play, but has its deficiencies too. As an account, it is probably better suited to the period during which EU action on migration and asylum initially developed in the 1990s, but has more difficulty accounting for developments since the 2000s, particularly after the Lisbon Treaty came into force in 2009 and 'normalised' migration and asylum as EU policy issues (Acosta and Geddes, 2013). The European Parliament is co-decision-maker with the Council and the CJEU exercises full jurisdiction over free movement, immigration and asylum.

A transgovernmental system

The result is that the EU is less corrosive of state power than allowed for by the 'losing control' account, but more substantive than allowed for by the 'escape to Europe' hypothesis. If both accounts offer insights, but both have limitations, then how can we explain the development of a common EU migration and asylum policy? There is a paradox: states seek new ways to control by moving to EU level, but cede power and authority in order to acquire this control. Our account of this paradox focuses on states as key actors within the EU project, but recognises, first, that state interests are not static and that they change (not least as a result of more than 60 years of European integration) while also identifying the dynamics that can arise as a result of interactions at EU level.

To capture these changes in this book we focus on, first, a change in the strategic context within which EU member states operate and interact on migration and asylum policy that can be understood as *transgovernmental*. The second is a territorial re-scaling of EU politics within a system of *multi-level governance*.

Transgovernmentalism arises when there are interdependencies, but where states also retain a significant degree of power. In the case of migration, some competencies have clearly been ceded to EU level and there are regular interactions between ministers and officials from all member states and non-member states plus other actors that are, to greater or lesser extents, involved in this policy area (such as international organisations, private companies, lobby groups, NGOs and think tanks) (Slaughter, 2009). These interactions have a strong sectoral focus, i.e. they are focused on the migration and asylum policy sector and change the strategic context within which policy-shaping and policy-making occur.

Multi-level governance is a term that describes the ways in which territorial relations in Europe have been restructured by the organisation of politics across levels of governance with a significant EU dimension (Taylor et al., 2013). Although more typically applied to regional development policy, there are significant interactions between sub-national, national and EU levels in the area of migration policy plus fairly extensive involvement by private actors such as business in the border security industry labelled by Andersson as 'Illegality Inc' (Andersson, 2014). The EU has devoted considerable effort and resources to the development of border security in new member states. It also offers funding to support projects and schemes to support migrant integration at sub-national (e.g. city) level. These can be seen as local–national–supranational linkages in a multi-level system.

Immigration policy

This section looks more closely at free movement and compares it with EU action on migration and asylum. Variation is shown to occur along two key dimensions: the level of *institutionalisation* (particularly the role of EU institutions in policy-making) and the degree of *constitutionalisation* (the role of supranational legal authority). As we see below, there has been greater institutionalisation and constitutionalisation of migration and asylum since the 2000s, but this does not compare with the much deeper processes that embed free movement within the EU legal, social and political framework.

Free movement

There is a high degree of both institutionalisation and constitutionalisation of free movement at EU level to which can be added greater politicisation particularly since the EU's ambitious waves of enlargements that began in 2004 and that, by 2013, saw 13 new member states join the EU. Existing member states were able to impose transitional measures lasting up to seven years before citizens of new member states could access free movement rights, but this can only be a temporary transitional limit. All EU citizens sooner or later acquire full access to this key EU right.

Free movement is central to the European project. One of European integration's founding figures, Robert Schuman, the French foreign minister between 1948 and 1953, said that an aim of European integration was 'to take away from borders their rigidity and what I call their intransigent hostility' (cited in Maas, 2007: 61). In contrast, opponents of European integration and immigration see merit in the intransigence of borders as markers of entitlement, belonging and identity. For opponents of free movement, enlargement opens the door for large numbers of people from new EU member states to move from poorer to richer countries with fears of so-called 'benefit tourism' as migrants allegedly move to more generous welfare systems, although the evidence is that people mainly move for work not benefits. Maas (2013) presciently notes that, unless member states maintain some authority over access to welfare entitlements then 'a backlash will result', but also notes that controls on free movement would 'hollow out' EU citizenship and lead to it being firmly placed in a subordinate category to national citizenship. Perhaps more importantly, one of the foundations of the EU – free movement – is compromised, which would be a very expensive price to pay for pro-EU states and EU institutions.

In contrast, for its supporters, free movement possesses both a strong economic rationale as a facilitator of growth and prosperity, but also plays a political and symbolic role in that it represents the core ideals of the European project. When people are asked what the EU means to them, it is common for the first answer to be 'free movement'. In a speech in London in February 2014, Commission President Jose Manuel Barroso highlighted free movement's link both to the EU's single market and to widening:

> You cannot have a single market without free movement of European citizens ... So we shouldn't disappoint now the new members of our union, it would be completely unfair. And if you think in economic terms, namely when you speak about European competitiveness, compared to the United States, or others, can you imagine a situation where goods, capital and services could move from New York to California, but people could not? It would be absurd. An internal market needs all these freedoms. If not, we are shooting in our own feet. And also, there must be no first and second class citizens in Europe, where only the highly skilled are able to move and work freely while the low-skilled are not. This would be a kind of social stratification, which is against all the principles of fairness and against the principle of non-discrimination.

Barroso's speech highlights free movement as a core aspect of the EU's identity. The EU's founding treaty, of Paris (1951) establishing the European Coal and Steel Community (ECSC), included free movement provisions for workers in these industries. The right to free movement was initially extended only to workers, but has since been extended across categories to become a more general right. For example, there is now movement within the EU by retired people from northern to Southern Europe protected by EU laws that allow them to take their pensions and other benefits with them while also accessing key services such as health care.

The CJEU has played a key role in protecting the right to free movement. Maas (2013: 20) highlights the centrality of a form of words used by the CJEU in its 2001 ruling in the case of Grzelczyk (Case C-184/99) that has been used repeatedly since:

> Union citizenship is destined to be a fundamental status of nationals of the Member States, enabling those who find themselves in the same situation to enjoy the same treatment in law irrespective of their nationality, subject to such exceptions as are expressly provided for.

How many people actually take up this right to move freely? It is instructive to compare the EU with the USA. Around 3 per cent of US citizens are mobile annually across the borders of states within the USA. The level of movement across the borders of EU member states has been much lower at about 0.3 per cent each year. Europeans are also less likely than Americans to move even within their own state (Favell and Recchi, 2011: 52). In terms of 'stocks', in 2012 there were 20.7 million non-EU migrants in the EU (4.1 per cent of the total EU population) and 13.6 million EU movers (2.7 per cent of the total population). Eurostat data for 2012 show that, of these movers, the largest numbers came from Romania (23 per cent of the total), Poland (16.6 per cent), Italy (8.8 per cent) and the UK (7.7 per cent) (Eurostat, 2015). It has also been found that 'positive selection' in free movement means that it is more likely to be the highly educated and highly skilled that move, which means that free movement may lead to more not less elite social reproduction rather than the democratising aspects highlighted by Barroso in his 2014 London speech, above.

The EU actively seeks to promote mobility. Recchi (2008) identifies three ways in which this occurs:

- a *constitutive* component is related to the place of free movement in the EU's constitution, i.e. in treaties, laws and CJEU decisions;
- *regulatory* approaches establish a level playing field for EU movers and involve things such as the recognition of professional qualifications, portability of social entitlements such as pensions, and attempts to harmonise higher education systems through what's called the 'Bologna Process';
- *distributive* policies include the allocation of EU resources to student exchange schemes such as the Erasmus programme, as well as funding for scientific researchers to move within the EU offered by the Marie Curie funding programme.

While levels of mobility in the EU remain low, there has been growth. Explanations for this have involved looking at how free movement symbolises an integrating social space as much if not more than it does an integrating economic space (Recchi, 2008). This is because movers often emphasise the identity and emotional aspects of movement, which is facilitated by lower costs of communication and transportation (e.g. high speed railways and low cost airlines) that allow them to stay in touch with home when living in other EU countries and also to get back to their home country relatively cheaply if they so choose. While the scale and economic impacts of free movement may not be as high as some advocates of European integration had hoped, their political and symbolic role may also be a particularly significant change, albeit one that is under attack from those who prefer borders to be decidedly more intransigent and hostile, to return to Robert Schuman's phrase.

Building Schengenland

Central to EU migration and asylum policy is the Schengen system named after a town in Luxembourg where an agreement was reached in 1985 that links free movement within 'Schengenland' to controls at the external borders of the member states and compensating security measures within. The risk could be that we now get lost in a miasma of EU laws, institutions and policies. To avoid this, a relatively simple question can be posed: how did we get from there to here. 'There' being the EU's founding treaty – the Treaty of Rome (1957) – which contained no provisions relating to immigration by non-EU nationals; 'here' being the Lisbon Treaty of 2009 which, after earlier work by the Maastricht, Amsterdam and Nice treaties (in 1993, 1999 and 2001, respectively), finalised the creation of a common migration and asylum policy with:

- Qualified Majority Voting (QMV, a weighted voting system in the Council of Ministers);
- co-decision on legislation between the Council and the European Parliament;
- full jurisdiction for the CJEU.

All these mean that those aspects of migration and asylum law and policy covered by the Treaty (N.B. not the numbers to be admitted) are 'normal' EU policy issues.

The Schengen Agreement of 14 June 1985 brought France, Germany and the Benelux countries together in a far-reaching attempt to abolish border controls with compensating internal security measures including immigration and asylum. A Schengen implementing convention was agreed in June 1990, which came into effect six years later. By 2014, 26 European countries were Schengen members. Britain and Ireland have opted-out mainly as a result of British insistence on maintaining passport controls. Iceland and Norway are associated with Schengen. All new member states are required to join as a condition of membership.

Schengen initiated intensive patterns of co-operation on free movement and internal security that the Amsterdam Treaty (1999) brought into the main Treaty. Monar (2001) described Schengen as a 'laboratory' for future developments within the formal Treaty structure and as demonstrating the willingness of member states to pursue more 'flexible' forms of co-operation and integration with smaller groups of member states pushing for closer integration.

Other important developments occurred outside the formal Treaty framework but later moved into EU law. In the area of asylum policy, the Dublin Convention of June 1990 provided that an asylum seeker would be required to make an asylum claim in the EU state in which he or she arrived. The Dublin Convention was an agreement in international law between the member states that required ratification in all member states, which was finally secured in September 1997. The Dublin Convention was then recast as EU law via a Regulation of 2003 that led to Dublin II and then was further renovated in 2013 to become Dublin III. The decision by the German government in summer 2015 to allow Syrians to make asylum applications in Germany irrespective of the country through which they entered the EU was seen as seriously undermining the Dublin system. The system had already come under heavy criticism because it effectively meant that countries proximate to trouble spots, such as Greece and Italy, would be bound to receive much larger numbers of asylum applicants while, until September 2015, there was no mechanism within the EU to promote solidarity and the sharing of responsibility.

Agreement in the 1990s on the Dublin system or the creation by the Maastricht Treaty (1992) of an intergovernmental pillar for Justice and Home Affairs (JHA) were weakened by inadequate decision-making structures and weak mechanisms for accountability and judicial oversight. There was also a baffling proliferation of non-binding measures concerning immigration and asylum of which there were more than 70 between 1993 and 1998.

While the EU policy focus has tended to be on external borders, much debate within the EU has focused on internal borders and the Schengen system of free movement. Once people are in the Schengen area – have cleared immigration control in a Schengen country – then they can essentially move freely in Schengenland including all EU member states except Britain and Ireland, but including the non-EU-member states Norway and Iceland. This right to free movement and the development of the Schengen system to support it are central to the EU. In summer 2015 and in light of very large flows of asylum seekers and refugees, a number of countries, most notably Hungary, reinstated temporary controls at their borders with EU member states. In the immediate aftermath of the Arab Spring in 2012, there had been disputes between France and Italy about movement of people from North African countries using Italian permits that allowed them to move to France. In March 2012, President Sarkozy even threatened to suspend French participation in Schengen. The Danish government that was holding the EU Presidency at the time brokered a toughened evaluation procedure to monitor implementation of the system plus a proposed Regulation that would allow the reintroduction of controls for a period of up to two years. The Danish Presidency also tried a complex legal manoeuvre that would reduce the role of the European Parliament from that of 'co-decision' to mere consultation in this area. The Parliament reacted furiously to this with the leader of the Parliament's centrist ALDE group, Guy Verhofstadt, calling it an 'attempt to renationalize Schengen' (Monar, 2013: 130). The Parliament sought to protect its own role and resist attempts to dismantle the open borders system. Sarkozy's intervention was influenced by impending Presidential elections and his concern about the erosion of his right-wing support by the FN (see Chapter 3). This rise of distrust also led to delays in the integration of Bulgaria and Romania into the Schengen system.

Pressure on the Schengen system increased further in the context of the refugee situation that emerged in 2014 and 2015. According to the Dublin agreement refugees would have to register in the countries where they first entered the EU; in reality many of them managed to find their way through EU countries like Greece, Italy and Spain to other destination countries, particularly Germany and Sweden, but also to Britain, France and the Netherlands. The reinstallation of border controls at EU 'internal' borders was significant. While, formally, the Schengen agreement does allow for border controls in exceptional circumstances and as long as the controls are not 'structural', this was a signal that went against the 'spirit' of Schengen. First France installed controls at the border with Italy, and also returned migrants it thought entered France via Italy. In September 2015, Germany installed controls at the Austrian border. This was a powerful signal from the German government that if Europe would not adopt a fair quota system for asylum migrants, then Germany would take appropriate measures. In November 2015 the Dutch, Austrian and German governments even launched the idea of narrowing 'Schengen land' to only those countries really willing and able to control their external border; a sort of 'Mini-Schengen' within Schengen.

The argument over substance

The Amsterdam Treaty (1999) defined the EU as 'an Area of Freedom, Security and Justice' with a new Title IV added that dealt with free movement, immigration and asylum. Title IV gave the Council of Ministers the responsibility to ensure within five years of Treaty ratification (2004) the free movement of persons and related external border control, asylum and immigration measures. Amsterdam also incorporated the Schengen Agreement of 1985 and Implementing Accord of 1990, plus all associated decisions (an 18-page list of 172 documents covering all aspects of Schengen's 142 articles). Schengen was incorporated either into the new Title IV (free movement, immigration and asylum) or into a recast 'pillar' dealing with judicial and police co-operation. The British government opposed this extension of EU powers and were appeased by allowing them to opt-out of the Treaty's Title IV measures that would impinge on the UK's ability to exercise border controls, as too were Ireland and Denmark.

The Amsterdam Treaty gave the European Commission something into which it could get its teeth. Prior to Amsterdam, there was no legal basis for EU activity. The Commission could be present at meetings, but its role was limited. After Amsterdam, the Commission could point to Title IV provisions and argue that this gave it the responsibility to bring forward proposals on migration and asylum. A Justice and Home Affairs task force was established within the Commission, which became a fully fledged Directorate General (DG) and, in 2010, as a reflection of the significant importance of the issues on the EU's agendas, was split into two DGs: one dealing with Justice and the other with Home Affairs.

At Tampere in Finland in October 1999, the member states agreed a five-year plan that set migration and asylum objectives. This was followed by subsequent five-year plans agreed at The Hague in 2004 and Stockholm in 2010, and 'Strategic Guidelines' issued in 2014. Back in 1999, the Tampere plan played a key role in delineating the scope for future action by identifying priorities for the development of both the 'internal' and 'external' dimensions of the EU's common migration and asylum policy.

Developing EU law and policy

We now look at the main features of policy and institutional development at EU level since 1999. We see significant development of EU competencies, but also that these have affected some policy areas more than others. We also see growing importance for the 'external' dimension, but here there are obvious legal and institutional limits to what the EU can do in non-member states. A good example of this was the role of Libya during the refugee crisis of 2014–15 when the effective absence of a national government led to a breakdown in internal security. Even so, the EU has sought to export policy objectives to non-member states with this aspect of policy present in all of the main EU policy declarations from the 1990s onwards (Lavenex, 1999, 2004) and affirmed by the EU's Global Approach to Migration and Mobility (CEC, 2011). The European Agenda for Migration took this external dimension even further with plans for military intervention to destroy smuggling networks by targeting their vessels (CEC, 2015).

The European Agenda was a highly significant development because not only did the Commission suggest mandatory quotas for the relocation of displaced people to the EU (up to 160,000 people) but because it also proposed military intervention to attack smuggling networks (CEC, 2015). The argument was that smuggling was criminal activity and needed to be dealt with forcefully. On the other side of the argument were those who worried about 'collateral damage', if migrants were literally caught in the crossfire. Doubt could also be cast on the basic reasoning because smuggling networks were the symptom of much deeper problems linked to conflict and oppression while EU measures attacked the symptoms but not the 'root causes'.

Asylum

Asylum applications to the EU are, of course, sensitive to conflict. The conflict in former Yugoslavia saw applications peak at 672,000 in 1992, with Germany the key destination. In 2001 numbers reached 424,000. There was a further spike in numbers linked to conflict in North Africa and the Middle East with 435,000 applicants in 2013 and 626,000 in 2014 rising to over 960,000 in 2015. Key origin countries for applicants in 2015 were Syria, Eritrea, Kosovo, Afghanistan and

Ukraine. In 2014, there were 123,000 applicants from Syria, or 20 per cent of the EU total. Germany was the number one destination with 203,000 asylum applications made in 2014 followed by Sweden (81,000), Italy (65,000), France (63,000), Hungary (43,000) and the UK (32,000).

The first phase of the CEAS was elaborated in the five years after the Amsterdam Treaty came into force (1999–2004). Member states reached agreement on a Dublin II Regulation that formalised, in EU law, the principles initially laid down at the beginning of the 1990s. In 2001, a temporary protection directive was agreed, followed in 2003 and 2004 by directives on qualifications (the setting of standards for identifying people in need of international protection); procedures (seeking common standards for safeguards and guarantees) and reception conditions (establishing common standards for reception). A recast EURODAC regulation developed the EU-wide biometric fingerprint database on failed asylum applicants while a European Refugee Fund (ERF) supported reception measures and resettlement programmes that had a €700 million budget between 2008 and 2013.

The first phase was criticised on many grounds. The directives on qualifications, procedures and reception conditions were seen as too vague and as allowing for the continuation of national standards that didn't achieve the directives' objectives. It was thus seen as a levelling down of standards. NGOs were particularly critical of a system that failed to add value as a European system of protection with too much scope for member states to evade or water down their responsibilities to asylum seekers. This criticism also reflected some tension within the EU's institutional system as the Commission had made the case for higher standards with backing from NGOs and influential international organisations such as UNHCR while the Council representing the member states was more resistant to rights-enhancing measures (Boswell and Geddes, 2011).

The second phase of the CEAS, completed in 2015, recast these directives with movement towards more tightly defined provisions and less scope for backsliding, with the aim to provide stronger protection to those seeking asylum. This second phase saw revised Dublin and EURODAC regulations plus recast directives on qualifications, procedures and reception conditions. There were tensions during the negotiation of the second phase between those member states more exposed to asylum flows such as Cyprus, Greece, Italy and Malta. These countries sought more sharing of responsibility but other member states preferred to try to reinforce capacity in points of arrival. Attempts were made to offset these tensions by agreement in the Council on a 'common framework for genuine and practical solidarity towards Member States facing particular pressures due to mixed migration flows'. This would allow European Refugee Fund (ERF) resources to be used to support resettlement. Within the €2.8 billion allocated to the Asylum, Migration and Integration Fund for the period 2014–20 were payments to member states of €6,000 per resettled refugee with €10,000 payments for those resettled from 'priority' countries such as Syria and Ukraine.

Central to the EU asylum system is the Dublin principle mentioned earlier, whereby an asylum application is made in the EU country that an applicant first enters. This became deeply controversial during the Mediterranean refugee crisis because countries such as Greece and Italy found themselves with hundreds of thousands of people arriving on their territory (see Table 1.1 for 2015 data). Asylum seekers themselves were also restricted in their ability to access asylum in the country of their choice. In September 2015, this led to hundreds of asylum seekers being prevented by police from boarding trains at Budapest station to travel on to Germany. The Hungarian authorities stated that they were applying the Dublin principle. The asylum seekers made it clear that they did not want to stay in Hungary or be returned to their country of entry. Most wanted to go to Germany, whose government had stated that people fleeing the Syrian conflict would be given protection.

The Dublin principle also assumes that all member states have efficient asylum systems capable of processing claims and respecting the rights of applicants. A consequence, albeit probably unintended but starkly illustrated by the Mediterranean refugee crisis, was 'burden-shifting' to southern and eastern member states. The unequal nature of relationships created by the Dublin system was made evident when, in 2012, the Italian government reported that 4,665 asylum seekers were transferred back to it under the Dublin system, but that only 14 were moved from Italy to other member states – a ratio of 1:333 (Monar, 2013: 125).

The asylum system was seen as a good example of the 'escape to Europe' argument as the initial steps during the 1990s were dominated by the executive branch of national governments with a strong focus on control, while EU institutions were largely excluded. But does this still apply following the 'normalisation' of migration and asylum in the 2000s, particularly after the entry into force of the Lisbon Treaty in 2009?

Enhanced standards for asylum seekers and refugees have been ensured by the Courts (El-Enany and Thielemann, 2011) and by the activities of EU-level NGOs (Kaunert et al., 2014). The CJEU decision in 2012 on the joined cases of N.S versus the UK government and M.E versus the Irish government (Cases C-411/10 and C-493/10) was of particular importance. The cases related to migration by Afghan, Algerian and Iranian nationals that entered the EU via Greece but sought to make asylum applications in other member states. The appellants argued successfully that there were serious deficiencies with the Greek asylum system, and that it could not be presumed that Greece's supposed adherence to the Dublin framework would mean respect for their rights. This echoed the decision made by the European Court of Human Rights in the case of M.S.S versus Belgium (Case ECtHR 30696/09) on the issue of sending an asylum applicant from Belgium to Greece. This weakness in a key entry point to Schengenland was one of the factors that contributed to break downs of trust within the Schengen system and arguments, such as those advanced by President Sarkozy of France, that there should be scope for reintroduction of controls in exceptional situations. Between 2011 and 2013, Greece received €19.5m of support from the ERF to help develop an asylum system that would conform to its EU obligations and, it was hoped, prevent future embarrassment in the courts.

The EU and the refugee crisis

The refugee crisis has been a key theme throughout this book. This section explores specific measures adopted by the EU and also the difficulty securing agreement between member states.

In May 2015, the Commission's European Agenda for Migration sought to specify a comprehensive EU approach to the crisis. Essentially, the Commission was presenting the member states with a series of hard choices that needed to be made if a genuinely common EU response was to develop. This included proposals made in December 2015 for creation of a European Border and Coast Guard. At the core of this was the plan to relocate up to 160,000 asylum applicants from Greece, Hungary and Italy to other EU member states. The aim was to ease some of the pressure on these three key destinations, but also ensure more solidarity within the EU rather than an imbalanced situation that saw most asylum seekers move to Germany and Sweden. The relocation scheme was agreed in the Council in September 2015, but by use of the qualified majority voting system which meant that opposition from governments such as Hungary and Slovakia was over-ridden.

In October 2015, the member states agreed to further measures:

- Amendment to the existing budget provisions to devote a further €1.7 billion to the refugee crisis, raising the overall allocation to €9.2 billion. The Commission also called on member states to commit resources to the UNHCR, World Food Organisation and other relevant organisations such as the EU Regional Trust Fund for Syria.
- Identification of 'hotspots' (the Greek islands of Lesvos, Chios, Samos, Leros and Kos and, in Italy, the island of Lampedusa and the ports of Pozzallo, Porto Empedocle, Augusta, Taranto and Trapani) where FRONTEX would help to co-ordinate increased resources devoted to the identification, registration and fingerprinting of asylum applicants.
- Implementation of the relocation scheme with asylum applications distributed according to a calculation of a country's reception capacity. Table 7.1 shows the allocations.
- Return of rejected asylum applicants.

A key concern regarding these plans is in the implementation. Controlling the vast EU border, including its 'sea-border', sounds more politically opportune than practically feasible. Especially when an important corridor passes through

Table 7.1 Relocated asylum seekers across EU member states (September 2015)

Member states	Relocation places
Austria	1,953
Belgium	3,812
Bulgaria	1,302
Croatia	968
Cyprus	320
Czech Republic	2,691
Denmark	n/a
Estonia	329
Finland	2,030
France	19,714
Germany	27,536
Greece	n/a
Hungary	1,294
Ireland	600
Italy	n/a
Latvia	481
Lithuania	671
Luxembourg	527
Malta	131
Netherlands	5,947
Poland	6,182
Portugal	2,951
Romania	4,180
Slovakia	902
Slovenia	567
Spain	9,323
Sweden	3,728
UK	n/a

Source: European Commission (http://europa.eu/rapid/press-release_
MEMO-15-5698_en.htm)

Greece, a country whose state apparatus has been devastated by the recent financial and economic crisis. For the actual implementation of the quota system for
the distribution of refugees, most countries also do not exhibit much enthusiasm. By January 12 2016, only 272 people had been relocated from Greece and
Italy meaning that there was a long way to go to reach the planned 160,000
(CEC, 2016). The ovious question is the extent to which the EU would be willing
to actually enforce the quota system on which member states had agreed.

Furthermore, of key importance to the EU response was relations with Turkey that, as will be discussed in Chapter 10, show the centrality of Turkey to EU migration and asylum policy.

Irregular migration

The EU and its member state measures devote considerable attention to border security and measures to restrict immigration. A key EU focus has been on the development of external frontier controls. These borders are those of the member states and not EU borders because the EU is not a state and does not have its own borders. The member states control admission to their territory by TCN migrants. The EU's role is on the operational side as it seeks to support policy development and border control capacity. New member states are required to demonstrate the legal and administrative capacity to regulate borders as a condition for membership (Geddes and Taylor, 2013).

A good example of the focus for EU action is the European Border Surveillance System (EUROSUR) that became operational on the EU's southern borders in December 2013 and on the EU's eastern borders in December 2014. The core issue at stake was highlighted in an open letter of October 2013 to the Justice and Home Affairs Council in which a group of NGOs disputed the idea that tougher border controls would achieve their objectives. They argued that:

> enhanced border controls, including through the establishment of FRONTEX, and the elaboration of new tools, such as EUROSUR, force more and more migrants and refugees to take increasingly dangerous routes, putting their lives at risk and that these measures, coupled with limited opportunities for regular migration and obstacles to seeking and obtaining asylum, are among the causes of the ever increasing number of people dying on Europe's doorstep in an attempt to reach its shores. (Cited in De Bruycker et al., 2013: 9–10)

There is a substantive EU legal basis for action in the area of return/expulsion that was agreed in 2008 when the Return Directive dealt with conditions related to the deportation of TCNs without the appropriate permission to stay in an EU member state. The directive included provisions allowing re-entry bans for periods of up to five years and detention for up to 18 months. It was the first measure to be agreed under the co-decision procedure with the Council and Parliament acting as co-legislators. Ripoll Servent (2011) analysed the Parliament's internal dynamics to show that a winning coalition was built that was close to the majority coalition of centre-right parties within the Parliament, the European Peoples' Party (EPP). She also looked at how more informal dynamics linked to the Parliament's more liberal framing of migration policy caused institutional tensions and led to pressure for behaviour that was more 'responsible', 'pragmatic' and 'mature', meaning, in effect, more closely aligned with the Council and member states' agenda for control (Ripoll Servent, 2011: 17).

The activities of the EU border agency, FRONTEX, have bolstered EU return efforts. In 2012, FRONTEX co-ordinated 39 joint return flights working with 20 member states plus Switzerland and Norway to return 2,110 returnees to Armenia, Colombia, Ecuador, Georgia, Ghana, Gambia, Kosovo, Nigeria, Pakistan, Serbia, Ukraine and Uzbekistan. In 2012, the Council adopted the 'EU Action on Migratory Pressures – A Strategic Response' that sought to strengthen co-operation with third countries of origin and transit, enhance border management, prevent irregular migration (particularly at the Greek–Turkish border), tackle abuse of regular migration and free movement and improve co-operation on return migration. As part of its approach to irregular migration, the EU has also by summer 2015 agreed readmission agreements with 13 countries with the intention that irregular migrants can be returned, although, in practice, this can be difficult.

The CJEU has also ruled in cases related to expulsion. The decision in 2011 in the El Dridi case (Case C-61/11) found that the Italian authorities had breached the terms of the EU's Return Directive when they had imprisoned an irregular migrant. In the case of Achughbabian (Case C-329/11), the French authorities were similarly found to be in breach of the directive. The CJEU ruled that imprisonment undermined the directive's purpose, which was to facilitate return. Similarly, in the case of Sagor (Case C-430/11) versus the Italian authorities, home detention was ruled admissible only if it came to an end when physical transportation of the individual from the member state became possible. This does not mean that EU governments are unable to deport TCNs, but it does mean that that they are subject to EU law and decisions of the CJEU in relation to their actions (Acosta and Geddes, 2013).

7.1 REPORTING ON EU BORDER SECURITY

Biannual reports on the functioning of the Schengen system area are sent to the European Parliament and Council. The May 2015 Schengen biannual report highlighted the large-scale loss of life in the Mediterranean and the return of radicalised foreign fighters to Europe.

In 2014, there were almost 284,000 detected irregular border crossings, with 60 per cent of these being across the so-called 'central Mediterranean route' towards Malta and Italy from key source countries such as Libya. This was nearly double the number in the previous peak year of 2011 and the highest since the gathering of data by FRONTEX began in 2007.

As in 2013, the main nationalities in 2014 of those detected were Syrians and Eritreans with growth too in the number of people from Kosovo. This led FRONTEX to provide support at the Serbian–Hungarian border while Austria and Germany also supported border controls at this border.

The external dimension

The EU has what is known as an 'external' dimension to its migration policy. The basic issue is that any external approach requires co-operation with non-EU member states and raises the issue of whether they would be willing or able to co-operate with the EU. This issue came starkly into focus as the death toll rose in the Mediterranean in 2015, but this was only a manifestation – albeit on a larger scale – of longer standing problems in what could be called the EU's 'international migration relations' (Geddes, 2005b).

7.2 OPERATION MARE NOSTRUM AND OPERATION TRITON

Some basic fault lines in responses to people smuggling in the Mediterranean can be seen if we examine the discontinuation of the Operation Mare Nostrum search and rescue mission compared to its more limited successor, Operation Triton.

Operation Mare Nostrum was an Italian operation that ran from October 2013 to October 2014 and involved more than 900 members of the Italian naval forces, 32 vessels, two submarines, helicopters, two drones and a patrol aircraft. The Italian navy reported that the Mare Nostrum mission involved 421 operations and rescued 150,810 migrants, as well as capturing 330 alleged people smugglers. The area covered by the operation was 70,000 square kilometres, involved 45,000 hours of active operations and occurred at a cost estimated to the Italian government of €9 million a month.

The costs were too high for the Italian government to sustain and it sought help from other EU member states. The UK government declined to offer assistance claiming that search and rescue missions were a 'pull' factor because migrants would embark on dangerous journeys knowing that there was a rescue operation.

Operation Triton was the successor to Mare Nostrum. Triton was co-ordinated by FRONTEX with support from 18 Schengen member states. Triton was primarily a border security mission covering a much more limited area than Mare Nostrum and not a search and rescue operation. It deployed two fixed wing surveillance aircraft, three patrol vessels, two coastal patrol boats and one helicopter at a cost of €2.9 million a month to assist Italy in coping with migration flows. Triton was launched in November 2014 and in its first two months of operation was involved in 109 search and rescue cases with 15,325 people found on boats that were in distress while 57 alleged smugglers were arrested.

Many boats ranging in size from small fishing vessels to larger cargo craft make the potentially perilous journey across the Mediterranean. Box 7.3 recounts the case of the *Ezadeen*. The people on board were lucky in the sense that they were rescued. More than 3,700 in 2015 alone were not so fortunate and lost their lives. FRONTEX seeks to promote and facilitate co-operation and also to gather intelligence about the main routes for irregular migration to Europe.

7.3 RESCUE AT SEA: THE *EZADEEN*

At 19.00 hours on New Years Day 2015 the cargo vessel, *Ezadeen*, flying the flag of Sierra Leone was intercepted 100 miles off the coast of the southern Italian region of Calabria. The *Ezadeen* was detected by Italian and Icelandic coastguard vessels working together in the FRONTEX co-ordinated Operation Triton border control mission. The ship had left Turkey a week earlier with 360 people from Syria aboard (232 men, 54 women and 74 children). The ship had previously carried livestock, which meant that steel cages were found below deck with rudimentary cooking and toilet facilities. The *Ezadeen* had no lifeboats and the engines and navigation system had been deliberately damaged by the smugglers to force the rescue of the people aboard. Two of the migrants had got reductions in their fare by agreeing to take the helm of the boat.

Central to the external dimension are what could be called the EU's 'international migration relations', which refers to the ways in which international migration becomes part of the relationship between the EU and non-member states. A basic problem is that the EU might lack the leverage to secure its objectives. After all, what incentives do non-member states have to act as agents of the EU? If, for example, they were asked to process asylum applicants then this could mean that they incur the costs and other disadvantages of hosting and trying to process potentially large numbers of asylum applicants. This might solve the problem for EU governments, but create quite serious problems for non-EU states. This is, of course, to say nothing about the human rights and protection issues that would be raised. One thing that the EU has been keen to do is establish dialogues on migration with neighbours to the east and South with the aim of promoting exchanges of views and information and, or so the thinking goes, fostering greater co-operation. To the east, the Prague and Budapest process seeks to build dialogue on migration while the Rabat and Khartoum processes look to build links with countries in North and West Africa and with countries in the Horn of Africa, respectively.

Family migration

The focus on the refugee crisis in 2015 can deflect from the fact that most people who migrate to the EU do so through 'regular' channels for admission as labour or family migrants. Family migration has long been and will remain a key flow to member states that has been targeted by national governments (for example by President Sarkozy in France, see Chapter 3). However, the right to family life has been recognised as a key human right and courts have struck down draconian attempts to restrict family migration.

It does need to be reiterated that EU has no competence to determine the numbers of family migrants to be admitted. In 2003, the EU Directive on the Right to Family Reunification was agreed. The title is misleading because there is no right to family reunification; rather, there are complex national systems that regulate the entry by family members for purposes of, for example, family reunification by children or new family formation as a result of marriage. The EU family reunion directive determines the conditions under which legally resident TCNs can exercise the right to family reunification. It also 'aims to highlight' the need for integration policy to grant TCNs rights and obligations comparable to EU citizens. The directive was agreed in June 2003 after a negotiating period of three years and after three different Commission proposals. The Commission's more ambitious stance was watered down by member states with Austria, Germany and the Netherlands to the fore. Because of their opt-out provisions the directive does not cover Britain, Denmark and Ireland.

The directive also makes a link between admissions and the integration of family migrants. The Commission's original proposals conceptualised 'integration' in relation to the promotion of social stability through access to training and education for family members. The Austrian and German governments were insistent on the inclusion of integration provisions in accordance with their national laws. The end result was a directive that recognises the rights of member states to impose conditions on family migration and gives them margin to do so in relation to factors such as the definition of the family, waiting periods and integration measures.

As with the asylum directives, there was criticism that the Family Reunification Directive allowed too much discretion to the member states and was a watering down of protection. This was confirmed by a Commission report (CEC, 2008), which showed that even the minimal standards laid out in the directive were being breached by member states by incorrect transposition or misapplication. This is a tricky issue for the Commission because of national sensitivities, but in 2011 the Commission began a process of consultation that saw responses from more than 120 organisations (CEC, 2011). The result was a decision not to re-open the directive, but to issue guidance that would allow member states to more effectively and accurately transpose the directive and meet their responsibilities. In the area of family reunion we also see a role played by the CJEU, as was seen in the Chakroun case (see Chapter 5).

Admissions

The EU has no say over the numbers of migrants to be admitted but can play a role in co-ordinating member state responses to particular forms of labour migration such as the highly qualified via the so-called 'Blue Card' directive as well as for migrants who are seasonal workers. There are also measures that link residence and work (the single permit directive of 2011).

An attempt in 2001 by the Commission to move to a common approach to admissions was rejected by the member states. This meant that a 'horizontal' approach applying across admissions policy generally was unworkable. Instead, the Commission developed a 'vertical' approach that focused on particular types of migration (such as the highly qualified) with the Commission required to demonstrate 'added value' to national approaches (Cerna, 2013). The Blue Card Directive of 2008 sought to approximate the rights of highly qualified workers from non-EU states and their family members. There were problems with implementation of the directive. In 2012, the Commission notified 12 member states that it intended to begin infringement proceedings for incorrect implementation. There was also delay introducing the legislation, with Germany, for example, only processing its first Blue Card application in August 2012 and insisting on a high income threshold of $44,800 for highly qualified migrants to benefit from the scheme (Monar, 2013: 128).

The 2014 directive on migrant seasonal workers seeks application of the principle of equal treatment for such workers in some areas, but does not affect the ability of member states to determine numbers. In pursuit of its 'sectoral' approach dealing with particular types of migration, a directive was agreed in 2014 covering people moving within multi-national companies (intra-corporate transferees).

The Commission continues to pursue a more developed EU labour migration policy and represents this as a 'tool for growth' and as a way to 'attract and keep top talent' (CEC, 2013). One argument is demographic because, at current migration levels the old-age dependency ratio between the retired and economically active population is projected to rise from 26.8 per cent in 2012 to 52.6 per cent by 2060. There are a number of ways to address this issue such as increasing the retirement age or improving female labour market participation. The Commission argues that 'well-managed migration may not be the panacea to this common challenge, but can play a positive role' (CEC, 2013: 4).

The EU has also extended rights to long-term residents. A 2003 directive establishes rights and freedoms for long-term TCNs that are granted after five years of continual residence, including access to employment and self-employed activity; education and vocational training; social protection and assistance; and access to goods and services. The directive also gives the right to move and reside in another member state. Article 5 on conditions for acquisition of secure status includes 'compliance with integration conditions provided for by national law'.

CJEU decisions have also shaped interpretation of the Long-term Residents' Directive. This again emphasises the point that any account of the EU must take account of judicial dynamics and see these as an extension of the rights-based politics that has been identified as a key dynamic in European immigration politics at national level. The 2012 decisions in the case of Kamberaj (Case C-571/10) provided for equal treatment in access to housing benefit, and in the case of the Commission versus The Netherlands (Case C-508/10) it was ruled that the Dutch government was charging excessive fees ranging from €188 to €830 for issuing residence permits. Even the lower end of the scale was seven times more than Dutch citizens would pay to renew an identity card. This was seen as contrary to the intention of the directive, which was to encourage TCNs to access the rights associated with long-term residence.

Admissions issues are also evident in the internal and external dimensions of EU migration policy in the form of the EU's Global Approach to Migration and Mobility. One example of this is the development of 'Mobility Partnerships' (as of spring 2016 with Armenia, Azerbaijan, Cape Verde, Moldova, Morocco and Tunisia). Mobility Partnerships reinforce EU policy priorities by working with sending countries to 'manage migration' and, in return, create access for labour migration to the EU. Mobility Partnerships are agreements in international law that do not bind member states. The Commission's role is limited to co-ordination while the European Parliament and CJEU are largely excluded (Carrera et al., 2011).

Immigrant policy

The EU does not have formal responsibility for immigrant integration. Article 79(4) of the Lisbon Treaty makes it very clear that this is a matter for the member states. National level integration policies do not apply to EU citizens exercising their right to free movement even though EU citizens may experience issues associated with language, housing, education and health care that are analogous to those experienced by non-EU migrants. The EU's role has mainly centred on two directives on anti-discrimination agreed in 2000 as well as provision for 'integration' measures in the directives covering family reunification and long-term residents. There are also 'softer', non-binding measures, such as the EU's Common Basic Principles on Immigrant Integration and other non-binding forms of co-operation such as funding for particular programmes and schemes (often at city level) that contribute to the idea that in this area of policy too there are interdependencies that require some form of collective response.

The Common Basic Principles on Immigrant Integration are shown in Table 7.2. They emerged as a result of discussion and reflect the changing focus of European integration policies. They were heavily influenced by a mobilisation led by a leading US-based think tank, the Migration Policy Institute, and by the input of academic researchers, particularly from the Netherlands. They were formally agreed during the Dutch Council Presidency in the second half of 2004.

Table 7.2 The Common Basic Principles on Immigrant Integration, adopted by the Justice and Home Affairs Council of 19 November 2004

1 Integration is a dynamic, two-way process of mutual accommodation by all immigrants and residents of Member States
2 Integration implies respect for the basic values of the EU
3 Employment is a key part of the integration process
4 Basic knowledge of the host society's language, history and institutions is indispensable for integration
5 Efforts in education are critical for preparing immigrants to be more successful and active
6 Access for immigrants to institutions, as well as to public goods and services, on a basis equal to national citizens and in a non-discriminatory way is an essential foundation
7 Frequent interaction between immigrants and member state citizens is a fundamental mechanism
8 The practices of diverse cultures and religion as recognised under the Charter of Fundamental Rights must be guaranteed
9 The participation of immigrants in the democratic process and in the formulation of integration policies, especially at the local level, supports their integration
10 Integration policies and measures must be part of all relevant policy portfolios and levels of government
11 Developing clear goals, indicators and evaluation mechanisms to adjust policy, evaluate progress and make the exchange of information more effective is also part of the process

Source: Council of the European Union, 2618th Council Meeting Justice and Home Affairs, Brussels, 19 November 2004

The result is a mix of binding and non-binding measures, but limited EU effects in a policy area that still remains strongly focused on the national and subnational levels. There are, however, 'multi-level' dynamics as we see EU funding for projects and activities that seek to promote migrant integration. There are also transgovernmental effects as there are frequent interactions between member states on issues related to migrant integration. For example, the Dutch approach to civic integration has been picked up by other member states. This is an example of the sharing of ideas between member states and not of some kind of 'one size fits all' common EU approach, which would be totally unfeasible given the diverse approaches of the member states.

It is fanciful to imagine that some kind of EU-wide migrant integration paradigm will emerge, but the EU's effects may be evident in other ways. For example, we have already seen CJEU decisions that relate to key issues such as the scope for 'integration abroad' measures in the Netherlands to affect family reunion, the right to equal treatment in access to housing benefits for long-term residents and prohibition of excessive charges inspired by long-term residents when they seek the necessary permits. The national setting will not be driven or determined by these EU actions, but EU laws do have effects and require adaptation.

Anti-discrimination

One area in which adaptation has been required is anti-discrimination law. The Amsterdam Treaty included a new Article 13 that extended the anti-discrimination provisions to include race, ethnicity, religion, age, disability and sexual orientation. The Commission was given the power to make policy proposals in this area with the Council making decisions on the basis of unanimity. Directive 2000/43/EC of 29 June 2000 implemented the principle of equal treatment between persons irrespective of racial or ethnic origin ('Racial Equality Directive') while Council Directive 2000/78/EC of 27 November 2000 established a general framework for equal treatment in employment and occupation ('Employment Equality Directive'). The Racial Equality directive (although some member states have not used the terms 'race' or 'racial' when transposing the directive in their national laws) applies to the public and private sectors, including public bodies, and thus eliminates the 'state action' hurdle, which had hampered anti-discrimination law enforcement in other contexts. The Employment Equality Directive applies to access to employment, including self-employment and occupation, vocational training and working conditions; social security and health care; social advantages; education; and the provision of goods and services which are available to the public, including housing. The Employment Equality Directive also creates scope for 'positive action' in order 'to prevent or compensate for disadvantages linked to racial or ethnic origin'.

The two directives went far beyond the provisions in many member states and represented a significant levelling up in provision. They drew from British and Dutch policy frameworks where legislation has focused on direct and indirect discrimination and where terms such as 'ethnic minorities' have acquired everyday policy currency. This was not a levelling down or a lowest common denominator policy. In fact, UK and Dutch standards with provisions on direct and indirect discrimination far exceeded those in many member states (Geddes and Guiraudon, 2004).

Between 2006 and 2008, infringement proceedings were launched by the Commission against 25 member states. Taking stock of the situation in 2014, a joint report of the Commission and European Parliament noted that all 28 member states had transposed the anti-discrimination directives. The report notes that the key issue is no longer the technical transposition of the laws into national frameworks, but the need to ensure that key actors within these national systems, such as judges, fully understand the directives and their implications. This provides us with another instance of transgovernmental co-operation where the Commission works with a network of European equality organisations (EQUINET), the European Fundamental Rights Agency, employers' bodies, trade unions and a wide variety of other organisations and agencies in the member states.

Another key issue was the lack of data. The directive does not require member states to gather equality data that could distinguish between people on the basis of their ethnic origin. This was because of the long-standing opposition of the French government to collecting such data (see Chapter 3). The Commission noted that without such data it was difficult to actually monitor the effectiveness of measures designed to tackle discrimination.

A final issue flagged by the Commission and Parliament is protection of the Roma, who are covered by the directive, but have been victims of significant discrimination in many member states. Figure 7.1 represents survey data for seven European countries that asks people whether they viewed Roma, Muslims or Jewish people either favourably or unfavourably and discovered widespread unfavourable attitudes to Roma and to Muslims with pockets of unfavourable attitudes to Jews.

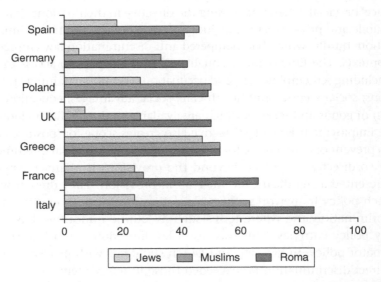

Figure 7.1 Hostility to Roma, Muslims and Jews in European countries (% unfavourable)

Source: Pew Research Centre, 2014

The Commission instigated infringement proceedings against the Romanian government for measures in its land planning law that appeared neutral across groups but could actually be discriminatory against Roma (i.e. indirect discrimination). The Commission also developed an EU Framework for National Roma Integration Strategies to cover the period to 2020. Particular attention is given to monitoring member state Roma integration strategies regarding education, employment, health care and housing as these are all areas that fall directly within the remit of the Racial Equality Directive.

Soft governance

As we have seen in the area of anti-discrimination, alongside binding legal measures exist 'softer' co-ordination, co-operation, monitoring and benchmarking activities. For example, the European Migration Network (EMN) composed of member states (mainly interior ministry officials) meets regularly and shares information about migration and integration. There are also the EU-wide Common Basic Principles on immigrant integration; funds to support networking, projects and research; and a European website on integration. These softer governance mechanisms can provide a forum for knowledge exchange and the development of new knowledge and understandings, but can also indicate poor practices that could potentially be subject to infringement proceedings and changes in practices in member states.

Between 2007 and 2013, the EU budget (within the General Programme 'Solidarity and Management of Migration Flows' with a total allocation of €4,032 million) set aside €825 million to TCN integration. This funding supported work that focused on links between admissions and integration and to break down economic, social, cultural, religious, linguistic and ethnic barriers. However, by 2012, the Commission was lamenting the clear evidence from across the EU that there remained significant problems. In 2012, unemployment rates for TCNs were 21.3 per cent compared to an EU average of 10.5 per cent. TCNs were much more likely to risk falling into poverty or social exclusion. Children of a migrant background were found to be much more likely to be 'not in employment, education or training' (NEET) (CEC, 2013: 8).

In summary, there is not an EU migrant integration paradigm and it is highly unlikely that one will emerge. There are, however, binding and non-binding measures at EU level that represent the transgovernmental and multi-level dynamics identified earlier in this chapter. These can change the strategic setting within which policy is made, but can also change the ways in which policy problems are understood. To some extent, migrant integration has also become a 'problem of Europe' requiring some form of European response.

Conclusion

This chapter has demonstrated the increasingly pivotal role played by the EU in the European politics of immigration. These involve both the development of responsibility, but also questions about the willingness of member states to work together and about the EU's capacity as an organisation to act. Clearly, there have been important shifts in both the organisational and institutional basis for action on migration, labelled as transgovernmentalism, coupled with changes in the territorial basis for EU action, labelled as multi-level governance, and that also extend beyond the EU into the realm of 'external governance'. These changes do not signify that member states have been written out of European immigration politics. Far from it; they remain central actors, but the point is that they now share power with each other and with other actors, such as EU institutions.

The effect is to change the strategic context. EU countries share power with each other and with EU institutions, but the overall EU framework is fragmented and lacks coherence. Both the numbers of migrants to be admitted and immigrant integration policy remain matters for the member states. Yet, we also saw that important steps have been taken in areas such as asylum, irregular migration, family migration, the rights of long-term residents and regular migration. These often confirm the emphases that are evident in national legal and policy frameworks, but the point is that they do so at EU level and expose the member states to different institutional dynamics. There are also extensive EU efforts backed by considerable and growing financial resources to build capacity for Europe-wide responses to asylum, migration, integration and border security, although these were sorely tested by the refugee crisis. Given the importance that has been ascribed to courts in protecting migrants' rights at national level, it is striking to see CJEU decisions in areas such as asylum, family migration and integration that can influence national practices.

At the beginning of this chapter it was asked why states would do all this. Does it, we asked, signify that member states have lost control? We have shown that this is not the case and that the EU can be understood as a way in which member states have sought to reassert control. Does it then justify the 'escape to Europe' thesis? We are sceptical on this point too because the development of legislative and judicial dynamics at EU level challenges the idea that the EU is merely a venue for the executive branch of national governments to avoid such checks on their actions. We have shown that the EU is shaped by its member states, but also how, in important and increasing ways, it is shaping the politics of immigration in Europe.

8

Italy and Spain: Opening Pandora's Box?

Introduction

Juan López moved to Spain from Peru and opened a small bar in the Aluche district of Madrid. Speaking with a *Financial Times* journalist in 2014, he said that: 'Half of the people I know have already left, and people are still leaving … I ask them: Why are you leaving Spain? The answer is always the same: there is nothing left here for me. If I have to be hungry, I would rather be hungry at home'. In the 1990s and 2000s Spain was one of Europe's key immigrant destinations with high levels of immigration associated with the growth and modernisation of the Spanish economy. The devastating effects of the economic crisis and austerity put an end to this. There were forecasts that Spain's population would fall by half a million each year until 2023 and reduce the country's population by around 5 million. This raised the possibility that the loss of young people would lead to a declining and ageing population unable to sustain its pension system (*Financial Times*, 2014b). Germany and the UK became the preferred destinations for Spanish emigrants (Fondazione Migrantes, 2014). This story of renewed emigration is similar in Italy, where in the face of economic crisis and austerity, 94,000 people left in 2013 (up from 71,000 in 2012). As in Spain, a concern was that the departure of young, often well-educated people, feeling devoid of economic opportunities at home, would weaken the Italian economy.

Both Spain and Italy have been strongly shaped by emigration, immigration, European integration and their effects. The two countries have also been the sites for some of the most powerful images of contemporary migration, such as the plight of thousands of people trying to make their way by boat from Libya to the shores of Sicily. These images give the impression of Europe under siege, although it is worth remembering that the vast majority of immigrants to Europe enter without problem through air and seaports and not via perilous sea crossings. The images also play into the idea that immigration is a challenge to governance, state authority and order. This book also suggests that we turn this image around and consider the ways in which the EU and European countries themselves shape and influence these migration flows. We see that Italy and Spain may be points of arrival, but this is strongly linked to their geographical position and place within the EU, and the relations between European countries, the EU and its neighbours to the South. We also see a more complex picture of new migration and emigration from both within and outside the EU that has been strongly shaped by institutional settings in both countries and, more recently, by the effects of economic crisis and austerity.

In the 1990s and 2000s, Italy and Spain could make very good claims to being Europe's most important immigration countries both in terms of the scale and impacts of immigration and also because of their centrality to common EU migration and asylum policies. For these reasons – and others – this chapter shows why it is important to break from analysis focused on 'older' immigration countries in North West Europe and broaden our view to include migration dynamics in Southern Europe. By doing so, we see that many key dynamics in the policy and politics of migration and free movement are playing out in Southern Europe.

What are these South European migration dynamics? A key element – and the starting point for this analysis – is the transition that both Italy and Spain experienced in the 1980s from being predominantly emigration countries to being predominantly immigration countries. Both countries have also been represented as 'frontline' states because of their proximity to major sending regions such as the Middle East and North Africa. Reliance on media coverage alone would lead to particular kinds of images of immigration policy and politics in Italy and Spain. Coverage of Italy has been dominated by images of people trying to enter the country crossing the Mediterranean by boat with a shocking loss of life. In one particularly shocking incident in October 2013, more than 360 men, women and children mainly from Eritrea, Somalia and Ghana died 120 kilometres off the coast of the Italian island of Lampedusa. Similarly, representations of immigration to Spain also tend to focus on border controls, although often in relation to the Spanish enclaves of Ceuta and Melilla on the north coast of Africa bordering Morocco. In June 2014, there were reports of more than 400 people, mainly young men from sub-Saharan Africa, trying to scale the triple-layer security fence separating Melilla from Morocco (Andersson, 2014). A photographer captured the image of two tourists playing golf while, in the background, young African men clung perilously to high border fences.

The South European 'frontline'?

Words such as 'frontline' and images such as those of hundreds of forlorn and desperate people crammed onto small boats or hanging from a security fence play to two powerful ideas that animate European immigration politics. First, that Italy and Spain are under siege from migrants (and the criminal gangs that facilitate their movement). Second, that they are Europe's porous southern border and a gateway to the rest of the EU. These ideas then play into domestic politics and have enabled in Italy a re-vitalisation of the xenophobic *Lega Nord* (Northern League) led by Matteo Salvini and into EU politics where member states squabble about the steps that should be taken.

The desperation of these migrants and the shocking death toll does actually suggest that the idea of porousness may well be misplaced and that, for many people, Europe's borders are powerfully exclusionary, if not deadly. This chapter shows that focusing on border security and its consequences is an important part of the contemporary politics of immigration in Italy and Spain, but it is not the whole story and risks reinforcing what De Haas (2007) called a 'myth of invasion'; namely, the idea that Europe is besieged by migrants and that immigration is a threat against which these societies must be protected. Such a narrative of invasion badly misses the point. For one thing, people fleeing poverty and conflict in parts of Africa and the Middle East move in vastly bigger numbers to neighbouring or nearby countries within these regions rather than to Europe. Another is that migration has played an important role in the social and economic transformations of Italy and Spain. Migrant workers have, for example, been central to the provision of social care in both countries and helped to sustain welfare provision (Arango, 2013). Understanding immigration policy and politics in Italy and Spain as being only about border controls would neglect the fact that immigration politics in both countries has played out against the backdrop of other important social and economic changes that have played a key role in giving meaning to migration as a social and political issue. This goes directly to the point made in this book's Introduction (Chapter 1) that it is a mistake to see immigration simply as some kind of external challenge or threat to European states. Instead, we need to understand how European countries have through the needs and requirements of their labour markets and welfare states, as well as their historical connections with sending countries, played a key role in shaping and defining international migration.

As with the other countries analysed in this book, this chapter is not predicated on the idea that Italy and Spain are exceptional cases and that we understand them only by digging into their national characteristics. As this book shows, all European countries have their own characteristics linked to the historical development of their own societies and to their international links. It is also highly relevant to explore the extent to which Italy and Spain conform with more general European patterns or, perhaps, whether there is a South immigration regime with shared characteristics (including also Greece and Portugal). Peixoto et al. (2012: 141) make precisely this point about a separate and distinct South European migration regime when they write that the 'timing of inflows, the position in the migration cycle, the level and type of labour demand, the socio-economic structures, the public perception and the immigration policies [in Southern Europe] are all significantly different' (from 'older' immigration countries in North West Europe). This contrasts with Freeman's (1995) view (discussed in Chapter 1) that there is wider convergence in types and forms of immigration politics in liberal democratic states, including all European countries based on tendencies towards clientelistic forms of politics when it comes to expansive admissions policies (essentially, that powerful, concentrated interests such as those of business hold sway over policy outcomes). It could be added that there is also significant diversity within this southern type. For example, compared to Spain, Italy has seen stronger anti-immigration/immigrant mobilisations in its domestic politics via, for example, the *Lega Nord*. Spain has not seen right wing anti-immigration politics on anywhere near this scale (Arango, 2013). In Spain the left-wing *Podemos* (which translates as 'We Can') political party received 20.7 per cent of the vote at the 2015 general election and, amongst other things, advocates an open and expansive approach to immigration and migrants' rights.

A key factor linking Italy and Spain with other European immigration countries is their relationship to common EU migration and asylum policies. EU law and policy has domestic effects on policy-making in Italy and Spain and wider implications for the future development of EU policy. Peixoto et al. (2012) see the South European immigration type as an impediment to the development of common EU migration and asylum policies because they introduce divergent interests and potentially erode the trust-base for co-operation, given concerns in 'older' immigration countries such as France, Germany and the UK about the efficacy of border controls in Southern Europe.

A factor that clearly links Italy and Spain is the significant scale of immigration that has made them two of Europe's key destination countries. In both countries, immigration was linked to social and economic transformation. In Italy in 1990 there were only around 100,000 resident foreign citizens, but by 2012 this number had increased to 4.3 million (Eurostat, 2014). Spain experienced high levels of economic growth during the 2000s that helped to fuel net immigration of around 500,000 people each year (Arango, 2013). This put Spain second only to the United States in terms of levels of immigration. The immigrant population in Spain increased as a share of the total population from 4 per cent (1.5 million people) to 14 per cent (6.5 million people) between 2000 and 2009 (Arango, 2013). As already noted, the post-2008 economic crisis had powerful effects on both these countries. In Spain the foreign population increased to 5.5 million, or 11.7 per cent of the population in 2012, but in 2013 fell back to just over 5 million people with the continuing effects of economic recession a key reason for foreigners leaving Spain (Arango, 2013). It was economic factors that had played a key role in driving migration to Spain during the boom year and the same factors – albeit in the context of recession – leading to a fall in admissions after 2008.

Informality and irregularity

Russell King (2000: 8–12) developed a model to capture the dynamic context underpinning the development of immigration as a social and political issue in both Spain and Italy:

- Diversion effects initially contributed to immigration in Southern European countries because of stricter controls in North Western Europe since the mid-1970s.
- Major cities in Southern Europe such as Barcelona, Madrid, Milan and Rome are relatively accessible because of their centrality to global communication networks of cities such as Barcelona, Madrid, Milan and Rome. Many irregular migrants enter legally, as tourists for instance, and then overstay, take employment when they don't hold the appropriate permit, or fall foul of bureaucratic procedures.
- Colonial ties linking Italy and Spain have underpinned some migration to these countries. That said, newer migration flows have lacked such strong political–historical structuring factors and led to a multiplicity of national origins of migrants in Southern Europe with particular recent growth from countries such as Romania.
- Rapid economic development in the 1980s and 1990s created labour market shortages while the relatively large informal sector created spaces for irregular migration. Domestic labour market changes have meant that immigrants (employed either formally or informally) are needed to do the jobs that native workers seem no longer willing to do. In Italy there are high levels of unemployment in the South, but southern Italians are less willing either to move north or outside Italy in search of work. The result is that high unemployment can co-exist with immigration, which suggests 'dual labour markets' with migrants inserted into those economic activities that native workers are less willing to do.
- A sharp demographic frontier has low-birth rate Southern European countries on one side and high-birth rate countries in North Africa and the Middle East countries on the other.

To King's list can be added the effect since the late 2000s of war and conflict in North Africa and the Middle East. As was the case with migration from the former Soviet Union in the early 1990s, it was as much the fear of mass migration rather than the reality that agitated EU member states. The vast majority of those fleeing conflict in countries such as Libya and Syria make relatively short distance journeys to the next safe place rather than risk trying to get to Europe. UNHCR data for mid-2014 shows that Lebanon, Jordan and Turkey have received much higher numbers of people fleeing conflict than EU member states. In mid-2014 the numbers of refugees in Lebanon, Turkey and Jordan was 1.1 million, 824,000 and 736,000 respectively. In contrast, Italy hosted just over 76,000 refugees and Spain 4,600.

Economic informality and irregular migration have been seen as key components of South European migration and are present in both the framework developed by King (2000) and in Peixoto et al.'s (2012) analysis of the South European immigration regime. They have important policy implications because they mean that socio-economic drivers of migration can play a more important role than 'migration management' and that policy may actually play catch-up with the reality of migration dynamics.

Economic informality can be defined as income-earning activities that are not regulated by the state in situations where similar activities are regulated and have played a particularly important role in Italy and Spain (Castells and Portes, 1989). A person can be employed on a building site or as a domestic worker either formally (taxes and social contributions paid) or informally (taxes and social contributions unpaid). Calculated across the period 1999 to 2007 the informal economy in Italy was estimated to account for 27 per cent of national income, while in Spain the figure was 22.5 per cent. This compares to estimates of 12.5 per cent, 15 per cent and 16 per cent in Britain, France and Germany respectively (Schneider and Enste, 2013).

Immigration did not cause economic informality. In the case of Italy, Reyneri (1998) argued that a heritage of informality has been linked to labour market rigidities, high labour costs, strict working regulations, low productivity growth, lax enforcement by public bodies, and low levels of social control, all of which led to a tolerance of free riders. Mingione and Quassoli (2000: 32) argued that informality is 'an element of continuity in the mode of [Italian] national economic organisation'. Martiniez Viega (1999: 105) made a similar point in relation to Spain when arguing that 'informal employment ... revitalised old traditions'. The irony is that this occurred when immigration could be seen as indicative of Italy and Spain's entry into a more advanced stage of capitalist development.

The advantages of informality and irregular migration arise from a trade-off between the lower costs for employers who avoid tax and social costs and the benefits for migrants who obtain employment and earn more than they would in their country of origin. For states, the tolerance of some informality can be less costly than strict controls and tight social regulation. Moreover, small and medium sized enterprises can have a more precarious cost base and depend on hiring and firing flexibility and thus benefit from employing irregular workers.

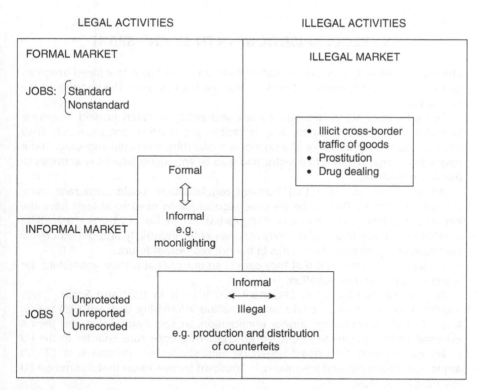

Figure 8.1 The constitutive markets of an economy

Source: Baganha, 2000: 176

This is law-breaking, but, if there is a weak workplace inspection regime then the chances of getting caught are low. In some economic sectors in Italy and Spain such as construction, the household economy, agriculture and tourism, there are particularly high levels of informality related at least in part to the continued demand for 'flexible' migrant workers and the difficult-to-regulate nature of these sectors.

These advantages are more than counterbalanced by the serious disadvantages of informality and irregularity that mean that governments find it hard to continue with a situation whereby large numbers of people are vulnerable to exploitation and are outside of much of the tax and benefits system. Informality can bring the state's regulatory capacity into disrepute and can also lead to a sense of grievance as irregular migrants may be seen as jumping the queue ahead of those who go through the proper channels. In the more extreme cases, irregular migrants can fall into the hands of smugglers and traffickers who exploit the demand for admission by offering control-busting and dangerous entry into Southern European countries. That said, most irregular migrants enter via legal routes using, for example, a short-term visa, and then overstaying.

8.1 REGULARISATIONS IN ITALY AND SPAIN

The most commonly used mechanism in both Italy and Spain to address irregularity has been regularisations that seek to manage the flow from the informal to the formal sector.

Regularisations are an attempt by law and policy to catch up with immigration that has already occurred. Regularisations are reactive, not proactive. They occur because the persistence of a pool of irregular migrants could encourage more migrants to enter the informal sector and lead to employers switching activities to the informal sector.

An argument against is that frequent regularisations could encourage more irregular migration. Thus to be effective regularisations need to at least have the impression of being one-off events. If regularisations are like city buses – there'll be another one along soon – then migrants can enter irregularly and be reasonably confident of regularising their status in the not too distant future.

An argument in favour is that they correct an unsustainable issue and reduce the scope for abuse and exploitation.

Regularisations have been important policy tools in Italy and Spain. These regularisations have more to do with prevailing informality than with EU policy. If regularisations encourage further immigration, as some argue they do, then a principal policy instrument employed in Southern Europe runs counter to the EU policy frame and is determined largely by domestic factors. Peixoto et al. (2012) argue that informality and irregularity in Southern Europe mean that a common EU response is less likely.

Between 1986 and 2014 in Italy and Spain around 2.6 million people – 1.4m in Italy and 1.2 million in Spain – had their status regularised. Almost half of these regularisations occurred between 2002 and 2005 (Finotelli and Arango, 2011: 498). In 2002 Italy regularised 634,000 people while in 2005 Spain regularised 578,000. The Spanish regularisation in 2005 led to protests from other EU member states because it was seen as creating a back door entry route.

Irregularity and informality raise three important points that highlight important aspects of the internal politics of immigration in Italy and Spain. First, irregular migration shows the pre-eminence of market and social factors, rather than the state, in labour migration and demonstrates limits to control. Second, key economic sectors in both countries have had strong demand for migrant workers. In Spain, prior to the 2008 economic crash, there was strong demand in the construction sector while in Italy, there was demand from small-scale manufacturing companies in the north, as well as from agricultural employers. In both countries, there is continued demand in the domestic and health care sectors that is strongly related to the structure of the welfare state and a reliance on family and household provision. This also leads to a gendered dimension in both countries with a strong presence of women migrants in the care and domestic sectors. Women migrant workers have played a key role in sustaining and reproducing this type of welfare and care provision in Italy and Spain. Third, irregularity and informality open the 'Pandora's box' of internal controls (Sciortino, 1999; Finotelli and Sciortino, 2009) because stringent implementation of labour market controls with the necessary levels of social control and intrusion would impinge not only on migrants (who have little political power) but also on employers (who tend to be well-organised and politically influential).

Immigration policy

The impression that Italy and Spain are besieged by migrants (the 'myth of invasion' referred to earlier [de Haas, 2007]), belies the impact of social and economic transformation as 'pull' factors drawing migrants to both countries as well as emigration from these countries both by TCNs and their own nationals.

In both Italy and Spain an effect of irregular migration has been to create 'back door' labour recruitment with market forces playing a more pre-eminent role than formal state policies. Attempts to develop 'managed' labour recruitment through the front door with the state playing the leading role have proven more difficult. In both cases the strong presence of the informal sector has constrained migration management. In the case of Italy this is also compounded by significant regional differences between the north and South of the country.

The key transition in both Italy and Spain was from being an emigration to an immigration country. There was large-scale emigration from both Italy and Spain to other European countries in the 1950s and 1960s with estimates of between eight to 10 per cent of the population of both countries moving. Of these, around half were prototypical free movers within the then European Economic Community mainly moving to North West Europe (Livi Bacci, 1972). The transition to being immigration countries began in earnest in the 1980s and accelerated in the 1990s accompanied by the development of immigration policy. The EU was a powerful external frame of reference for both countries as they put in place immigration policies (discussed more fully below).

Historically, workers from Italy and Spain were an important component of the 'reserve army' of labour that fuelled post-war economic reconstruction in countries such as Belgium, France, Germany and Switzerland (Castles and Kosack, 1973). It was also at the pressing of the Italian government that free movement for workers was developed as a core EU principle in the 1950s (Maas, 2007). There were also important internal migrations within Southern European countries. Internal controls meant that Italy managed to create the category of an illegal internal migrant because a fascist law of 1939 (repealed in 1961) sought to curb urbanisation, but meant that many of the hundreds of thousands of people that moved from the rural South to urban northern cities in the

1950s fell into the category of illegality. This further weakened their social and economic position (Ginsborg, 1990: 218–9). South to north internal migration in Italy created the forms of social and welfare support that have then been sustained by immigrant workers from the 1990s onwards.

Responses in Italy

Italian governments in the 1990s adopted the key elements of EU policy and in March 1998 joined the Schengen area. To its chagrin, Italy had not been a founder of Schengen in 1985 because there were some doubts among the founding five members about Italy's capacity to attain Schengen obligations. During the 1980s, Italian immigration policy concentrated on legalising and regularising migrant flows rather than reducing them (Pugliese, 1998: 5–28).

The first piece of immigration legislation was the Martelli Law of 1990, which was mainly focused on irregular migration. It created a visa system in an attempt to limit inflows while also strengthening border controls and making provision for increased deportations. The Martelli Law also extended the right to asylum to include people from non-Soviet bloc countries and initiated a regularisation. The basic failing of the Martelli Law as identified by Reyneri (1998: 314) was that it did not tackle irregular migration and sent out a message that Italy was relatively open to irregular immigration.

Attempts to manage policy were undermined by the arrival of large numbers of Albanians after 1990 with renewed flows after 1997. So-called *scafisti* would pilot high-powered boats (*motoscafi*) from Albania to Italy's Adriatic coast. It was, however, difficult for the Italian government to legislate between 1992 and 1996 because of the political transition from the first to the second republic following the *mani pulite* (clean hands) corruption scandals of the early 1990s. A 1995 decree, introduced by the technocratic government of Lamberto Dini, mainly dealt with expulsions and frontier controls. The Dini Decree was renewed either in part or in full five times during 1995 and 1996 but never acquired the parliamentary approval necessary to become law.

The Turco–Napolitano law of 1998 introduced by the centre-left government maintained the repressive elements linked to Italy's EU obligations through reinforced measures dealing with entry, residence and expulsions. The law also sought to move away from back door recruitment to a system of 'managed migration' via an annual immigration quota and a sponsorship scheme that allowed Italian citizens, legally resident foreigners, regions, local administrations, unions and voluntary organisations to sponsor migrants who would be issued with a temporary permit. Provisions on family reunification were also broadened to include relatives of the 'third degree' such as uncles, aunts and great grandchildren. Reception centres were introduced for irregular immigrants. The right-wing parties had wanted illegal entry to be classed as a crime.

The left resisted this. Reception centres were a compromise and were open to significant regional variation in implementation.

The tension between right and left and the politicisation of migration is a feature that has distinguished Italy from Spain. In 1998, the centre-right government led by Silvio Berlusconi's *Forza Italia* party had opposed the Turco–Napolitano law and, on coming to office, immediately sought to replace it with a more repressive set of measures focused on border controls. The legislation was presented to Parliament in the names of Umberto Bossi, leader of the xenophobic, regionalist *Lega Nord* and Gianfranco Fini, leader of the 'post-fascist' *Alleanza Nazionale* (National Alliance). The Bossi–Fini law heralded a much more security-driven approach with the abolition of the sponsorship scheme and the linking of work and residence permits in the form of a *contratto di soggiorno* that would last only as long as the contract of employment. Further, the length of time during which suspected illegal entrants could be detained in reception centres was to be increased from 30 to 60 days. If undocumented migrants were arrested for a second time then they could face between six months and a year in prison. A third arrest could lead to between one and four years behind bars. The provisions on family reunification were also tightened. Only foreigners with work contracts would be able to back family members for admission. Finally, it was proposed that the period for the acquisition of permanent residence be increased from five to six years.

The tension – or contradiction – is that all this tough talk and security-driven legislation was accompanied by a large-scale regularisation. A key issue is whether the move towards a greater emphasis on security and border controls only reaffirmed the importance of back door recruitment to dodge these controls and led to a growth in irregular entry. If it did, then it would indicate limits to measures focused on external controls. There were already hundreds of thousands of migrants living in Italy – many of them with jobs – but that were in an irregular situation without the necessary work and residence permits. The Berlusconi government initially proposed a regularisation only for those employed in domestic work and the provision of health and social care, but this was extended following pressure from employers' organisations and the Catholic Church to a more general regularisation for more than 630,000 people (Geddes, 2008b). In 2006, a further *de facto* regularisation occurred when a so-called *maxi decreto* (maxi decree) allowed entry for 470,000 foreign workers. This was a *de facto* regularisation because most were already in Italy. This was followed by smaller scale decrees in 2008 and 2009 plus a regularisation in 2009 aimed at only domestic and care workers. These showed that regularisation was still seen as 'the most suitable instrument to repair the disfunctionalities of the Italian migration regime and ... an important element of continuity between the policies of centre-left and centre-right governmental majorities' (Finotelli, 2013: 49–50). Regularisation then provides a basis for family reunion and a stabilisation of the immigrant population (Einaudi, 2007). We thus see the impact of economic and social factors within Italy on migrant recruitment, which, in turn, points to limits on state capacity to regulate admissions.

The focus on control also necessarily raises questions about implementation, which has an external dimension (external frontier controls and relations with sending states) and an internal dimension (regulation of society and the labour market). While public debate can often be fixated with border controls, the internal dimension is particularly important. Jahn and Straubhaar's (1998) analysis of 'the political economy of illegal immigration' focuses on what they call the 'economic market' for migrants and the 'political market' for regulation. If we accept this conceptualisation of the policy process – with some echoes of Freeman's (1995) work – then debates about illegal immigration will centre not so much on the content of legislation, but on the extent to which it will be implemented as a result of balancing the interests of those who call for more migrants and those who call for tighter regulation. If this is the case, then some irregular migration will be tolerated because up to a certain point the costs of control outweigh the costs of illegal immigration. This could be seen as relevant, in the case of Italy, in the sense that well-entrenched informality and a contin-ued demand for migrant workers impinge very directly on the political market for regulation in ways that could hinder the state's ability to tackle economic informality. The internal controls necessary to tackle relatively high levels of informality could be politically costly because they would impinge on the lives of employers (employing migrants in their businesses) and ordinary Italian citi-zens (employing migrants in their homes). As Sciortino (1999: 249) puts it: 'To focus on internal control is to take a political risk'.

This gives us a slightly different take on Hollifield's (2000b) argument that domestic ideas and institutions will constrain the control capacity of states and lead them to prefer external measures, such as EU co-operation, where these constraints may be less pronounced. The point here that Hollifield was making was that external co-operation via the EU can help to make states stronger because it allows them to achieve objectives that they would not be able to achieve acting alone. The EU can also give external credibility to domestic reforms because political leaders could claim that 'we have to do this because the EU tells us to'. In Italy, the EU has been seen as a *vincolo esterno* (external constraint) empowering technocrats and giving credibility to domestic reforms (Dyson and Featherstone, 1996). This was enabled by the fact that the EU was generally more popular and credible than Italian governments. Since the end of the 2000s a more Eurosceptic tone comparable to that in other European coun-tries has been evident in Italian politics in the form of the *Lega Nord* and the fast-growing anti-system *Movimento 5 Stelle* (5 Star Movement) led by Beppe Grillo. Under the leadership of Matteo Salvini, the *Lega Nord* saw a resurgence in support, also outside its traditional northern heartlands of the Lombardy and Veneto regions.

The literature on European immigration politics does discuss the potential constraining effects of institutions and ideas. Writing about France, Hollifield's reference point is a country where the extent of state penetration of society is far deeper than in Italy. Yet, in Italy too, ideas and institutions can inhibit control capacity, albeit as a result of a lower level of state penetration of society creating more space for informality and irregular migration. Sciortino (1999: 256) also injects a note of healthy caution when considering the 'crisis' of control, which he links to unrealistic expectations and vicarious fears (of immigrant criminality and ensuing moral panic, for instance) rather than a structural feature of the real processes. At the same time, he acknowledges that the problem in Italy – and other Southern European countries too – remains relatively weak internal controls, which point to the 'special, well-entrenched mode of relationship between the Italian state and Italian society'.

From low to higher intensity immigration politics in Spain

There are important points of convergence between Italy and Spain in terms of the timing of the transition from emigration to immigration countries and also the strong presence of the informal sector creating space for irregular migrants. There are, however, also important differences. Spain was hit very hard by the post-2008 financial crisis with the effective collapse of key sectors (such as construction), huge cuts in government spending and more than a quarter of the workforce unemployed. In March 2012, 36 per cent of the immigrant origin workforce was unemployed (Arango, 2013: 6), yet there was no breakthrough by anti-immigration/immigrant movements. Arango (2013) links these to three factors. First, the economic contribution made by immigrants. Second, immigrant demography meant that most immigrants were young and in employment meaning that issues around longer-term settlement had not arisen. Third, the Spanish political culture that emerged in the period after the transition from the fascist Franco regime in the mid-1970s contains a strong anti-populist norm that militates against anti-egalitarian parties or movements.

Like Italy, Spain too became an immigration country in the late 1980s and joined the EU in 1986. By the 2000s, immigration was seen as becoming a hotter political issue with implications for what Arango (2000: 247) argues had been a 'low intensity, low tension model of immigration in the 1990s'. Yet, by 2013, Arango was able to write that many of the characteristic features of Spanish immigration politics had been maintained with a relatively liberal approach and an absence of anti-immigration mobilisation. He saw this as particularly remarkable given the devastating effects of the post-2008 financial crisis on the Spanish economy and society, but also suggested that there were some signs that Spain might still eventually follow the same path in terms of the form of immigration politics evident in other European countries (Arango, 2013).

There has been some policy fluctuation depending on whether the centre-right or centre-left has been in power, but Spain has maintained a comparatively liberal policy approach to both admissions and migrants' rights. In 1991, for instance, it recognised that it was a country of immigration. This becomes more impressive when it is borne in mind that it had barely become one, while other longer-standing countries of immigration such as Germany could not at that time bring themselves to admit this. Spain swiftly brought its immigration and asylum legislation into line with that of other EU member states and with the requirements of EU policy on external frontiers. Spain is a member of Schengen, is signed up to all the EU *acquis* on migration and asylum, participates in FRONTEX and in associated border control measures such as the EUROSUR surveillance scheme.

While migration dynamics were closely linked to the socio-economic transformation of Spain, policy development was associated with EU requirements, which became the driving force behind immigration policy (Cornelius, 1994; Arango, 2000). That said, the liberal approach to admissions and the prevalence of irregular migration do challenge the EU focus on external border controls. As noted above in the case of Italy, the EU frame impinges most directly on external frontier controls rather than opening the 'Pandora's box' of internal controls and state–society relations. In Spain, as in Italy, irregular migrants can find work and have played a key role in the Spanish economy and in the provision of welfare services. Spain does not have implementation problems to the same extent as Italy because regional differences are less pronounced with a greater degree of social and political consensus and a more efficient administrative structure (Finotelli, 2013).

Between 1985 and 2000 the number of immigrants in Spain increased fourfold. The legislative frame was put in place very early. Arango (2000: 267) linked the 1984 Asylum Law to more general administrative modernisation because there were actually very few asylum seekers in Spain at that time. The rules of the game for the entry, admission, residence and work of non-EU foreigners were regulated by the 1985 *Ley de Extranjería* (Foreigners Law). As Solé et al. (1998: 339) argue, the effect of the legislation was to create 'the legal category of "immigrant", which in turn created the category of "illegal" immigrant because most immigrants were unable to regularise their situation'.

The 1985 law created three routes into Spain. First, applying for a visa from abroad with evidence of a job offer. The application would be made to the Spanish consulate in the country of origin and then passed to the Spanish Foreign Ministry. The Foreign Ministry would then forward the application to the Ministry of Labour and Social Security, which would request a report from its office in the province where the migrant proposed to work. For the permit to be issued the investigating authorities would have to be satisfied that there were no Spaniards or EU nationals capable of doing the job. This could be a lengthy process and perhaps it's not surprising that irregular migrants could shortcut this process by securing work in the informal sector. Second, Spain employed a quota system for new migrants (the *contingente*). Third, regularisations ushered irregular migrants from the informal to the formal economy. Spain had six regularisations between 1985 and 2005.

Although there was some variation between the centre-right and centre-left, the general thrust of Spanish policy was very open to new admissions both formally and, as a result of strong economic demand, informally too. Interestingly, one indication of the differing approaches of centre-right and centre-left was the allocation of departmental authority within government for the issue. For the centre-left, it was an employment issue; for the centre-right it was a matter for the interior ministry (Balch, 2010).

As in Italy, a key issue was the relationship between border controls and its relationship to migration management. To return to the analogy used for Italy, there were attempts to close the 'back door' and move to a system of 'managed migration'. This became most evident following the election to power in 2004 of the centre-left PSoE party, which tried to move to a more market-driven approach combining a shortage list for occupations that needed migrant workers, tougher workplace inspections and a 2005 regularisation for 570,000 people.

The economic crisis had powerfully negative effects for the PSoE government and, in 2011, the centre-right PP swept to a landslide victory. Not surprisingly, one of its first acts was to rename the Ministry of Labour and Immigration as the Ministry of Employment and Social Security and to give responsibility for migration to the Interior Ministry, which has tended to focus on border control and security.

The EU's impact

Migration, immigration and policy change have been strongly shaped in both Italy and Spain by the EU. But if both countries were seen as merely passive recipients of immigrants and EU policies then this would badly neglect the ways in which they are both also key and influential EU member states that have sought – working with other member states – to attain (or not) their objectives at EU level. It would also neglect how, particularly in Italy, scepticism about the EU has been evident in the form of the resurgent *Lega Nord* under Salvini's leadership and Grillo's 5 Star Movement. This means that it is also highly relevant to focus on other dimensions of EU impact such as the ways in which EU law and policy work their way into national law and policy and the effects they can then have.

As was discussed in Chapter 7, it has been argued that the EU can be an external and alternative venue to which EU member states 'escape' so that they can avoid domestic constraints, particularly from courts (Freeman, 1998). This view emerged in the 1990s to correctly characterise a situation when the EU institutions such as the Commission, European Parliament and CJEU had severe limits on their role in migration and asylum policy. As Chapter 7 showed, things have changed since the Lisbon Treaty came into effect in 2009. Co-decision now makes the European Parliament the co-legislator on migration and asylum policy with the member states in the Council of Ministers while the CJEU has full jurisdiction (Acosta and Geddes, 2013).

For the case of Spain, Cornelius (1994) argued that immigration policy arose almost entirely as a result of EU pressures. Similarly, Pastore (2001: 1) argued that the links between Italian and EU policy are 'systematic and profound'. Freeman (1995) and Baldwin-Edwards (1997) both noted that EU pressures have been a general feature of policy development in all Southern European countries. In the case of Italy, Zincone (1999) contends that the EU's impact has been particularly noticeable on the 'repressive' aspects of policy such as external frontier controls. This reflects that the EU has no scope to intervene in matters related to the numbers of non-EU migrants that are admitted because the EU Treaty specifically precludes it from doing so. This means that the EU tends to focus on regulatory issues associated with border control, but not with the more complex distributive issues that arise when determining entry levels and what happens once migrants are 'in' (Geddes and Taylor, 2013).

This could give the impression that the linkages essentially flow in one direction from the EU to Italy and Spain and that these countries are largely passive recipients of EU laws and policies. This is far from being the case. As was discussed in Chapter 7, Italy and Spain are key EU member states because of the scale of migration flows and also because of their proximity to major sending countries and regions, particularly from North Africa and the Middle East. The scale of arrivals in Italy – or to be more precise, particular places in Italy such as the island of Lampedusa – led Italian governments to call for greater solidarity between EU member states in the sharing of responsibility for asylum seekers and refugees. With financial support from the EU, Italy launched a major search and rescue operation after the October 2013 tragedy referred to in this chapter's Introduction when more than 360 people lost their lives off the coast of Lampedusa. This operation – *Mare Nostrum* as it was known – was scaled down in late 2014 because other EU member states were unwilling to continue with their financial support. For example, the British government justified its decision to cease its participation by arguing that *Mare Nostrum*, which was estimated to have rescued around 150,000 people, was a 'pull' factor encouraging the smuggling gangs to keep on moving people to Europe. The scaled back operation was a much more limited border control mission referred to as Operation Triton with support from 18 other EU member states (see Chapter 7).

As Chapter 7 showed, from both Italy and Spain there have been frequent calls for greater EU solidarity in terms of providing financial resources to help cope with migration pressures, but also to think about mechanisms for the more equal sharing of responsibility for migrants across member states.

Another dimension of EU effects that has become evident since the time of the Lisbon treaty of 2009 is the potential constraining effect of EU law on the executive branch of national governments. This is highly significant because, as we have seen in other chapters, national courts have played an important role in protecting migrants' rights by, for example, protecting family reunification and guarding against arbitrary or excessive use by state authorities of their expulsion powers. The Berlusconi-led government elected in 2008 saw the introduction of tough security-focused immigration measures by the Interior Minister Roberto Maroni from the *Lega Nord*. These included controversial proposals – later dropped – for fingerprinting that were seen as targeting Italy's Roma population. There were also provisions for the imprisonment of irregular migrants. This became a matter for the CJEU, which ruled that imprisonment was not compatible with the requirements of the EU's 2008 Return Directive. The CJEU ruled that migrants either needed to be returned or given the conditions under which they could stay. Detention was not consistent with the provisions of the Return Directive. This did not mean that the Italian government could not deport irregular migrants; but it did mean that EU law could protect migrants from the arbitrary and excessive use of their powers by state authorities in ways that were not consistent with EU law (Acosta and Geddes, 2013).

Immigrant policy

This section analyses the crucial importance of background institutional factors such as the organisation of the welfare state and the labour market effects arising from the strong presence of the informal sector. It also highlights the centrality of state and local (particularly city level) policies and the very limited EU role.

As with other European countries, it can be quite hard in both Italy and Spain to locate a 'national paradigm' or 'model' into which migrants are supposed to integrate. For example, there are significant regional differences within both Italy and Spain. Italy and Spain are hardly unusual in this respect either because all European countries of immigration have their own particularities. As with other European countries, it is vital to establish the social, economic and historical context within which immigrant policies have been formed and to think about the factors that have driven policy development. As will be seen, these factors are primarily domestic as there is only a very limited role for the EU in integration policy. We also see that issues of immigrant integration have most frequently played out in major cities in both countries, which is where the immigrant population is particularly concentrated.

As with other European countries, the welfare state plays a key role in immigrant policy. It has been argued that there is a Southern European welfare state model that derives from a combination of 'occuptionalism' (a maintenance system linked to employment) with universalism (in the provision of health care) that is not found in other parts of Europe (Ferrera, 1996). Because of relatively low levels of coverage there can be a reliance on non-state institutions such as voluntary organisations as well as moral obligations within the family that particularly fall on women. For instance, Saraceno (1994) argues that the Italian 'familialist' welfare system is based on the perception of the family as a unit of income and resources with women having a primary responsibility in the provision of care. Both Italy and Spain had relatively low levels of female labour market participation. As this increased then there was higher levels of employment of (mainly) women migrants in domestic work and social care.

The welfare system interacts with the relatively high levels of economic informality in both countries. In 'older' European immigration countries, the point of reference has been states with a relatively high level of penetration of society (such as in Sweden or the Netherlands where relatively extensive welfare states require highly organised societies with the state playing a key role). What form do debates about immigrant integration take when the state's penetration of society is not at such a high level, where state avoidance, lax enforcement and free-riding are more prevalent, and where expectations of the role of the state and its capacity to 'deliver' benefits for its citizens are not as deeply embedded?

In Italy as in other Southern European countries there has been a remarkable local divergence because much of the responsibility for dealing with migrants falls on towns and cities that can be more or less well equipped to deal with these issues. In Italy, Zincone (1999) argues that the diversity of the response had the beneficial effect of allowing a thousand flowers to bloom and for some of the better ideas from the periphery to inform practices at the centre. This was further enabled in 2000 by the creation of the *Fondo Nazionale per le Politiche Sociali* (FNPS, National Fund for Social Policies). Italian regions – the first being Emilia Romagna in 2004 – could create their own laws relating to migrant integration. These emphasised access to employment and to key services such as housing and education, as well as efforts to combat discrimination. Access to health care proved controversial when, in 2009, the Berlusconi government proposed that medical staff be required to alert the police to any irregular migrants that they treated. This proposal – that would breach the ethical commitments of doctors – was withdrawn following criticisms from medical professionals and civil society. Finotelli (2013: 62) wrote that: 'Due to the weak presence of the state, municipalities and regions have become the most important integration actors in Italy', but this has been challenged by the economic crisis which saw big cuts in the FNPS.

In both Italy and Spain there have been relatively high levels of labour market participation by immigrants with rates above those of native workers reflecting the young age profile of the migrants but also the strong demand in certain sectors for migrant workers leading to sectoral concentrations, gender effects in employment patterns (such as the employment of female migrants in social care and domestic work) as well as residential concentrations in large cities.

As well as sharing some important characteristics, there are also some important differences between the two countries. We have already seen that Spanish policy has been more expansive in terms of its approach to admissions and more inclusive in terms of its extension of rights. One important difference – and an area in which Spain has had a very liberal approach compared to other European countries – is the Spanish system of *arraigo* (rootedness) that allows individuals to regularize their status after 3 years residence.

In contrast, Italy has over time aligned itself with the values and attitudes that inform immigrant policies in other EU member states. The 1995 Dini Decree extended access to emergency health care, the treatment of serious accidents and free preventative medicines to irregular migrants. The 1998 Turco-Napolitano Law extended the right to free public health care to include the children of irregular migrants. The Turco-Napolitano Law also proposed to extend local voting rights to legally resident foreigners, although this was ruled unconstitutional by the Legal Office of the National Assembly and the plans dropped. To become Italian citizens, legally resident foreigners have to wait at least 10 years before they can apply. In another move that reflects development elsewhere in Europe, in 2011 provision was made for Integration Agreements between the individual migrant and the state. These would require that migrants learn Italian, respect the basic constitutional principles of the Italian Republic and fulfil their legal and civic duties, such as sending their children to school (not that there was any evidence that they didn't do this already). Migrants would also be required to sign the *Carta sui valori della cittadinanza e dell'integrazione* (Charter on the Values of Citizenship and Integration) that had been put forward by the then Interior Minister Giuliano Amato in 2006 and attend a ten-hour course about life in Italy in which they needed to score a mark of 30 or better. Those that don't reach this level would have to extend their contract another year and scoring a mark of zero could mean expulsion.

As with its early recognition that it was an immigration country, Spain was also a relatively quick starter on integration policy. In 1994, the Spanish government published a 'Plan for the social integration of foreigners', although this was a statement of good intentions rather than a practical plan of action. It did, however, create the Forum for the Social Integration of Migrants comprising representatives from employers' organisations, trade unions, local authorities and government ministries. It must be consulted before immigration or immigrant integration policies are adopted. In 2007, the government introduced a three-year plan for citizenship and integration (the PECI), which was renewed in 2011. As in Italy, the main focus for policies is the areas in which migrants live, particularly the major cities. Provision was made in 2007 for funding for municipalities to develop their own approaches to integration, although these funds were severely reduced in the government spending cuts introduced in response to the financial crisis. Spain has not followed other European countries in requiring immigrants to sign 'integration contracts' or demonstrate proficiency in the Spanish language. Only in Valencia were such plans suggested, but did not come to fruition.

In the face of austerity and the landslide election victory of the centre-right PP party in 2011 the inclusive approach to migrants' rights was challenged. Since 2000, irregular migrants had been able to access health care, but the PP government proposed to remove this right by requiring proof of residence. Access to health care for irregular migrants would be limited to pregnant women, emergencies and children under the age of 18. The proposals ignited a wave of opposition, which was indicative of the deeply entrenched egalitarian norms in Spanish society that have informed the approach to migrants' rights. The regional governments of the Basque Country, Navarre, Andalucia and Catalonia said that they would not comply with the legislation, as too did associations of doctors.

The Treaty of Lisbon affirms the exclusion of the EU from matters relating to immigrant integration, but this does not mean that the EU is absent from these debates. As we have already discussed in Chapter 7, EU money from the 'European Integration Fund' (€825 million between 2007 and 2013) provided funds for local schemes – particularly at city level – addressing issues related to immigrant integration. This can help with particular projects and also, because these projects involve a range of participants, they can also provide a base for the sharing of ideas and experiences. It would be an enormous leap, however, to claim that these mean that the EU reshapes the dynamics of immigrant integration policy. Rather, the EU is an actor, albeit a relatively marginal one.

Conclusion

A core theme within this chapter has been the extent to which developments in Southern Europe conform or not with patterns of migration policy and politics seen in other European countries. To contrast a stylised 'North' with an equally stylised 'South' would be to miss the particularities and important contextual factors that are evident across Europe. In the same way that there is not a typical 'North' or 'older' European immigration country, there is not a single type of South European immigration country. As we saw, for example, an important point of contrast between Italy and Spain has been the scope for anti-immigration/immigrant mobilisations with movements such as the *Lega Nord* enjoying some success in Italy, but no breakthrough for similar movements in Spain. While we saw similarities between Italy and Spain, there are also points of difference. This emphasises the importance of being attuned to the importance of contextual factors in each country.

That said, there are also some important points of similarity, of which four are particularly salient.

- Both Italy and Spain experienced a migration transition and the onset of immigration only from the late 1980s onwards.
- Immigration was set against the backdrop of wider social and economic transformations. Migration did not drive these transformations but did play an important role in facilitating economic and social change.
- Immigration occurred in countries with well-embedded modes of economic informality that provided space for the economic incorporation of irregular migrants.
- Both Italy and Spain were strongly influenced by the EU policy setting in the initial development of policy in the 1970s and 1980s and in current dilemmas of border security and solidarity/responsibility sharing within the EU.

In terms of immigration policy, this has meant adhering to the EU focus on border security although, as was also shown, the EU has much less involvement in the issues that arise once immigrants are 'in' – that is, on the state's territory and interacting with the labour market, welfare state and with political institutions at local and national level.

In short, there are some differences between Italy and Spain and the dynamics of immigration and immigrant policy that we see elsewhere in Europe. It may be that the issues are, essentially, of time and timing and that the politics of immigration in Southern Europe will 'catch-up' with those seen in Northern Europe. Arango (2013) suggests as much in his analysis of Spain when saying that he expects greater similarity over time. It could be argued that Italy is already showing some similarity in terms of anti-immigrant mobilisations, but also the adoption of measures such as 'integration contracts'.

Time will tell whether there is 'catch-up' and the kinds of convergence that Freeman (1995) identified as a key component of immigration policy and politics in liberal states. What is clear, however, is a point that is central to this book's analysis, namely the centrality of specifying the role and effects of background institutional conditions. Immigration cannot simply be understood as some kind of external challenge or threat; rather, immigration and emigration are defined as social and political issues in both countries by key institutions and organisations. As with other European countries, it is not possible to understand the meaning of emigration and immigration without setting them against this historical, legal, social, economic and political backdrop. It is here that we see the key differences between Italy, Spain and other European countries that relate strongly to the organisational basis of work and welfare, well-entrenched patterns of informality and irregularity, and the domestic pre-conditions for debates about immigration control and immigrant integration. These underpin not only the relationship between states, citizens and migrants in these countries, but also have implications for common EU migration and asylum policies. Southern European countries have sought greater solidarity while Northern European countries have been concerned about what they perceive as lax controls in Southern Europe. As the politics of migration in Europe repeatedly demonstrate, perceptions can have very real and powerful effects.

9

In the Shadow of the 'Fortress'? Migration Dynamics in Central and Eastern Europe

Introduction

Central and East European countries could be seen as 'policy takers', accepting the requirements of EU migration and asylum law and policy as a condition for membership. The refugee crisis in 2015 showed that they had also become policy 'shapers' and 'makers' as they responded to and, to some extent, tried to resist, the large flows of people across their borders (many moving towards Germany of course). The Czech Republic, Hungary, Romania and Slovakia all opposed the mandatory EU scheme for the relocation of asylum applicants from Greece, Hungary and Italy, but were outvoted in the EU's Council and the scheme went ahead. This chapter shows how Central and East European countries developed migration and asylum policies in the absence of migration (but in the presence of the EU) and how this then helped to shape responses to the refugee crisis.

Between 2004 and 2013, 11 Central and East European countries joined the EU. Accession brought with it access to free movement rights, the Schengen zone, as well as the need to implement EU requirements on migration and border security. The complex relationship between open borders within the EU and controls on movement by non-EU nationals that we have analysed in earlier chapters also became evident in 2015 when Hungary, Slovenia and Slovakia all played a central role in the refugee crisis.

This chapter identifies important differences in the factors that have shaped immigration and immigrant politics and policies in Central and East European (CEE) countries compared to Northern and Southern member states. A key concern, as will be shown, has been the position of 'national' as opposed to migrant minorities while nationality, citizenship and migration are closely connected to the historic diasporas developed by countries such as Poland and Hungary in Europe and beyond (Faist and Bauböck, 2010).

In policy terms, the chapter shows an EU-induced emphasis on strict border controls combined with membership of an intra-EU open borders framework. We assess the extent to which these changes have occurred in the shadow of so-called 'fortress Europe'. By this, we mean that policies and laws have been shaped by a restrictive impetus emanating from the EU that potentially impacts upon immigration policies, free movement, minority rights and diasporic politics. We show too that law and policy cannot be separated from the EU context, but that the 'fortress' metaphor does not capture the rather more complex dynamics that have emerged, including the dynamics and impacts of free movement and their interplay with the position of minorities and with diasporas in Europe and beyond. Linked to an assessment of the EU's role, we also ask whether there is evidence of convergence in immigration and immigrant politics and policies or whether there are important national contextual factors that mean that CEEs need to be understood as separate and distinct. As with the previous chapter, we show that stylised representations of 'old' and 'newer' or 'Western' and 'Eastern' immigration countries can fail to capture the complexities of developments. We also show that the development of immigration and, to a lesser extent, immigration policy occurred as a requirement of EU membership even though most of these countries had only small immigrant populations. The result is that EU policy models and ideas about borders, security and insecurity have been exported to CEE countries even before these countries became significant destinations. The EU induced these countries to become countries of immigration policy before they were countries of immigration.

Stepping out of the EU's shadow

The end of the Cold War had huge effects on both former Warsaw Pact countries that underwent a transition to liberal democracy as well as on the EU. The Maastricht Treaty of 1992 was a response to the new Europe and also marked a significant advance for European integration with its plans for a single currency, as well as the creation of a Justice and Home Affairs pillar covering immigration and asylum (see Chapter 7). The EU would become both 'deeper' in terms of the level of integration and 'wider' with new members. Europe would be re-made and reunited. The scale of the challenge was immense.

Co-operation between the EU and CEE countries on immigration and asylum in the 1990s was driven by the fear of large-scale flows from former Soviet bloc countries. The scale of flows arising from the break-up of the Soviet Union and its sphere of influence in Central and Eastern Europe did not, however, materialise on anywhere near the scale that some had foreseen. The intention on the part of existing member states to ensure that CEEs were able to control their borders was also very clear.

The first steps towards control occurred during the 1990s when a web of bilateral ties between the EU and CEE countries developed, as too did the EU-inspired idea of the 'safe third country', which meant that these bilateral agreements included provision for migrants in the EU to be sent back to a CEE country through which they had passed, because these countries were deemed safe (Lavenex, 1999). In the 1990s, countries such as Poland and Hungary became, in effect, part of a Central European 'buffer zone' for the EU (Geddes, 2008a). Then, as they moved closer to accession there were very specific requirements in the area of migration and border security within Chapter 24 of the EU accession framework, known as the *acquis communautaire*. Table 9.1 shows the countries that joined the EU after 2004 and the dates on which they joined.

Access to the EU labour market and free movement within Europe was, of course, a key reason for these countries to join the EU and a tangible benefit of membership for citizens of these countries (Favell and Hansen, 2002). After 1989, but especially since EU membership, the numbers of people moving from countries such as Poland to EU member states such as Britain, France, Germany, the Netherlands and Sweden has increased significantly (Black et al., 2010). Some studies predicted moderate levels of movement from CEE countries after EU accession. Chapter 2 showed that a study for the UK Home Office predicted 5,000–13,000 people a year, although this was based on the assumption that other EU members would open their labour markets too. Actual numbers moving to the UK were more than ten times this figure running at around 170,000 a year in the 10 years after the 2004 enlargement (see Chapter 2).

While within the EU and more generally CEE countries themselves have tended to be countries of emigration rather than immigration, Table 9.2 shows that

Table 9.1 EU enlargements in Central and Eastern Europe after 2004

Date	Accession states
May 2004*	Czech Republic, Estonia, Hungary, Latvia, Lithuania, Poland, Slovakia, Slovenia
January 2007	Bulgaria, Romania
July 2013	Croatia

* Cyprus and Malta also joined in May 2004

Table 9.2 Total population and immigrant population in CEE member states (2014)

Country	Total population	Total immigrant population ('00s)	Immigrants by country of birth ('00s)		
			Native born	EU citizens	Non-EU citizens
Bulgaria	7,246,677	14.1	5.1	3.7	5.2
Czech Republic	10,512,419	34.3	8.3	10.6	15.4
Estonia	1,316,819	2.6	0.9	0.3	1.4
Croatia	4,246,809	9.0	0.9	1.5	6.5
Latvia	2,001,468	13.3	9.6	1.0	2.7
Lithuania	2,943,472	19.8	15.6	1.7	2.6
Hungary	9,877,365	33.7	4.9	13.5	15.3
Poland	38,017,856	217.5	120.4	39.7	57.4
Romania	19,947,311	167.3	132.3	6.3	26.8
Slovenia	2,061,085	15.0	1.9	2.2	11.0
Slovakia	5,415,949	5.4	0.8	3.8	0.8

Source: Eurostat (http://ec.europa.eu/eurostat)

relatively small numbers of immigrants have been arriving from outside the EU. This can include labour migration to rural areas on the eastern borders of countries such as Poland and Romania where there can be an interest in maintaining migration links because of the supply of relatively cheap labour from countries such as Belarus, Ukraine and Moldova. CEE countries were initially less exposed to the refugee crisis that drove the European Agenda for Migration of 2015 (CEC, 2015).

Table 9.3 shows that across Central and Eastern Europe generally there were low numbers of asylum applications. Of the EU total number of applicants in 2014 of 625,000 (a 45 per cent increase from 2013), just 66,700 were made in the 11 EU member states in Central and Eastern Europe. The conflict in Ukraine has also led to increased flows of refugees that might not have attracted the attention as those in the Mediterranean, but have grown in numbers increasing from just over 1,000 in 2013 to over 14,000 in 2014. Table 9.3 also shows particular concentration in Hungary where growth in anti-immigrant sentiment has been linked to not only the rise in asylum applicants, but to the actions of the nationalistic, right-wing government of Victor Orban and his *Fidesz* party, and by the extreme-right political party *Jobbik* (meaning Movement for a Better Hungary) (Korkut, 2014). Just over half of the asylum applications made in Hungary in 2014 came from people from Kosovo, the vast majority of which were rejected. Indeed, in 2014, Hungary offered protection status to fewer than 10 per cent of cases upon which a decision was reached. In contrast, Bulgaria received just over 11,000 applications in 2014, the majority of whom were from Syria and, for the cases upon which a decision was reached, protection status was granted to 94 per cent of applicants.

Table 9.3 Asylum applications in CEEs (2014)

Country	Number of applicants
Bulgaria	11,080
Czech Republic	1,145
Estonia	155
Croatia	450
Latvia	375
Lithuania	440
Hungary	42,775
Poland	8,020
Romania	1,545
Slovenia	385
Slovakia	330

Source: Eurostat (http://ec.europa.eu/eurostat/statistics-explained/index.php/Asylum_statistics)

While, generally, immigration has not been as strongly politicised in CEE countries as in other EU member states, there are some exceptions. In Hungary, Prime Minister Orban exploited concerns about immigration by proposing to issue a questionnaire to all Hungarian citizens over the age of 18 that would ask a series of highly leading questions on immigration, such as whether people thought that 'the mismanagement of the immigration question by Brussels may have something to do with increased terrorism?' To reinforce the point of the questionnaire, a covering letter from Orban himself made it very clear that the questionnaire's results had already been decided as he wrote that 'Economic migrants cross our borders illegally, and while they present themselves as asylum seekers, in fact they are coming to enjoy our welfare systems and the employment opportunities our countries have to offer ... We shall not allow economic migrants to jeopardise the jobs and livelihoods of Hungarians' (*EU Observer*, 2015). It doesn't require an advanced training in semiotics to understand that the 'framing' of this letter represents immigration squarely as a threat to security and resources. Orban's right-wing nationalism combined with the presence of *Jobbik* (which secured 20 per cent of the vote in the 2014 national elections) has contributed to a hostile environment in Hungary to immigrants and foreigners. This applies in particular to Muslim migrants who have been viewed with hostility. Similarly, the Slovakian government indicated that it did not wish to receive non-Christian refugees. Hungarian Prime Minister Orban, his *Fidesz* party and *Jobbik* make links between two key issues that are a standard component of right-wing Euroscepticism in the EU – hostility to 'Brussels' and to immigrants (Korkut, 2014).

The EU presence looms large in Central and Eastern Europe, but has changed as a result of membership. No longer are CEE countries the supplicants seeking to satisfy EU requirements, as they are now member states that play a role in shaping policy. Orban's hostility to the EU and to immigration is an extreme example, but other CEE countries have also expressed scepticism about aspects of the EU role in migration. While the numerical implications of the EU relocation system were small, looming in the background were concerns about ceding sovereignty on migration. This led to confrontation with Germany that advocated such a system. Slovakian and Hungarian ministers blamed Germany, and Angela Merkel in particular, for having been too open in their policy towards asylum applicants. Hungary, located along a key route for Syrian and Afghan refugees on their way to countries such as Germany and Sweden, closed its border with Serbia and built a security fence.

Chapter 7 explored EU free movement and the position of countries such as Austria, Britain, Germany and the Netherlands that have raised the idea of limits on access to welfare benefits. The European ministers of Hungary, Poland and Slovakia all stated that free movement was a 'red line' issue for them, on which they would not be prepared to budge (*Financial Times*, 2015b).

While it is fairly easy to identify the impetus the EU has given to policy developments – led by the wish to join the EU – it is also important to identify the changes in political dynamics that arise as a result of membership. As this chapter shows, the overall effects of engagement with the EU have been much stronger in the area of immigration policy than for immigrant policy because of the need to comply with the Schengen border security framework as a condition for membership. There has been less urgency in the area of immigrant policies with many CEE countries having highly developed forms of diaspora politics to maintain links with their citizens that have migrated abroad. There is some evidence of influence for the EU in immigrant integration through its 'European Integration Fund' that played some role in the development of immigrant integration measures and did, at least, get these issues onto the domestic agenda as well as stimulating the exchange of information and ideas with other member states. That said, there is concern about discrimination against Roma minorities within CEE countries – although this extends to other EU member states too – which has contributed to tensions between European countries and between CEE countries, the EU and other member states. Here too the issues are complex.

Immigration policy

CEE countries became countries of immigration policy before they became countries of immigration. Immigration policy was directly derived from the obligations of EU membership. Perhaps because of this and because of the restrictive emphasis of EU policies, eastwards enlargement of the EU and the development by CEE countries of the immigration and asylum *acquis* helped breathe new life into the term 'fortress Europe'. Indeed, some saw the EU as drawing a new iron curtain as it extended its immigration and asylum policies eastwards and installed new 'hard' borders on the eastern and southern frontiers of its member states and potential member states. These types of metaphors are excessive for some reasons that have been touched upon in earlier chapters and others that will be explained during this chapter. Even so, as Heather Grabbe (2002) notes there can be inherent tensions because:

behind the oft-used rhetoric of 'not putting up a new iron curtain' lies a complex set of compromises whereby each country has tried to navigate between EU pressures and other policy concerns, both domestic and external.

Patterns of migration

As Table 9.2 showed, immigration to Central and East European countries remains at a very low level when compared to Northern, Western and Southern member states. Several forms of immigration (and emigration) can be distinguished, which apply in different degrees to various CEE countries. During the period of Communism, there was some migration between communist countries, but this also was at a relatively low level. This involved immigration from communist countries in the neighbourhood as well as sometimes from abroad. For instance, this explains why several CEE countries have a rather significant Vietnamese migrant population (Iglicka, 2001a). Particularly the Baltic States, Estonia, Latvia and Lithuania, also have a very sizeable Russian population, as a heritage of the period during which these states were part of the Soviet Union. While these countries have small immigrant populations, they have large foreign populations because of the significant presence of Russian nationals. We discuss this issue below when assessing nationality laws.

9.1 MIGRATION DURING THE COMMUNIST PERIOD

During the communist period after the end of the Second World War until 1990, CEE countries often had very specific migration patterns. This involved primarily migration to and from other CEE countries that were part of the Soviet bloc, and to and from the Soviet Union itself. This included large scale migration of Russians within the Soviet bloc. Some exchanges between communist countries were also

(Continued)

(Continued)

actively promoted by the Soviet Union. In some cases, this contributed to diaspora formation in Eastern Europe, including a large Russian diaspora that is still very significant, particularly in the Baltic States.

On a relatively small scale, there was also refugee migration from CEE countries to Western European countries during this period. At times, this migration was more significant, such as around the Hungarian revolution against the Soviet occupation in 1956, the Soviet crushing of the Prague Spring and the Polish expulsion of Jews in 1968.

Soviet efforts to promote relations between communist countries also contributed to the arrival of several specific migrant groups in Central and Eastern Europe. Perhaps the most significant of them in terms of size and visibility today is Vietnamese migrants, many of whom have settled permanently in Europe. Current numbers of Vietnamese in the Czech Republic are estimated at around 80,000 with around 50,000 in Poland. Former East Germany also has a sizeable Vietnamese community. In Prague and Warsaw predominantly Vietnamese quarters have developed with the national governments relatively supportive when it comes to Vietnamese language instruction.

After the collapse of the communist regimes in CEE countries, levels of immigration as well as emigration increased. Overall, there was increased migration between CEE countries, particularly to Poland, Hungary, the Czech Republic and the three Baltic States of Estonia, Latvia and Lithuania. There was also significant return migration from their national diasporas. Historically, Poland in particular has seen the development of a large diaspora. The term 'diaspora' has also become linked to policy debates with, for example, EU discussion about immigration control linked to the effects of the diaspora (Weinar, 2010). The transition from the Soviet bloc to EU membership created opportunities for return to Poland. This included relatively small numbers of those who had fled and secured refugee status during the Cold War, but who now felt able to return. Levels of migration to Western Europe countries remained low immediately after the end of the Cold War. Levels increased gradually before EU accession in the context of so-called 'labour tourism' (Iglicka, 2001b: 8). Germany and the Netherlands also introduced specific schemes to facilitate labour migration for specific labour market segments. In 1999, for instance, there were 200,000 seasonal Polish workers in Germany.

EU accession brought a further new impetus to both emigration and immigration. While transitional arrangements of up to seven years could be imposed on free movement from new member states, such restrictions were bound to expire. There has been debate in some EU states about free movement. Political leaders in these new member states have criticised what they see as distorted representation of EU free movement from new member states, particularly if such distortions inform changes at either national or EU level that restrict the right to free movement. Romania's Ambassador to the UK warned of the danger of racist attacks if there was continued use of inflammatory language about his co-nationals (*Daily Telegraph*, 2013).

As a corollary of EU accession and free movement within the Schengen area, restrictions were installed at the EU's external border with countries such as Belarus, Ukraine, Moldova and Russia. The Europeanisation of migration meant, for example, those EU regulations concerning border control had to be applied and inhibited, including seasonal cross-border migration to rural areas at the eastern borders of CEE countries. However governments, such as that of Poland, established special programmes that allowed for temporary labour migration in their border regions, especially with Ukraine and Belarus. As a consequence, an East–West pattern of 'chain migration' emerged, where Belarusian and Ukrainian labour migrants moved to Poland, whereas Polish labour migrants moved to countries such as Germany, the Netherlands and the UK.

Europeanisation

The relatively rapid development of a migration policy context during the 1990s led to four potential sources of strain. Firstly, unpredictable migration pressures could lead to perceptions of loss of control, particularly if the rhetoric of control and the maintenance of 'hard' borders are stoked-up in conditions that are not conducive for attainment of this objective, as became clear during the refugee crisis in 2015.

Secondly, the scale and extent of borders means that policing them is costly. Poland, for instance, has 'green' (i.e. relatively unpopulated) borders of 407 km with Belarus and 526 km with the Ukraine. These costs of control occur, it should be remembered, in relatively poor countries where there are other calls on the public purse.

Thirdly, the development of new controls at the EU's eastern frontier can confound other objectives such as cross-border migration for trade purposes. Cutting off this movement can cause domestic social and political pressure. Ease of movement can be a pressure valve.

Finally, state and nation-building in Central and Eastern Europe illustrate the point that nation and state are rarely fully coinciding. Most CEE states are comprised of various ethnic groups. Three million Magyars, for instance, live not in Hungary but in neighbouring states. Substantial numbers of Russians live in the Baltic States. Roma are present in most CEE countries.

EU accession also meant adaptation to EU laws and policies. Among the myriad obligations contained within the 80,000 pages of the EU law, the CEE countries were required to adapt to the EU *acquis* on free movement, immigration and asylum as a condition for membership. The CEE countries were placed on a steep learning curve and looked towards practices and ideas in other EU member states. While the free movement *acquis* was clear (albeit with some reluctance to allow CEE countries to benefit from it until a transition period of up to seven years was served), the immigration and asylum *acquis* was less clear even though this was the area where adaptational pressures were strongest. To facilitate adaptation, formal EU links were supplemented outside of formal EU structures that provide venues for ministers and officials to meet, as well as forums for the diffusion of policy ideas. Migration dialogues such as the 'Prague Process' and the 'Budapest Process' provide a forum for the exchange of ideas and information.

At its most basic, the deal between existing member states and applicant states was quite simple: EU membership was to be accompanied by tight control of the borders of new member states with non-member states. This could be seen as contradictory because tightly controlled borders run counter to the free movement framework that is a defining feature of European integration. Yet, as has become clear in earlier chapters, European integration has boundary removing features while also establishing new boundaries. This reflects broader dilemmas raised by the openness of economies to flows of capital and money, but not to people. EU member states seek a balance between closed states and open economies. The incorporation of the CEE countries further tests this balance and raises the salience of issues associated with borders, boundaries and frontiers in an integrating Europe.

Discussing borders and frontiers in Central and Eastern Europe makes us think about the nature of these borders and their relation to 'the European project'. The EU itself does not have external frontiers. Its borders are those of its member states. It is the member states that retain responsibility for policing them. The EU's notional external frontiers are not fixed. They 'moved' with four previous enlargements of the EU in 1973, 1981, 1986 and 1995, which brought nine new member states into the Union and moved again in 2004, 2007 and 2013. These borders are also more than just a line on the ground or on a map. Borders have a formal, legal meaning but also represent practices and ideas associated with these lines. According to Anderson (1997), borders involve agreements between neighbouring states, the management of these borders by police and customs authorities, and arrangements between neighbouring states on cross-border co-operation. Within these practices are ideas about the role and purpose of these borders, with the effect that policy-makers, border zone inhabitants and the population more generally all have ideas about their meaning and significance. The EU's single market is, of course, centred on a frontier-free EU within which people, services, goods and capital can move freely; but this is also predicated upon control of the single market's external frontiers and ideas, for instance about 'good' movement and 'bad' movement within the European space.

The boundary issues are migration in its various forms and its interaction with the dynamics of European integration. These issues are not exclusively related to Central and Eastern Europe. The argument is not for Central and East European exceptionalism in the same way that there was not an argument for Southern European exceptionalism in Chapters 8 and 10. The argument is that the politics of migration and immigration in Central and Eastern Europe shows how international migration relations between European countries have been reconfigured with a key role played by the EU. The migration policy dilemmas in Central and Eastern Europe are writ large because of

- the scale of the enlargement;
- the experience of international migration in its many forms;
- debate about the meaning and significance of borders;
- ideas about security and insecurity;
- the position of minorities within and beyond these countries;
- new patterns of interdependence and integration to which European integration contributes;
- an emerging political debate about the costs and benefits of EU membership.

Immigration policies in CEE countries

Whereas CEE countries have now clearly developed into important actors in defining EU immigration policies, as illustrated by their role in the European refugee crisis after 2015, their EU accession in the 2000s certainly also involved a coercive element to the development of immigration policies because the migration *acquis* was an obligation of membership. The adaptational pressures were strong and there was little scope for new member states to influence the migration policy requirements of EU membership.

If policy mechanisms are analysed then we can say that EU accession involved a largely one-way process of policy transfer with significant immigration and asylum policy implications. This prompted a rapid process of policy learning coupled with efforts to transpose the *acquis* into national laws and practices. However, the distinction between *making, becoming* and *seeming* European is useful in the sense that adapting to the requirement of EU membership can be motivated by external imposition, by a desire to join the EU, and by institutional mimicry in order to accord with the requirements of EU membership.

At the same time, a key difference with the development of immigration policies in many other European countries is the lack of politicisation of immigration. Low levels of immigration and the concentration on emigration and intra-EU mobility have meant that immigration had not become an issue that provoked high levels of political concern or wider public concern, although this was tested by the refugee crisis after 2015. Hungary already appeared an exception with Orban's government and his *Fidesz* party focusing on the immigration issue despite the relatively low numbers of migrants in Hungary (Korkut, 2014). This was also evident during the refugee crisis where Hungary built fences at its borders and sought to stop refugees moving across Hungarian territory on their way to other EU member states. In Slovakia too there was evidence of increased politicisation with protests against refugee migration.

This relatively modest politicisation is set against the significant administrative challenge of implementing the very complex EU migration and asylum *acquis*. In effect, this largely meant the transposition of EU legislation into national law (Weinar, 2006). Implementation of the *acquis* has been relatively uncontested and was treated primarily as a technical and administrative issue (Canek and Cizinsky, 2011; Taylor et al., 2013). Further, with the growing importance of labour migration across the EU's eastern borders, immigration policies in countries such as Poland and the Czech Republic in particular have been influenced by business interests and their labour needs.

Mirroring the EU's asylum and migration policy, all new member states in Central and Eastern Europe now have a restrictive immigration policy in place. Because of the relatively low levels of immigration (see Table 9.2), the impact of this restrictive regime is, however, difficult to establish. For labour migration there has been a demand for foreign workers linked to, first, the reliance on cross-border seasonal migration in sectors such as agriculture coupled with the shortages in the domestic labour market resulting from the large-scale emigration of workers to other EU member states (Engbersen et al., 2010). Specific schemes were developed for seasonal labour migration from non-EU member states in Eastern Europe. For example, Poland established a special scheme for providing access to its labour market for seasonal workers that would spend no more than 6 months annually in Poland and for whom the employer promised employment. In 2011, there were 260,000 people admitted under the provisions of this scheme, the majority being from Ukraine but with others also from Belarus, Moldova, Georgia and Russia too (Kepinska and Kindler, 2014).

As already noted, the Baltic States are in a different position because of the sizeable Russian minorities, of which there were more than a million across these three countries in 2016. Following their independence in the early 1990s, all three countries implemented restrictive immigration policies with the intention of curtailing immigration from CEE countries.

Finally, a distinctive characteristic of immigration policies in some CEE countries, perhaps most notably Poland, is its migration policy for co-ethnics or 'repatriates'. To some extent, this policy can be compared to German policies towards *Aussiedler* (see Chapter 4), facilitating the return of Polish emigrants, some of whom had left Poland generations earlier. The revival of national identities in CEE countries in the 1990s also revived the notion of return to these countries, closely connected to the strength of *jus sanguinis* as the principle of access to nationality in many CEE countries, discussed more fully below. Poland had special regulations for returning Poles by the early 1990s, targeted specifically at the Polish diaspora throughout the former Soviet bloc, where people of Polish origin had been forced to renounce their Polish citizenship in the past. A Polish Charter of 2008 defined a number of categories of members of the Polish diaspora that meant exemption from paying for visas for entry into Poland and access to the labour market on an equal basis with Polish nationals (Kepinska and Kindler, 2014). Similar policies have been adopted in Hungary aimed at the many Magyars living across the border.

Immigrant, minorities and diaspora policies

The observation that, generally speaking, immigration had – at least until the refugee crisis – triggered little political or wider public concern in CEE countries, applies even more strongly to the issue of immigrant integration. We have already seen that there are relatively small immigrant populations in CEE countries, although these countries often maintain close ties with their diasporas. Furthermore, as a legacy of the complex process of state formation and boundary changes over the past centuries, many CEE countries do host sizeable national minorities. As in the area of immigration, the EU has been an important motor behind the development of national policies regarding immigrants and minorities. However, as we will discuss below, in the absence of a clear and firm EU legal framework, pressures for Europeanisation have not been so directly applied. This can be seen by exploring two minority groups that played a key role in immigrant policies and in their relation with the EU: the Roma and the sizeable Russian minorities.

Migrants and minorities in Central and Eastern Europe

The discussion in CEE countries differs from that in Northwest and Southern Europe in that it is less about the formation of immigrant communities (although it is about this too), than about the position of minorities within CEE countries. Kymlicka (1995) argues that national minorities have the right to preserve their culture and that this places obligations on the state regarding legal protection, the provision of services to these national minorities (such as education in their language) and representation. The definitions of national minorities can be arbitrary. The Slovenian constitution guarantees two seats in its parliament for minorities with one for the Hungarian minority and one for the Italian minority. There are no seats for the larger Croatian minority because they are defined as an immigrant group (assumed voluntary entrants) rather than a national minority. The Roma too receive no seats in the Slovenian parliament.

As already noted, Estonia, Latvia and Lithuania have very sizeable populations with Russian citizenship amounting, on average, to around one-third of the total population in these countries. Though rather ethnically homogenous countries until the Second World War, the ethnic composition of these countries changed dramatically during the German occupation and especially in the subsequent Soviet period. The Soviets pursued an active settlement policy, bringing migrants from many different parts of the Soviet empire to particularly the industrialising areas of the Baltic states (such as North East Estonia and the area around Riga). When these countries regained independence, most of these post-Soviet migrants stayed. Some of them even opted for Russian citizenship rather than citizenship of the Baltic states in which they had lived, often for several generations.

Immigrant policies are relatively new developments in most CEE countries. The low number of immigrants meant there was a lack of urgency. The Czech Republic, one of the states to receive relatively high numbers of immigrants, was amongst the first to develop such a policy. Strongly influenced by international legislation, the Council of Europe and the EU, it established a formal immigrant policy in 2000. Until then, as in most CEE countries, responses to the arrival of refugees, labour migrants and repatriates had been mainly *ad hoc*. Poland established an interdepartmental working group for the preparation of a Migration Policy only in 2007.

Since the 2000s, there has been a gradual institutionalisation of migrant integration policies in most CEE countries. However, in sharp contrast with many other European countries, it has remained largely an administrative concern, with very little politicisation (Cernik, 2014).

The main stimulus for the development of migrant integration policies in CEE countries seems to have come from the EU. Partly this involves spin-offs from EU legislation in the areas of asylum and migration (such as the Long Term Residence Directive). As Chapter 7 showed, the EU does not possess many 'hard' governance tools in the areas of either immigration or immigrant policies. It does, however, have various mechanisms through which it can promote policy convergence, such as the European Integration Fund and networks that facilitate the exchange of information and ideas. Pawlak (2014) observes that, since 2009, many Polish governmental and non-governmental organisations have received funds from the European Integration Fund and that this triggered a steep increase in activities in the area of migrant integration. As such, the Integration Fund was a lever for policy development in this area. Besides the EU, other international organisations such as the Council of Europe, the IOM and the International Centre for Migration Policy Development (ICMPD) all played important roles.

An implication of these various sources of policy change and development is that the influence of external factors is multivalent, meaning that there are many sources of change and that these do not all arise from the EU. For example, the Council of Europe has powerful human rights standards that have fed into minority and immigrant policies.

An issue that also looms large in debate is implementation. Adaptation to EU requirements could induce a tick-box mentality where legislation is introduced but without this leading to real change such as in the way officials understand the issues. Superficial change can be understood as an instrumental adaptation to EU requirements because it is a necessity to adapt if EU membership is to occur and the obligations of membership are then to be respected. This contrasts with more deep seated engagement that can lead to more profound change in national ways of doing things. This point becomes clear when bearing in mind Cernik's (2014) observation that there can frequently be a gap between policy and practice when it comes to migrant integration. Pawlak (2014) observes that many initiatives in the area of migrant integration had been driven primarily by a desire to secure EU funds, such as from the EIF. In practice, it is a range of organisations operating at a local level such as churches and local welfare organisations that play a key role when it comes to immediate integration concerns.

There is evidence that CEE countries have been exposed to ideas about immigrant policy and also that they conform to some important Europe-wide policy trends. For instance, since 2012 the Czech Republic and Poland have introduced language tests as a condition for naturalisation. Another area where some, but only very incremental, convergence has taken place concerns citizenship and naturalisation policies. The citizenship policies of most CEE countries are firmly rooted in the principle of *jus sanguinis*, providing access to citizenship via family relations. This has been beneficial for the integration of repatriates, but has made it difficult for others to obtain full citizenship. A new act on Polish Citizenship of 2009, although enacted in 2012, makes naturalisation easier for migrants that have been resident in Poland for more than three years.

Diaspora politics mean that countries develop policies that facilitate access to citizenship and re-integration as much as possible for co-ethnics that live in other countries. For instance, regulations regarding dual nationality have been relaxed in Poland to facilitate return migration, and a special fast-track toward naturalisation has been established for people married to a Polish national. Article 6 of the Hungarian Constitution (revised in 1989) provides that: 'The Republic of Hungary bears a sense of responsibility for the fate of Hungarians living outside its borders and shall promote and foster their relations with Hungary'. In 2001, the Hungary parliament passed a Law on Hungarians Living in Adjacent States in 2001 (Toth and Sik, 2014) that facilitated access to visas, residence permits and border crossing. Romania has also facilitated access to Romanian citizenship for people (and their descendants) who have lost Romanian citizenship in the past, of whom many were in Ukraine, Serbia or Moldova. Some concerns have been raised in the EU concerning diaspora politics, access to citizenship to co-ethnics in surrounding countries and consequential access to EU citizenship and the Schengen area. Fears are that this would provide a back door route to EU citizenship. At the same time, in CEE countries, there have been concerns about how EU membership may strengthen borders between CEE countries and surrounding countries, thereby weakening connections with co-ethnics in bordering non-EU member states.

9.2 *THE POLISH PEASANT IN EUROPE AND AMERICA*

Emigration and diaspora formation are nothing new. This is clearly reflected in a book that is considered one of the classics of sociology: *The Polish Peasant in Europe and America*, by Florian Znaniecki and William I. Thomas (first published in 1918). The book presents a study on the incorporation process in the United States of nineteenth century Polish migrants, stressing the role of group formation amongst the Polish diaspora in strengthening their position. It also shows how gradually mixed identities emerge, such as Polish–Americans.

The book's analysis remains relevant when assessing the position of the contemporary Polish diaspora, which is large and widely dispersed across the world. One important change is that, since EU accession in May 2004, the context for the Polish diaspora in Europe is very different. Within the EU, the Polish are no longer migrants (at least not from a legal perspective). Rather they are mobile EU citizens making use of their right of free movement. Some sociologists speak of the rise of 'liquid mobility', a situation where migrants, particularly labour migrants, often continue to be on the move rather than settling permanently in one place (Engbersen et al., 2010). As such, the situation for the Polish migrant may be very different now than it was in the days of Znaniecki and Thomas' study.

Besides targeting co-ethnics in neighbouring states and the broader diaspora that migrated over the last century due to the many conflicts and disputes in Central and Eastern Europe, the relevance of diaspora politics has been increased tremendously by the large-scale movement of people from CEE countries to other parts of the EU. These migrants can be an economic source of great significance for CEE countries with efforts to reinforce the 'circular' and 'temporary' character of this migration and ensuring that ties with the home country are maintained. Okolski (2001) speaks in this respect of 'incomplete migration', by which he refers to often temporary migration with different degrees of legality and connected to work in secondary parts of the economy. Wallace (2002) applies the term 'mobility' rather than migration, capturing what she sees as the dynamic and temporary character of this form of migration. Similarly, Engbersen et al. (2010) identify 'liquid migration' that involves movement from one country to another but without necessarily involving permanent migration and settlement. Whether these ideas play out in reality is another matter. In a sense, the EU is designed to enable mobility, fluidity and 'liquidity', but people are not simply factors of production to be circulated around the EU on a temporary basis wherever the labour market and requirements of capitalism dispatch them. This will provide an interesting test of the 'character' of EU mobility and whether it translates into permanent settlement or retains a more temporary, circular and liquid character. While it's unlikely to be simply one or the other, there do seem to be tendencies towards settlement as marked, for example, by family reunification and new family formation.

Russian minorities

While the emphasis on *jus sanguinis* and diaspora politics in many CEE countries has inclusive implications for co-ethnic repatriates, the consequences for minorities can be very different. One instance of this is the sizeable Russian minority in the Baltic States in particular. Estonia, Latvia and, to some extent, Lithuania did not allow automatic access to national citizenship for former Soviet citizens after their independence as they effectively re-installed their national constitutions from before the Second World War. This meant that former Soviet citizens, mostly Russians but also Belarusians and Ukrainians, had to enrol in naturalisation procedures if they wished to obtain citizenship of the newly independent Baltic States. This left many Russians stateless with many opting for citizenship of the new Russian Federation, or one of the other states from the former Soviet bloc. In 1995 no fewer than 29 per cent of the Latvian population belonged to the category 'Latvian non-citizens', which had decreased to 14 per cent in 2012 (Supule, 2014). After EU accession of the Baltic States (in 2004), many Russian minority members also moved to other EU countries, such as the UK.

The naturalisation policies adopted in the Baltic States involve relatively high demands not just in terms of language comprehension but also in terms of basic knowledge of society. In Latvia this requires knowing the national anthem while in Lithuania an oath of allegiance to the Republic must be sworn. Language tests can be problematic for the Russian minorities, some of whom have been living in the Baltic countries for several generations and are used to being able to speak Russian. Also, the tests on basic knowledge of society involve efforts by the Baltic States to define a clear national identity after decades of occupation, triggering reluctance on the part of Russian minorities to take part in these tests. At the same time, resentment against the Russian period is obviously the key driver for these Baltic States to impose such a high threshold on access to full citizenship. This has also led to strong tensions between the Russian government and those Baltic States, exacerbated by conflict in Ukraine and concern about the wider ambitions of Russian President Putin.

In spite of the gradual emergence of policies toward immigrant and national minorities, Russian minorities remain excluded in various respects. As many of them are non-citizens, they are excluded from public office, do not possess voting rights at local or national level, and thus lack representation in the national political arena. There are NGOs that address the concerns of Russian speaking minorities, although this does not make up for limited formal political representation. A specific issue of concern in all three Baltic States is schooling and language training in the Russian language. A 2012 law in Estonia established Estonian as the language of instruction in all public secondary schools, thereby effectively undercutting the rationale for Russian language secondary schools that had previously coexisted alongside Estonian language schools.

Ethnic tensions emerged between the Russian minorities and the native population of the Baltic States following their independence, which continue to exist until today. Russian speaking minorities have been depicted as a 'fifth column' with loyalty to Russia, and in the early 1990s there were some efforts to encourage emigration of Russian speakers. Since the mid 1990s, there has been a more constructive dialogue, also stirred by concerns about stabilising relations with the Russian Federation. That tensions seem to persist is clearly illustrated by the traumatic events of 'Bronze Night' in Estonia in 2007 (referring to the relocation of a monument for Soviet soldiers – the 'bronze' soldier) which triggered riots in Tallinn and attacks against government institutions (Lagerspetz, 2014).

EU institutions have frequently raised concerns about the position of Russian minorities in the Baltic States. Guaranteeing basic rights and counteracting discrimination have been important EU concerns, especially during the accession period. Beyond the EU, another regional organisation that played a role in softening the relations between Russian minorities and the Baltic States was the Organisation for Security and Co-operation in Europe (OSCE), within which the High Commissioner on National Minorities played a key role in instigating a dialogue on this contested topic. This OSCE role indicates that external sources of change need not emanate only from the EU.

The Roma

A minority population with strong roots in Central and South Eastern Europe in particular, but also increasingly dispersed throughout other parts of Europe, is the Roma (or Romani) people. There are not precise figures for the total population, but estimates of the Roma population include a presence in Bulgaria (between 4.7 and 10 per cent of the population), Romania (between 3.3 and 8 per cent), Serbia (between 2 and 8 per cent), Hungary (between 2 and 7 per cent), Greece (between 1.8 and 2.5 per cent) and Spain (between 1 and 2 per cent). The Roma population is difficult to measure because the population is not fully settled and because of fears about disclosing identity to the census authorities because of the racism and discrimination that could result (Cahn and Guild, 2010).

Discrimination against the Roma is one of the most pressing minority rights issues in CEE countries. The Roma have no homeland to press their concerns and do not seek a homeland. In terms of the usual models of ethnic politics there have also been problems because Roma are less likely to engage in the kinds of state-oriented terms that are recognisable to students of ethnic mobilisation. This means that there have been problems acting coherently as an ethnic bloc in national and EU politics. Even if mobilisation were to occur then there is a risk of a backlash from nationalists, which further reinforces the need for the consolidation of social, administrative, legal and judicial practices founded on principles of non-discrimination.

This has resulted in an excluded and very weak social position for Roma in various CEE countries. Few Roma children complete secondary education, labour market discrimination has been widespread, and little effort has been made to give Roma people a formal representative voice. In recent history, numerous cases of violent persecution or forced adaptation have occurred. In Romania, the Roma were particularly subject to violent persecution in the years after the fall of the Ceausescu regime with anti-Roma pogroms reported between 1990 and 1993. In 2010, the Romanian government dismantled a large Roma settlement, leaving many people homeless. The Czech Republic was reported to have continued a policy of sterilisation of Roma women until well into the 1990s. In Italy there have been various incidents, often triggered by specific criminal acts committed by Roma that sparked tensions and violence against the wider Roma population.

Since accession, EU institutions have been very critical of the social position of Roma and discrimination against them. EU membership has, at least, enhanced the legal framework of minority rights and protection in CEE countries, although the gap between policy and practice can be very significant. The fact that Roma have no clear country of origin that can defend their rights, that they are a mobile group and that their ethnicity is sometimes difficult to grasp, has not helped their position. There is, however, some hypocrisy in EU claims and demands regarding the position of Roma in CEE countries, as Roma in many West European countries (such as in France, Italy and Spain) encounter major difficulties and have experienced, at times, violent persecution (Parker and López Catalán, 2012).

Over the last decade or so, concerns about Roma have increasingly been broadened from a CEE concern to a wider European issue. The end of the Cold War and the EU's expansion have not only enhanced the rights of this minority, but also increased their already significant potential in terms of mobility (Cahn and Guild, 2010). Roma with passports from CEE countries have exercised their right to free movement in the EU although data on the scale of this movement are lacking because they may be classed by their national origin (Romanian, Slovak, etc.) rather than their ethnic identity as Roma.

Conclusion

This chapter has shown the development of immigration policy in CEE that occurred largely before the experience of immigration. This paradoxical situation is linked to the context of EU accession. There was no way that CEE countries could join the EU unless and until they demonstrated that they could control their borders. Once in – and once any transitional period had been surpassed – people from new member states that joined the EU after 2004 could move freely. Common EU migration and asylum policies led to restrictions that were designed to strengthen the EU's eastern border in the face of 'unwanted' migration flows. Given the low numbers of immigrants, immigration has largely been an administrative rather than a wider political concern with scope for implementation gaps.

In spite of the much weaker EU framework for immigrant policies, the EU has had some influence. Whether driven by a desire to be seen as 'European' and mimicry to satisfy the requirements of membership, at least on paper, as well as by coercion from EU laws, immigrant policies have developed in CEE countries, such as the requirement to introduce anti-discrimination legislation following from the EU's two anti-discrimination directives of 2000.

While the EU does provide a powerful impetus to convergence and a range of other external pressures from, for example the Council of Europe and OSCE reinforce this pressure, there are also elements of distinctiveness. First, countries such as Poland have been concerned to maintain specific migration measures that allow for labour migration. Second, we saw the importance of diaspora politics and the centrality of the emigration experience both in the more distant history of countries such as Poland and more recently as a result of EU membership. Nationality laws with a strong base in *jus sanguinis* are designed to facilitate return and maintain connections to the diaspora. Third, concerns about migration and in particular about integration have been much more focused on national minorities than on immigrant minorities. Due to the many border changes amongst CEE countries over the last century, many co-ethnics were placed in neighbouring countries (such as millions of Magyars, or ethnic Hungarians). More insidious is the situation of the Roma minority that is dispersed across Europe and whose social position is highly vulnerable. Since EU accession, the Roma issue has increasingly been upscaled towards the EU, triggered by events such as the forced repatriation of Bulgarian and Romanian Roma by France in 2010 (see Chapter 3). With an eye on the conflicts in the Ukraine, the position of Russian speaking minorities in Baltic States is of growing concern.

In short, the chapter has shown the shadow cast by the EU and its influence on immigration politics, free movement and diasporic politics. We see too some undercurrents of Euroscepticism and anti-immigration sentiment, which became more evident during the European refugee crisis. While the picture is not one of straightforward convergence, there are some important points of similarity with developments in other EU member states. These link quite closely to the EU's role as a source of law and policy, as well as both actually and potentially a bone of contention in domestic politics. The chapter also showed that the relation between CEE countries and European immigration policies has changed from one characterised by coercive adaptation in the context of EU accession, to a relationship in which CEE countries have become increasingly important actors in the definition of EU immigration policies or opposition to aspects of the policy, such as the mandatory relocation of asylum seekers.

10

Greece and Turkey: New Migration Dynamics in South East Europe?

Introduction

War, poverty and oppression have been the key – but not the only – drivers of migration towards South East Europe through what has been called the 'Eastern Mediterranean corridor' linking Asian countries such as Afghanistan and countries in the Middle East and Horn of Africa to Turkey and Greece. For example, in the space of ten days at the end of May 2015, around 1,500 people arrived on the Greek island of Kos, a popular holiday destination. These 1,500 people formed part of the total of around 39,000 people who arrived in Greece by sea between January and May 2015 (compared to 45,000 who arrived in Italy by sea). In September 2015, 130,000 people arrived on the island of Lesbos, which lies only 10km from Turkey, with a further 30,000 arriving in the first week of October. By the end of 2015, the IOM was estimating that more than 845,000 refugees and migrants had entered Greece via Mediterranean routes. The UNHCR estimates there will be 1.7 million refugees in Turkey by the end of 2015, due to the displacement caused by the conflict in Syria. Of these, just under 220,000 were housed in 22 camps with UNHCR praising the protection offered by Turkey in the face of such huge inflows of people fleeing conflict.

These developments in 2015 help to demonstrate that many of the key migration challenges faced by the EU arise at Europe's southern and eastern borders. This chapter asks to what extent are these new dynamics? Clearly, the impact of displacement related to conflict is on a very large scale. It is shown, however, that there are points of comparison in terms of policy and legal development that link Greece and Turkey to newer immigration countries in Southern and Central Europe. For example, we see that the EU, Council of Europe and UNHCR have all played important roles in policy development. There are also similarities between Greece, Italy and Spain (see Chapter 8) in terms of the timing of immigration, the relationship to the informal economy, the use of regularisations and the EU's influence on policy. What is new, and alters the dynamics of migration policy and politics in Europe, is the emergence of Turkey as a destination country. A key aspect of this has been people displaced by conflict, but there are other types of migration happening: settlement by labour migrants and family members, particularly in major Turkish cities; so-called 'transit migrants' who find themselves in Turkey, although that might not have been their intended destination; and forms of temporary or 'circular' labour migration.

The effects of conflict and displacement

As already noted, of particular importance since the early 2010s, especially in Turkey, have been the devastating human effects of conflict in countries such as Libya and Syria that have led millions of people to flee in search of safety and protection. Some of these people have moved to Europe, although far more have moved to neighbouring states such as Jordan, Lebanon and Turkey rather than move a long way from home and risk the more costly and potentially dangerous journey to Europe. It would be wrong and entirely misleading to imagine that the millions displaced by conflict in the Middle East and North Africa are all potential migrants to the EU. The history of displacement caused by conflict demonstrates that most people flee to the 'next safe place' with the intention or hope of returning home. In addition, for vulnerable groups amongst the displaced such as women, children and elderly people it can be difficult to move much further unless resettlement programmes facilitate their movement away from danger.

It would also be wrong to see Greece and Turkey simply as so-called 'transit' countries, meaning countries that people move across to go elsewhere. The reality is far more complex. As this chapter shows, Greece and Turkey are simultaneously sending, transit and destination countries (as indeed are most European immigration countries). As discussed later, it can be difficult to understand migration and migrant decision-making as conforming to ideas such as 'transit', although defining the issue in such terms can shape and influence policy responses.

Greece and Turkey have been divided by tensions but also share a land border. In 2012, the Greek government completed a 12km barbed wire fence along the Evros River, which is the land border with Turkey, designed to tackle irregular border crossing. It is essential to explore these border dynamics to not only understand developments in these countries, but also to enhance our perspective on migration dynamics and border relationships in a part of Europe that is, and will continue to be, central to the EU's future. We also see how and why the EU has been a key driver of immigration policy and politics with a strong emphasis on strengthening external frontiers and attempting to develop enhanced operational capacity. In Greece this has led to migration laws that have focused primarily on securing external frontiers. In Turkey, pressure from the EU as well as from the Council of Europe and UNHCR led, in 2013, to the country's first comprehensive legislation on migration and international protection.

In both Greece and Turkey, the immigration issue is nested within much bigger debates. In Greece, the dominant issue since the economic crisis post-2008 has been the hugely negative economic and social consequences of austerity and, linked to it, the transformation of the Greek party political system. In contrast, Turkey has seen, since the 2000s, high levels of economic growth, and has been seeking EU membership since 1959 with membership negotiations beginning in 1963, but by 2015 accession seemed no nearer. The result is that debate about borders, migration and asylum in Turkey have been framed by this ambivalent relationship with the EU, as well as by important social, demographic and political transformations in Turkey. There are a few issues to bear in mind here:

- Turkey has a large and growing population that is projected to rise to 100 million by 2050.
- There remains significant wealth inequalities between Turkey and the EU, but, since the 2000s, Turkey has experienced rapid economic growth and a demographic transition marked by movement from very high, to lower, birth and mortality rates.
- In 2010, Turkey experienced a migration transition when the number of immigrants entering the country exceeded the number of emigrants leaving (İçduygu and Kirişçi, 2009: 1). This means that Turkey is becoming an immigration country, which suggests it is too simplistic to imagine that there are millions of Turkish people sitting on their suitcases ready to move to an EU country, although this has been a sub-text for those EU member states that oppose visa liberalisation. Instead, we see migration to Turkey, across Turkey (so-called 'transit migration') and movement out of Turkey.

Migration and borders in South East Europe

As with other chapters, the analysis that follows is centred on the effects of borders because, as has been shown throughout this book, it is territorial, organisational and conceptual borders that make international migration visible as a social and political issue (Zolberg, 1989). Much of the EU focus in its relations with both Greece and Turkey has been on external frontiers, immigration control and on the scope for co-operation both within the EU and with neighbouring states on border controls and security.

10.1 REGULATORY AND DISTRIBUTIVE QUESTIONS IN GREEK AND TURKISH IMMIGRATION POLITICS

Border controls can be understood as *regulatory* questions that concern who can and cannot enter the state territory and on what basis. A key issue is then the state's regulatory capacity with high levels of irregular migration a potential indicator of capacity limits.

Immigration issues don't simply stop at these external frontiers. Instead, there arise complex *distributive* questions once migrants are 'in' that concern who gets what and on what basis. These relate to, for example, access to the labour market, social rights and welfare benefits.

As also seen in other chapters covering countries that are all EU member states, for non-EU migrants the EU's remit does not extend so directly to these internal distributive questions: welfare systems remain national while the approach to integration is specifically identified by the EU treaty as a matter for the member states.

There are, of course, important differences between Greece and Turkey; not least that one is inside and the other outside the EU. One point of similarity is the strong EU-driven policy focus on regulatory, external frontier issues compared to the much more limited EU reach into complex distributive questions that arise once migrants are on the state's territory (Geddes and Taylor, 2013).

A further challenge to the border and boundaries of Greece as a member state and Turkey as a candidate state is from European integration, which has important effects on border relationships including by creating an area of free movement for EU citizens (including Greeks, but not Turks) and, concomitantly, pushing for stronger controls at the external frontiers of the member states. The chapter contributes to what is by now becoming a familiar story. Adaptation to the EU is not some kind of smooth, linear process of adaptation. Analysts of developments in Greece and Turkey talk of 'critical' or 'contested' Europeanisation (Tolay, 2012; Triandafyllidou, 2014). Criticism and contestation of the EU has also become a more familiar picture in other member states too where variants of Euroscepticism, including about the migration-related effects of European integration, have become important domestic political questions (in Britain, France and the Netherlands to name only three as Chapters 2, 3 and 5 have shown). By exploring the Greek and Turkish cases we are better able to understand how the EU works its way into domestic politics simultaneously, as both an opportunity and a problem. To do so requires a focus on both 'external' and 'internal' borders and their effects. Taking our analysis from earlier chapters and applying it to the cases of Greece and Turkey means that we can identify three aspects of these effects:

1. The EU and its member states enter into what can be called a 'sovereignty bargain'. By joining the EU, member states agree to ceding some of their sovereign authority with the understanding that they become stronger as a result of the EU's collective strength.

Greece entered into such a sovereignty bargain upon joining the EU in 1981 and, with negative effects, when it joined the Euro in 2001. The essence of Turkey's claim for membership is that it too intends to strike such a bargain, but thus far there has been resistance from some member states to Turkish membership as well as questions about Turkey's political direction and orientation under the leadership of Recep Erdoğan who was Prime Minister from 2003 to 2014 and became President of Turkey in 2014.

2. Membership also involves a 'capacity bargain' whereby access to EU resources, know-how and collective decision-making can strengthen the ability of states to achieve their objectives (Geddes and Taylor, 2013). This focus on capacity has been a clear component of responses to migration in Greece since flows from Albania and other Balkan countries increased in the early 1990s. For a non-member such as Turkey the EU frame for law and policy has had important effects on the organisation of institutions and policy with acceleration after 2008. Capacity is not a neutral term as its meaning will heavily depend on the perception of the challenge to which capacity building is then seen as a response.

3. The EU introduces new elements into domestic politics that are not necessarily stable because they can change power relations by, for example, strengthening some actors and weakening others. It may strengthen pro-EU actors, but it is also plausible that anti-EU actors can be emboldened as a result of European integration. It should not necessarily be assumed that the end result is some smooth process of adaptation by nation states to the EU and its requirements. There are a variety of outcomes that could include resistance to EU effects. The literature on Europeanisation suggests that it is likely that we will find 'adaptation with national colours' and not some kind of identikit European response (Green Cowles et al., 2000). This highlights once again the importance of looking at how national political systems channel the effects of European integration both at national and local levels.

These three points can be applied across the EU and to non-EU states such as Turkey and demonstrate three key components of the relationship between the nation state and European integration. They also help with understanding of how, why and with what effects European integration becomes an issue in domestic politics and also how it can become a matter of contention – a political question – and not some bland, technocratic process of adaptation.

Greece

According to the 2011 census there were 913,000 foreign residents in Greece, of which 713,000 were TCNs and 199,000 were EU nationals (OECD, 2014: 258). Table 10.1 provides data on immigration to Greece and on the country's foreign born and foreign population.

Greece has been classified as a South European type of immigration country along with Italy, Spain and Portugal because of the relatively recent onset of immigration (since the 1990s) and with a key component of this classification being the relationship between economic informality, high levels of irregular migration and three major regularisations (Peixoto et al., 2012).

Table 10.1 Immigration and the foreign born population in Greece

	2000	2005	2011	2012
Immigration per 1,000 inhabitants	n/a	5.9	2.1	2.6
Foreign-born population (percentage of total population)	n/a	n/a	6.7	6.6
Foreign population (percentage of total population)	2.8	5.0	6.8	6.9

Source: adapted from OECD, 2014

Peixoto et al. (2012) also highlight that there is a tension between Southern EU member states and 'older' immigration countries in Northern Europe that centres on issues such as responsibility sharing and might actually undo common EU policies, or at least make their further development less likely.

For geographical reasons linked to its location, and to the scale and extent of its borders (including 6,000 islands of which 227 are inhabited), Greece has become central to the people-smuggling networks within the EU (and on its borders) along what is known as an Eastern Mediterranean corridor. A tension within the EU has been the sharing of responsibility for measures that seek to tackle these networks. The issues that are raised can also be complex because migration flows are often 'mixed', i.e. containing people who fall into different migration categories. The dilemmas were made evident in a quote reported from an official based in Greece from a leading international organisation: 'A small boat arrives at Greek islands where there are no police officers. In the same boat you might have asylum cases, trafficking cases and legal cases. So, if the receivers are not trained, they put everybody in the same room and they have the same treatment and reception' (cited in Geddes and Taylor, 2013: 62).

Such 'mixed' inflows present bureaucratic and administrative challenges, which, of course, will be exacerbated if the state concerned has been hit hard by austerity and public spending cuts, as has been the case in Greece. High levels of economic informality combined with irregular migration are also connected to public hostility towards migrants while ethnic-based citizenship laws made it difficult for non-Greek migrants to get citizenship. Reforms to naturalisation procedures were introduced by the PASOK-led government in 2010 leading to an increase in foreigners acquiring Greek citizenship (14,600 in 2012; 20,500 in 2013) (OECD, 2014: 258). The radical left-wing government led by the SYRIZA party that was elected in 2015 announced its intention to reform Greek laws to make it far easier for migrants and their children to acquire Greek nationality.

Immigration as a security issue

Initial legislative responses in Greece to immigration were draconian with a focus on security and restriction. For example, an early response was the 1991 Immigration Law introduced by a centre-right government led by the New

Democracy political party, which made irregular immigration an offence punishable by between ten days and five years in jail. The law was a response to Greece moving from being an emigration to an immigration country in the early 1990s, but the effect was to criminalise immigrants at a time when there was limited scope for regular entry, but also increased numbers of immigrants and strong labour market demand for migrant workers.

Patterns of migration in the 1990s were influenced by Greece's geographical position and by instability and conflict in neighbouring states. A key issue in the 1990s was migration caused by economic instability in Albania. By 2012, Albanian migrants comprised 60–65 per cent of the total foreign-born population in Greece. The militarisation of the Greek–Albanian border in the 1990s was seen as redolent of the 'border games' played on the US–Mexican border – another border separating relative prosperity from high levels of deprivation (King et al., 1998; Andreas, 2000). Albanian migrants in Greece were linked to crime, and the stereotype of the supposedly criminal Albanian immigrant acquired resonance in social and political debate. While it was the case that Albanians were more evident in police arrest figures and Albanian gangs were active in the smuggling of people, drugs and guns, the high level of arrests of Albanians also reflected police targeting of areas with large Albanian populations. Also, many Albanians were irregular immigrants and thus already breaking Greek law because of their irregular status.

Another key characteristic of migration to Greece in the 1990s, as in other European immigration countries, was its spatial concentration in big cities, particularly Athens. This interacted with irregularity and tendencies towards employment in the informal sector to create what was seen as:

a prototype for the trends towards informalisation of work and the increased social inequality and restructuring of consumption into high-income and very low-income strata. (Iosifides and King, 1998: 223)

The result was severe strains on the public administration with over-burdened municipalities picking up the bulk of the work because they were where the bulk of the migrant population was concentrated, particularly in and around Athens. This can then lead to significant capacity problems because as Adam and Devillard (2008: 272) put it:

The immigration department personnel in local administration authorities admit that there is a lack of the necessary human resources for the provision of services envisaged in the current legislative framework on migration.

An interview with a Greek public official cited in Geddes and Taylor (2013) demonstrates the effects of overload on local authorities where there may only be a small core staff with the result that there can be *many clashes because some institutions represent a sense of rationality while others represent the not necessarily rational demands of local centres of power or financial power, like, for example, the big agricultural lobbies that primarily use migrants as a workforce and play a crucial role in exercising pressure on policy-makers.*

The pressures can be more intense on local government because it is more immediately subject to political pressures and political costs. This can then translate into implementation difficulties that have been evident, for example, when seeking to regularise migrants as this has also been primarily implemented at local level.

Reform of Greek local government in 2010 (the so-called *Kallikratis* reforms) introduced a one-stop shop with 55 'Decentralised Administration Authorities' and also set up Migrant Integration Councils in Greece's 352 municipalities to include elected local representatives and migrants with the intention that these play a consultative role. In 2014, the *Code for Migration and Social Integration* brought together all previous legislation and relevant EU law into one single source.

The reliance on regularisations

The lack of an immigration policy regulating admissions during the 1990s and into the 2000s meant that many immigrants were pushed into Greece's informal economy. As in Italy and Spain, this can create an unsustainable situation with hundreds of thousands of people outside of many of the normal regulatory structures of a society while also being open to abuse and exploitation at work. As we saw in Chapter 8 on Italy and Spain, the use of regularisations has been seen as a policy response that typifies the Southern European migration type. The purpose of two Presidential decrees in 1997 was to attempt to deal with some of the regulatory problems caused by large-scale immigration. One decree introduced a so-called 'White Card' which gave temporary settlement rights to the large irregular population. This was followed by a 'Green Card' that granted more permanent status. Things did not run entirely smoothly because of administrative problems mentioned earlier. As was noted by an interview with a Greek public official (cited in Geddes and Taylor, 2013: 62) this was 'altogether a terribly confusing administrative mechanism [but] in the end quite beneficial because it brought the administration into contact with the whole mass of migrants in Greece'. Baldwin-Edwards (2009: 298) argues that the regularisation was 'not the result of popular movement or planned policy, but represented an emergency measure or admission of policy failure'.

For Linos (2002) the political puzzle that became evident in the 1990s was why Greek governments tolerated irregular migration when the public were intolerant of this irregularity. She argues that this toleration arose because the then Greek 'cartel' party system saw dominance by two parties, the Greek

Socialist Party (PASOK) and the centre-right New Democracy party. A cartel party system means dominance by political parties that use the state's resources to maintain this dominance (Katz and Mair, 1995). This can include finding jobs in the public sector for party supporters. Until the economic crisis of 2008, the dominant positions of PASOK and New Democracy made it difficult for challengers to break through because their control of the executive branch of government had allowed them to effectively co-opt state institutions. The result was that the dominant parties become less dependent on voters' preferences meaning that it was 'possible to conduct unpopular policy with less fear of electoral loss' (Linos, 2002: 20). There was broad similarity between the approaches of PASOK and New Democracy to border security and immigration control, although PASOK was more liberal on integration and citizenship than its conservative opponent.

The 2001 Immigration Law introduced by a PASOK government maintained the highly restrictive focus of Greek immigration legislation. It linked work and residence in a way that seemed destined to maintain high levels of irregularity, particularly because it increased the dependency of migrants on the workings of the Greek bureaucracy, which had experienced major problems coping with the numbers of people who came forward in the first regularisation of 1998. The legislation was also controversial because it limited family reunion and access by irregular migrants and their children to essential public services such as health and education. The 2001 legislation failed to tackle many of the issues that arose from the 1998 regularisation, which had allowed irregular migrants to apply for a temporary 'White Card' permit and then for a more permanent 'Green Card'. The Green Card process was riddled with bureaucratic obstacles and requirements that many migrants found impossible to fulfil. This led to calls for a second regularisation because of the numbers of people who managed to register with the Greek Organisation for the Employment of Human Resources, but then did not manage to submit their application due to the onerous bureaucratic requirements (Baldwin-Edwards, 2009).

The overall effect was that routes for regular entry to Greece were extremely limited and controlled by government quotas. In such a situation with the state attempting to regulate entry but with relatively weak state regulatory capacity, it was highly likely that irregular migrants would be able to enter Greece and find employment in the informal economy. Observers saw Greek policy as ineffective, harsh and offering inadequate protection to migrants while doing little to assuage social attitudes that were generally quite hostile to immigrants (Lazaridis, 1996; Triandafyllidou, 2000). The result was an inability and/or unwillingness to deal with the major administrative and political issues that concerted attempts to regulate the economic informality would have both for migrants and Greek citizens. There are clear similarities here with the situation in Italy and Spain that was assessed in Chapter 8. In all three countries, we see the importance of

Sciortino's (1999) observation about the 'Pandora's box' of internal controls that potentially impinge upon both migrants and citizens.

The EU's influence

In Greece there was clearly an external impetus to reform from the EU – at least in terms of border controls – but there were major domestic implementation challenges. Again, as was also seen in both Italy and Spain, there were attempts in the 2000s to create an immigration system that established mechanisms for the regulation of entry. The 2005 Greek Immigration Law had bold ambitions. It sought to

- plan migration flows in relation to social and economic life;
- ensure greater administrative consistency;
- protect the employment rights of migrant workers;
- introduce an immigrant integration policy;
- avoid the uncontrolled entry and exit of foreigners;
- incentivise foreign investment;
- and allow TCNs to exercise rights.

These are bold objectives and all are closely linked to state capacity to actually achieve these objectives. The 2005 law also incorporated EU Directives on family reunification and the rights of TCNs who are long-term residents. There was also some EU influence on the general framework for immigrant integration policy through the incorporation of the EU's *Common Basic Principles on Integration*. Writing about the 2005 framework, Adam and Devillard noted that:

> *Even though the ... legislative regime does represent a marked improvement compared to the previous regime, one still feels that 15 years after Greece became a (proportionally speaking) major host country, it continues to experiment with a workable regulatory framework. (2008: 272)*

As we saw for Italy, Spain and new member states in Central and Eastern Europe, immigration law and policy in Greece was strongly influenced by the EU. It wasn't until Bulgaria joined the Union in 2007 that Greece actually shared a border with another EU member state. In terms of policy, the EU and other member states provided a template for the kinds of legislative developments that were required, but, as flows from the Middle East and North Africa increased after the 'Arab Uprisings' post-2012, there was also a sense that other EU member states needed to demonstrate greater solidarity to their South European partners who were subject to increased pressures on their borders arising from the operation of smuggling networks. The 2015 European Agenda on Migration contained specific provisions on relocation of asylum applicants across the EU from countries facing large inflows and, in September 2015, brought forward proposals for relocation of up to 160,000 such applicants from Greece, Hungary and Italy (CEC, 2015). While often seen as a weak link in EU border security, Triandafyllidou (2014: 412) found disappointment amongst Greek officials with the EU, and a feeling that it was, in fact, other EU member states that were non-compliant because of the absence of solidarity. By adopting this position, Greek elites 'indirectly seek to counteract the discourse that ... sees Greece as ... to blame for its problems and for the problems it causes to the entire Eurozone'.

The effects of crisis

After 2008, the effects of the economic crisis and of severe austerity led to a fragmentation of the Greek political system. A further effect was to lead to renewed emigration from Greece with increased numbers of Greek people resident in Germany, Britain, Sweden, the Netherlands and Switzerland. A survey of Greek emigrants suggested that the majority were men (up to two-thirds) and that most were highly educated to at least university degree level (Triandafyllidou and Gropas, 2014).

The crisis had dramatic effects on the Greek labour market and society with high unemployment rates for natives that were exceeded by those for immigrant workers. In 2012, unemployment for immigrant men was 34.5 per cent, which was more than 14 points higher than the figure for Greek workers, while the unemployment rate for immigrant women stood at 32.6 per cent, which was five points higher than native-born women (OECD, 2014: 258).

One immediate effect of the crisis occurred in 2009 with a harshening of policy towards migrants, particularly after the 2009 European Parliament elections in which the extreme right LAOS party did relatively well receiving just over 7 per cent of the vote and getting 2 MEPs elected. The New Democracy government stepped up efforts by the police to apprehend and deport irregular migrants under the controversial *xenios zeus* programme, although this was strongly focused on apprehending irregular migrants in public places such as at stations and squares rather than in factories and other work places (Triandafyllidou and Ambrosini, 2011: 260). There are some similarities with the Italian case as the demand for migrant workers in sectors such as construction, agriculture, tourism and domestic work/care meant that the official Greek government admissions policy via quotas did not meet the actual needs for workers in these sectors and could then contribute to irregularity. Even during the economic crisis and deep austerity when the Greek government was arguing that the country couldn't take any more immigrants, there was, according to Triandafyllidou and Ambrosini (2011: 262), continued demand for migrant workers by families and businesses.

To illustrate this point, we can consider the quote below from an interview in 2008 with a Greek public official who succinctly captured the competing demands that can affect policy-making, with policies then reflecting an intentional jumble, or 'fudging', of different goals and priorities (Hall, 1986). Rather than necessarily being coherent, policies may actually be designed to keep different interests happy, appearing to be quite inconsistent or contradictory (Boswell and Geddes, 2011):

> Two years ago [2006] on the island of Lesvos there was a fight between some locals and some Albanians who were working in their village, so the municipal council decided that all Albanians would be persona non grata in their village and sent them away. Then the season came when they needed to collect the olives. So, this is the confusion in public opinion and with policy-makers who reflect on the conflict between recognising that they need migrants, but having to face a public that doesn't want them. (Cited in Geddes and Taylor, 2013: 67)

The fragmentation of the Greek political system in the aftermath of the economic crisis led to challenges to mainstream parties from the far left and right. In 2015, the far left SYRIZA party led by Alexis Tsipras became the largest party in the Greek Parliament securing 36.3 per cent of the vote and 149 of the 300 seats. It then secured a second mandate in September 2015. SYRIZA drew most of its support from its opposition to austerity, but also advocated a changed approach to immigration, as marked by the appointment of the country's first ever Immigration Minister, the human rights lawyer Tasia Christodoulopoulou, who promised to close detention centres, stop arbitrary arrests under the controversial *xenios zeus* programme and reform naturalisation laws to allow children raised in Greece to become Greek citizens.

From the extreme right, both LAOS and its anti-democratic and Nazi-sympathising successor Golden Dawn experienced some electoral success. Golden Dawn was Greece's third largest party at the 2015 general election when it won just over 6 per cent of the vote (17 of the 300 seats) despite its leader, Nikolaos Michaloliakos being in pre-trial detention at the time of the election for his alleged involvement in the murder of an anti-fascist.

In summary, developments in Greece demonstrate a strong focus on external border controls with weaker domestic regulatory reach, which is related to the capacity and reach of the Greek state. Policy has tended to be highly centralised with the Interior Ministry very dominant, although there have been centre–periphery tensions and hostility to migrants. The economic crisis has led to increased emigration from Greece, particularly by higher skilled people. The setting against which migration policy and politics have occurred has been strongly influenced by the economic crisis and its devastating social effects, as well as by the deterioration of the situation in the Middle East and North Africa that led to hundreds of thousands of migrants entering Europe via Greek Islands. One result of this has been increased irregular migration (including to Greek holiday islands) at a time when the Greek state has been subject to severe cutbacks as a result of austerity policies. At the same time, more northerly EU member states were reluctant to accept responsibility for redistribution of asylum seekers and refugees. The effects of crisis were also evident within the political system where the previously dominant PASOK and New Democracy parties saw their votes collapse as the far left SYRIZA party entered government promising a more open and liberal approach to immigration and reform of Greek nationality laws. Such concerns were, however, of a lower order of importance compared to the Euro crisis and the question of Greek's membership of the Eurozone within the EU.

In terms of wider points that can be taken forward from this overview of immigration policy and politics in Greece, the refugee crisis showed the vulnerability of the EU's southern and eastern member states to migration and refugee flows and the issues that are raised about solidarity within the EU. The chapter has also shown the difficulty of ensuring regulatory capacity at external borders and dealing with the complex distributive issues that arise once migrants are 'in'. As has also been evident in other chapters, we can understand more about how the effects of European integration can be contested or criticised in domestic politics because they play out in relation to both these regulatory and distributive aspects.

Turkey

The situation in Turkey differs in some important respects from the developments in Greece, particularly in that Turkey's first ever immigration law was not agreed until 2013, coming into effect in 2014. Turkey tends also not to be included in analyses of European immigration politics, but, as this section shows, this is an omission that needs to be challenged because of the links between immigration politics and policy in Turkey and those in other EU member states, as well as the EU's influence on policy and institutional development. Table 10.2 shows the foreign population in Turkey between 2010 and 2012.

Turkey has also received very large numbers of refugees from Syria, estimated at up to 2 million by the end of 2015 according to UNHCR. Turkey became central to the EU's response to the refugee crisis. In October 2015, the EU proposed an action plan for Turkey, the details of which are in Box 10.2, below.

Table 10.2 Foreign population in Turkey 2010–12

Year	Total foreign population
2010	177,000
2011	217,000
2012	267,300

Source: OECD, 2014: 304

10.2 EU–TURKEY ACTION PLAN

In October 2015, the EU offered Turkey a series of measures to reinforce practical co-operation on migration, asylum and border security. The aim was to stop the flow of refugees and migrants from Turkey to the EU. There were three key elements:

- up to €3 billion in assistance to Turkey to aid with reception and accommodation of refugees;
- visa free travel to Europe for Turkish citizens;
- re-opening of membership negotiations.

An important linkage between Greece and Turkey is the EU's influence on the control aspects of policy even for a non-member state, although, as was seen in Greece, there are limits on the EU's ability to directly affect the more complex distributive questions that affect migrants and Turkish citizens on the state's territory. We also see in Turkey that the EU's effects can be contested or resisted in domestic politics and also that the EU is not the only player in town. In Turkey, both the Council of Europe and the UNHCR have had important influences on migration and asylum law and policy while broader strategic considerations linked to Turkey's geo-political position have influenced its domestic and foreign policy.

Since 2010, immigration became a more pressing issue in Turkey with a growing presence of migrants and refugees from Iraq, Syria, Afghanistan, Pakistan and China in Turkey. This led to immigration rising up the Turkish political agenda with the governing AKP party seeking reform of migration policy, which was finally realised in 2013 in the form of the country's first comprehensive immigration policy. There were three policy issues that underpinned legal and policy development: readmission of irregular migrants; visas; and asylum. The first two of these were strongly framed by the EU while asylum law and policy were strongly influenced by the UNHCR, the Council of Europe and the European Court of Human Rights (ECtHR). The Council of Europe is entirely separate from the EU, is an intergovernmental body with a much wider membership than the EU (47 member states in 2016) and is chiefly known for its human rights standards.

These external influences, such as those emanating from the Council of Europe, UN and EU will also interact with domestic political institutions. At the beginning of this chapter, we said that one effect of EU influence might be to empower some actors (those in close connection with the EU) while weakening others. The chapters in this book have also shown that it is likely that adaptation will occur 'with national colours' (Green Cowles et al., 2000). One lesson that has been strikingly clear from all the previous chapters, and is even more the case in a non-member such as Turkey, is that it is wrong to see any country as a passive recipient of EU demands. They will always be filtered through domestic politics and can shift the balance in domestic politics.

It is also important to adopt the correct perspective on migration to, from and across Turkey. It is narrow and Eurocentric to simply label Turkey as a new immigration country and to then think of it only in relation to EU migration and asylum policy. If we change the perspective then we can see that Turkey occupies an important geo-strategic position 'at the crossroads between Asia, Africa and the EU' (İçduygu and Aksel, 2014: 338). Kirişçi (2012: 65) points out that Turkey 'has long been a country of immigration especially for Muslim ethnic groups', such as people moving from the Balkans. Similarly, İçduygu and Aksel (2014: 358) emphasise the importance of historical legacies in Turkish immigration policy 'all influenced by relations with Europe. Yet, European influence over these policies and practices was often intensely contested'. In the post-war period, the prominence of Turkish migrants and the formation of large Turkish origin communities in the Netherlands and Germany (in particular) have been shown. There has also been emigration to the USA, Canada, Central Asia and the Middle East because of employment opportunities. The result, as Tolay (2012) sees it, is that Turkey possesses 'multiple identities' as an immigration country. It is a point of destination, point of arrival and a country that people move across in transit to their final destination. After the end of the Cold War there were increased flows from East European countries such as Bulgaria and from the Middle East, with a huge increase in the scale of refugee flows after 2010, linked to the Syrian conflict. This movement placed pressure on the legal framework given the absence of migration laws, policies and institutions.

10.3 POTENTIAL DIMENSIONS OF CONTESTATION IN TURKEY OF EU INFLUENCE

In the area of migration and asylum policy, it is accurate to note that laws, policies and institutions in Turkey have been shaped by the EU context leading to some Europeanisation, but this has been referred to as 'critical Europeanisation' (Tolay, 2012: 41). Being critical can mean a selective adoption of EU standards 'transformed into a truly "Turkish" approach to migration and asylum ... the feeling that they can do "better than the Europeans", or be more "European than the Europeans"'. This fits with Turkey's 'ambivalent historical perception of Europe'. In Greece too we saw critical or contested Europeanisation and, in other chapters, we saw the ways in which connections between the EU and immigration have fuelled Euroscepticism.

There are six possible dimensions along which the EU's influence could be contested (Tolay, 2012: 52–54).

1 There can be disputes about the level of investment needed to make the required changes as this can be costly.

2 Inter-state power relationships can be affected as Turkey must adapt to the EU border security framework set out in the Schengen *acquis* if it is to become a member state. The resultant power imbalance could mean limited leverage for the Turkish government and a subsequent imbalance between the EU and Turkey that could be a cause of resentment.

3 The EU approach may contain contradictions that are difficult to resolve in law and policy. For instance, the EU seems to be saying that it wants members and aspiring members to be tough on irregular migrants, but to offer protection to refugees. A problem is that tougher border controls make it more difficult for people to access the protection system.

4 EU policies may be contested by, for example, civil society organisations if they are seen as harsh, unfair and driven by narrow security concerns.

5 There may be concern that EU member states are seeking to offload responsibility for migration and asylum to countries on the EU's southern and eastern border so that they become a 'buffer zone' or 'dumping ground'.

6 There could be a feeling within Turkey as an applicant that there is hypocrisy when the EU extols the virtues of free movement and the benefits of visa free travel while denying these benefits to Turkish people.

These potential dimensions of contestation were evident in the debate within the Turkish government in the run up to the new migration law agreed in 2013 and entering into force in 2014 which reflected a 'desire to do things for ourselves' as the world's sixteenth largest economy, while at the same time there was a greater sense of senior officials 'associating oneself with the broader international community dealing with asylum issues' (Kirişçi, 2012: 79).

As was seen in other chapters, the term 'immigration' is much too broad to capture the complex and numerous flows of people across state borders. For example, Memişoğlu (2014) identifies various types of migration flow with significant variation in terms of purpose and duration. Shorter duration migration can take the form of 'circular' or 'shuttle' migration by people moving on a temporary or short-term basis, often from post-Soviet countries and the Balkans. A term that has acquired high policy relevance is 'transit' migration with people moving from African and Asian countries and the idea behind the term being that they then move on to Europe. Turkey is thus a staging post in an onwards migration movement. As Düvell (2014) notes, the term transit migration is a blurred and politically contested concept that may well not capture the effects of migration on migrants themselves. For example, an intention to move on may not actually turn into reality if onward movement is difficult. The result can be that so-called transit countries such as Turkey become points of arrival, although that was not the original intention. Chapter 8 showed that 'diversion effects' because of immigration controls in Northern Europe contributed to increased settlement by migrants in Southern Europe. Migration has led to increased settlement and formation of immigrant communities in large cities such as Istanbul. Finally, and of great importance in the formation of Turkish migration policy, has been movement by people seeking protection from conflict and oppression. By March 2015, UNHCR was estimating there to be 1.65 million Syrian refugees in Turkey alone. To give an idea of how large numbers of people may arrive in short spaces of time, around 200,000 arrived in Turkey after the so-called 'Islamic State' assault on the Kurdish enclave of Ayn al-Arab/Kobane in northern Syria in mid-September 2014. This relatively sudden displacement of very large numbers of vulnerable people requiring protection can lead to major pressure on Turkey to provide proper protection for these vulnerable people.

The development of Turkish migration law and policy

A key issue for the Turkish government as it considered the development of migration law and policy was the so-called 'geographical limitation' from the provisions of the 1951 refugee convention, which still applies. The limitation means that only European nationals are entitled to attain refugee status while for non-Europeans the Turkish government works with UNHCR on reception and resettlement.

Initial responses to immigration were post hoc responses to flows rather than attempts to put in place a system to regulate those flows. The 1994 Regulation on Asylum reflected security concerns in the wake of the large inflows of asylum seekers from Bulgaria and Iraq in the early 1990s. This allowed non-Europeans to apply for asylum in Turkey, but then to be resettled elsewhere if their status as refugees was recognised. İçduygu and Aksel (2014) see this as having the effect of making Turkey a transit country for migrants from outside of Europe. In this way, we can see that legislation can create the categories into which migrants are placed that then become defined as policy problems. It's not so much the case that 'transit migrants' were particularly evident prior to 1994, but that an effect of the 1994 law was to create 'transit migrants'.

Policy development has been framed by engagement with the EU, although this far precedes the onset of these post Cold War migration flows. Turkey became a member of the Council of Europe in 1949 and first applied for associate membership status of the then EC in 1959, which was agreed in 1963. A customs union agreement was signed in 1995 and an application for full membership was made in 1999 with negotiations commencing in October 2005, although membership appears a distant prospect. A visa liberalisation dialogue did commence at the end of 2013 because of the anomalous situation that the customs union agreement allows freer movement of goods, services and capital between Turkey and the EU, but not of people. A crucial issue for Turkey in the negotiation of the migration aspects of the EU is that membership would require lifting the geographical limitation, but 'the greatest nightmare for them is one in which they would find themselves lifting the geographical limitation without Turkey's membership being taken seriously by the EU' (Kirişçi, 2012: 74). The fear would then be that Turkey would become a 'dumping ground' for refugees unable to access the EU.

Turkish laws related to the status of foreigners have long contained a strong focus on Turkish national identity. In 1934 the Settlement Law made it clear that only a 'person of Turkish descent and who is attached to Turkish culture' could migrate to and settle in Turkey. This definition was maintained by a new law on settlement introduced in 2006, although this refers only to migrants and not to refugees. This then leaves the category of 'foreigners' who have no citizenship bond with Turkey (Memişoğlu, 2014: 4). Their status was regulated separately until the 2013 Law on Foreigners and International Protection.

Legislative change

There has been a rapid development of laws and institutions on migration and asylum since the 2000s with a strong EU influence playing a key part in these developments. As seen in other chapters, we see here too that adaptation to EU requirements is not a smooth and linear process of adjustment. Rather we see scope for the contestation of EU standards in Turkey along the dimensions sketched in Box 10.3 above.

In 2002, the Turkish government toughened its trafficking and smuggling laws with increased penalties introduced in 2005. In 2003, new legislation covered Work Permits for Foreign Nationals to try to tackle irregular work. Memişoğlu (2014) sees these legislative developments as indicators of compliance with EU standards. Similarly influenced by the EU's membership criteria was the creation of (in 2002) a Task Force that was composed of three groups dealing with migration, asylum and external border controls. The results of the deliberations of these groups then formed the basis for the National Action Plan for the Adoption of the EU *acquis* in the Field of Migration and Asylum that was published in 2005. A part of the process of EU accession is the sharing of ideas and knowledge between member states and applicant countries. Turkey was, for instance, involved in 'twinning' exercises with EU member states (including with the UK and Denmark on asylum and with France and UK on Integrated Border Management).

The publication of the National Action Plan in 2005 then led to what Tolay (2012: 44) calls a 'period of adjustment' that was then followed by a period of more comprehensive reform after 2008. Central to this process was the Asylum and Migration Bureau in the Interior Ministry, which was created in 2008. The Asylum and Migration Bureau drafted the 2013 Law on Foreigners and International Protection, which covers: entry rules; visas; work and residence permits; protects the rights of asylum seekers and refugees but, importantly, maintains the geographical limitation; and creates a Directorate General for Migration Management in the Ministry of the Interior (Memişoğlu, 2014: 13). The law was seen as 'a remarkable turning point towards the establishment of an effective institutional and legislative framework for migration management' in which the EU played a 'pivotal role' (Memişoğlu, 2014: 1).

In addition to asylum, two other issues have been central to the development of Turkish migration law and policy. The first of these is visa policy. In 2002, Turkey became compliant with what is called the Schengen 'negative' list. This list is of those countries whose nationals require a visa to enter the EU. However, the Turkish authorities stopped imposing visa requirements on further countries after 2005, and started to reverse its approach after 2009 when it lifted visa requirements for Syrians, Libyans, Jordanians and Albanians in 2009 and then Russians, Lebanese and Serbians in 2010. These countries were all on the Schengen negative list. The reason why Turkey adopted this approach relates to a point made earlier about the influence of broader strategic considerations and, in particular, its foreign policy objective of 'zero problems with neighbours'. An explanation for this is that, since 2002, visa policy has seen Turkey reaffirm its 'neo-Ottoman ideology as an alternative normativity to the EU, as reflected in Turkey's latest visa liberalisation policies to countries which have been negative listed by the EU' (İçduygu and Aksel, 2014: 346).

The second key issue is re-admission, which means taking back Turkish nationals and TCNs that entered the EU via Turkey. Provisions for readmission are a central component of the external dimension of EU migration policy. A lengthy negotiation process between the Turkish government and the EU Commission began in 2005, but was blocked between 2006 and 2010 because of Turkish refusal to open its air and seaports to vessels from Cyprus. Agreement was eventually reached in December 2013 and, simultaneously, there was an agreement to begin a dialogue on visa liberalisation. This is not unusual, the *quid pro quo* when a readmission agreement is reached is for it to be accompanied by visa liberalisation as, for example, happened with Serbia, Montenegro and Macedonia in 2009 and 2010. The EU Commission favoured liberalisation, but key member states such as France and Germany were opposed. There is another side to this as Kirişçi (2012: 74) notes because 'Turkish officials are also conscious and deeply affected by the European public resistance to EU membership'. This led to the initiation of a visa dialogue with no guarantee that the end result would be visa liberalisation. There were concerns on the Turkish side that they would become a 'buffer zone' or 'dumping ground' for TCNs entering the EU via Turkey. There were also divisions within the Turkish government with the Ministry of the Interior more reluctant to sign up to the readmission agreement 'because of their conventionally and traditionally conservative perspectives based on security concerns' and fears about 'burden shifting' compared to the Ministry of Foreign Affairs with the agreement seen as a 'tool of migration management and a question of "burden sharing" with the EU' (İçduygu and Akjsel, 2014: 360).

The readmission agreement is an interesting example of the EU's international migration relations. As already noted, readmission is central to the external dimension of EU policy. The issue is the readiness of a country such as Turkey to agree to such a measure given the fear that it may be a means for the EU to solve a problem with the risk that Turkey becomes a 'buffer zone' or 'dumping ground'. There needs to be some incentive for Turkey to agree to readmit. This could be membership or, more likely, an effort to liberalise the visa regime between Turkey and the EU (or, to be more precise, the Schengen area). In his analysis of the negotiation, Bürgin (2012) argues that a key role was played by the Commission that offered a visa dialogue – albeit with no guarantee of membership – as a way to unblock the negotiation: 'the fact that the Commission has embraced the Turkish position was crucial to finalising the deal, which, in turn, forced reluctant governments onto the defensive' (Bürgin, 2012: 897). Bürgin (2012) then identifies three reasons why there will be increased pressure on the opponents of visa free travel: (i) the Commission will be an ally of Turkey and will continue to advocate it; (ii) the management of irregular flows through the Eastern Mediterranean route will require concessions to Turkey; and (iii) CJEU court decisions such as the Soysal case of 2009 were seen as chipping away at the credibility of a restrictive visa regime. The Soysal case referred to two lorry drivers working for a Turkish company but driving lorries owned by a German company. They were denied visas by the German authorities, but the CJEU ruled in their favour because of the provisions of the association agreement related to the freedom to provide services and the right of establishment.

There are divided opinions within the EU about visa liberalisation, with Germany, France, Austria and Cyprus reported to be opposed while Italy, Britain, Finland, Poland, Sweden and Spain were seen as in favour (İçduygu and Aksel, 2014: 354). The fear is that visa liberalisation would lead to mass migration. Turkish President Erdoğan addressed these concerns in a December 2013 speech when he stated that: 'no one should be concerned when the visas are lifted. Thanks to the country's dynamic economy over the past ten years, Turkey is no longer an exporter of labour; instead, the country has now become a destination for job seekers'. As İçduygu and Karaçay note, however, Turkey would be the poorest member state and has a population growth rate that far exceeds (by 13 times) the EU average. To offset this, the Turkish economy was growing rapidly at the end of the 2000s and 2010s at between 6 and 9 per cent a year, but is relatively poor when compared to other EU member states.

There has been a clear EU influence on policy development, but the EU is not the only player in town. We can distinguish between the various policy areas: on visas and readmission the key dynamic is related to the EU's influence, but on asylum the key role has been played by the UNHCR and more recently by decisions of the ECtHR. The influence of these non-EU factors should not be underestimated. Kirişçi (2012) shows how the cases instigated changes. In particular the Abdolkhani and Karimnia case in 2009 found violations by the Turkish authorities in their attempts to deport two Iranian refugees. This decision became a turning point as it was followed by 12 other cases leading to convictions and compensation claims (Kirişçi, 2012: 77). This helped drive the major shake-ups in the government that followed the creation of the Migration Bureau within the Interior Ministry that then drafted the 2013 migration law. The important point here, as Kirişçi (2012: 79) notes, is that the new migration law 'needs to be seen as a function of as much the socialisation effect of the UNHCR and ECtHR on Turkey as harmonisation with the EU *acquis*'.

Conclusion

This chapter has sought to further broaden the book's focus by drawing in analysis of immigration policy and politics in two South East European countries that are at the heart of contemporary debates about the future of European and EU migration policy and politics as well as the wider responsibilities of EU member states to refugees and displaced people. There are some important similarities with what has been seen as a 'South European immigration type' in the form of, for example, the interactions between economic informality and irregular migration, as well as pressures and tensions at external frontiers. In order to understand how these impact and how they become political issues, a distinction was made between regulatory and distributive concerns with the EU seen as much more present in the former area and having much less influence over the latter. We also saw that in relation to both regulatory and distributive aspects of policy, there is the potential for the effects of European integration and the EU to be politicised both positively and negatively and, in both countries, there has been evidence of a critical approach to the EU and a contestation of some of its effects. At the very least, European integration can change the balance of power in domestic politics, strengthening some actors and weakening others. In both countries we saw the importance of accounting for external influences such as – but not only – the EU and also to understand how these then interact with domestic politics. The fragmentation of the Greek party system provided a good example of the importance of identifying the centrality of these kinds of interactions between the EU and domestic politics.

Finally, the chapter has affirmed a more general point made by this book that it is important to account for the geo-political widening of European immigration politics and not focus on a small group of 'older' immigration countries in North West Europe. The future development of European and EU immigration and immigrant policy and politics is and will continue to be strongly influenced by developments in South East Europe.

Conclusion

11

Introduction

In June 2015, in another apparent blow to common EU migration policies, Italian Prime Minister, Matteo Renzi, proposed to offer temporary permits to asylum applicants in Italy with the idea that they could then move on to other EU member states. This was in response both to tightened border controls exerted by France and Italy as well as pressure within Italy from the anti-immigrant Northern League political party. It was a potential blow to a common EU approach because such a move seemed likely to exacerbate rather than ease tensions, and may well have been a move made by Renzi to draw attention to the unsustainability of the current situation of relatively large-scale arrivals in Italy (more than 153,000 in 2015, see Table 1.1). These events also help to illustrate four points that are central to this book's analysis of the politics of migration and immigration in Europe.

European immigration politics are now also European Union immigration politics

By this we mean that the EU shapes the strategic setting within which European immigration policy and politics are made and unmade, while the actions of the member states also shape this EU setting. No analysis of developments in European immigration policy and politics could be complete without some assessment of the EU's role, but without also accounting for the key role that is still played by the member states. This book has shown that it would be misguided to imagine that some kind of simple teleological narrative of 'ever closer union' could be used to explain the development of EU migration and asylum policy. The reality is more complex, more hybrid and a mix of both intergovernmental and supranational elements with clear evidence of both vertical pressure to adapt to the EU *acquis* and 'horizontal' learning between member states (perhaps using the EU as a forum) as, for example, with the idea of 'civic integration'.

We sketched this EU role along two dimensions. The first concerns the *institutionalisation of Europe*, by which we meant the ways in which common EU policies have been established and developed and within which member state concerns, primarily about border security, have played a key role. This also necessarily includes the consolidation of a free movement framework encompassing all 28 member states that effectively means open borders for EU citizens moving within the EU. It also means the more partial institutionalisation of common migration and asylum policies. They are partial because, as was shown in Chapter 7, they do not include the numbers of migrants to be admitted, which remains a matter for the member states to decide. Chapter 7 showed that EU policies have tended to be more focused on external border controls and less on the issues of admission and integration that have tended to be the stuff of immigration and immigrant policy and politics in the member states. This does not mean that the EU is irrelevant, in fact, far from it. Taken together, free movement, migration and asylum have become central to the European project in recent years and will doubtless maintain their salience as key priorities. More than this, they have also worked their way into domestic politics in the member states through what we called *the Europeanisation of institutions*, by which we mean the ways in which EU influences on immigration and immigrant policies work their ways into domestic politics. A key finding demonstrated throughout this book is that it would be entirely mistaken to imagine that this is some straightforward and linear process of adjustment. The EU 'appears' in domestic politics in the member states both as an opportunity, as a challenge and, for some, as a threat. For example, the EU can change the balance of power in domestic politics by empowering some actors and weakening others. We have also seen that free movement and immigration have become central components of Eurosceptic politics in Britain, France and the Netherlands. Chapters on Southern, Central and Eastern Europe showed that EU influence can be welcomed and embraced, but can also be contested, criticised or resisted. The wider point is that the EU needs to be understood as a political system with associated processes and not merely as a technical concern. While the language of EU politics can be dry and technical, the issues raised by EU free movement, migration and asylum policy strike right at the heart of key debates in the EU, which, as we showed, relate not only to the territorial borders of the member states, but also to their organisational and conceptual borders.

The search for solidarity

The term responsibility-sharing and the closely related idea of solidarity have become very much associated with common EU migration and asylum policies. In a certain sense it is an indication of how far these policies have come that we now seek to understand the ways in which 28 countries have agreed to share some aspects of their power and authority on international migration and thus expose themselves to a debate about the sharing of responsibility. The European Commission's Agenda for Migration of May 2015 made it clear that some form of solidarity needed to be evident if a meaningful approach to the Mediterranean refugee crisis were to be found. Commission proposals for a scheme to work with the UNHCR to relocate up to 160,000 asylum applicants from Greece, Hungary and Italy were agreed in September 2015 in the face of opposition from some member states such as Hungary and Slovakia with important question marks about how relocation on such a scale would actually be implemented. The basic dilemma is that, to be meaningful, common EU policies need some operative principle of responsibility-sharing otherwise the risk is that EU member states compete with one another to offload or shirk responsibility. As has been shown, a dividing line appears to be opening between those countries that see themselves as being 'frontline' member states such as Greece, Italy and Spain, and other member states (particularly those in North West Europe) that would see the further development of control capacity beyond the EU in non-member states, as well as in these EU destination countries, as the best way to deal with migration and refugee flows. These tensions lead to the third theme that has been central to this book's analysis.

The drivers of domestic immigration politics

Renzi's idea of issuing temporary residence permits arose from both the failure of EU member states to act collectively, but also because of the tensions within Italian domestic politics caused by the resurgent *Lega Nord* capitalising on anti-immigration sentiment not only in its northern Italian heartlands, but also in previously solid areas for the centre-left, such as Tuscany where the *Lega* secured 20 per cent of the vote in the June 2015 regional elections. While patterns are not uniform – Sweden being, to some extent, an exception as Chapter 6 showed – there is evidence across the EU of both increased support for extreme right or populist political parties and increased influence by those parties on governing parties. A powerful component of the appeal of parties such as UKIP in Britain, the FN in France and the Freedom Party in the Netherlands is that they all make connections between immigration and European integration and meld these into forms of Eurosceptic politics that resonate with some sections of the electorate in European countries. Governments may look anxiously over their shoulders and feel that they need to be seen to 'do something' – which usually involves being seen to get tough on immigration and immigrants. One risk of this analysis is that it does ascribe autonomy to public opinion and would see public hostility to immigration as a driver of policy. Another is that parties such as UKIP and the Dutch Freedom Party are seen as driving policy. In both Britain and the Netherlands, UKIP and Geert Wilder's Freedom Party have been able to capitalise on, as much as they have created, anti-immigration sentiment. This would entirely neglect the ways in which public opinion is shaped by elite discourses and practice on immigration as well as the ways in which immigration is represented in public debate and the media. It would be too superficial to simply argue that governments are pushed by electorates that are hostile to immigration without also thinking about the source of these hostile attitudes. It can be far more instructive to look beneath this headline data and to think about how opposition to immigration connects with other important social and political dynamics. Here we can see the importance of the link between opposition to immigration and a more general lack of confidence and trust in political institutions and political leaders. Put simply, the immigration issue can be a cipher for those who feel let down, left out and left behind by modern politics and this 'cultural divide' in European societies can help to explain the rise of the populist and extreme right (McLaren, 2012).

Immigrant politics are local

As Renzi raised the possibility of issuing temporary residence permits to asylum applicants, there were important political dynamics within Italy at that point to the centrality of what in this book we have labelled as immigrant policies concerning themselves with immigrant integration. In response to Renzi, the governor of Lombardy, Roberto Maroni, from the anti-immigrant *Lega Nord*, threatened to cut funds from towns in his region that accepted relocated asylum applicants. Here we see the importance of the oft-stated truism that all politics are local. This is particularly true of immigrant policies that play out in the towns, cities and neighbourhoods within which immigrants reside.

A key general trend that this book identifies is the tendency for immigrant integration to move away from measures targeted at specific immigrant groups and, instead, see more effort to 'mainstream' immigrant integration into general policy areas, such as education, employment and housing. The result is a diminished focus on categories that mark the distinctiveness of immigrants such as ethnicity and more on what is seen – usually by governments – as holding society together leading to a greater focus on socio-economic and linguistic adaptation. This book has shown this to be closely related to what we called 'background institutional conditions', by which we mean the effects of broader restructuring of welfare states and labour markets as well as of new ideas that animate these changes, such as a greater focus on self-reliance and less 'hand-holding' as a Swedish minister put it (see Chapter 6). This convergence is related to the restructuring of (neo)liberal capitalism in Europe, with effects on the ways in which these societies then make sense of immigration-related diversity. To be 'integrated' means to be productive as measured by economic contribution, with the other side of this being that asylum seekers (who are often excluded from work) or family migrants are downgraded and devalued.

In contrast to the convergence that we signalled in the field of immigration policies, there is not a strong EU signal directing convergence in immigrant policies. Most immigrant policies are decentralised to the local level. Although here there is a role for the EU – albeit limited – as it supports city networks that aim to promote the sharing of ideas and policy learning.

We also discussed a tendency to ascribe changes in immigrant policies to the influence of populist and extreme right political parties. We have, however, sought to demonstrate that the resurgence or rise of these parties is as much a symptom as it is a cause of these changes and that we must also factor into analyses the ways in which mainstream parties have led (or failed to lead) debate on these issues and not simply assume that they are driven along by more radi-cal or extreme parties.

Taking Renzi's statement about issuing temporary permits has allowed us to survey some of the themes assessed in this book. To make sense of the issues requires understanding the centrality of borders to the study of international migration. International migration is made visible by the borders of states, and it is at these borders that decisions are made about who can enter and who can-not, on what basis, for what purposes and for what duration. It is also at these borders that categorisations are made that are central to the analysis of immigra-tion politics because they determine not only the formal rights and status of international migrants, but also how that migration will be understood – as an asset or opportunity or as a threat or drain on resources. This book has focused on the ways in which European countries have made sense of international migration and thus necessarily reflects a destination country bias that may well not be attuned to the reasons why people move from one country to another. EU responses to the Mediterranean refugee crisis, for example, reflected the desire of member states to stop the flows rather than to deal with the underlying causes of movement which were grounded in much more difficult to resolve questions of poverty, inequality, oppression and conflict. Whether European countries will be able to further develop their co-operation on immigration and immigrant policy is a key question for the future, but also brings us back to a question posed at the start of this book about convergence.

Convergent politics?

Is there evidence that European and EU immigration and immigration politics and policy are converging? This book has shown the importance of emphasising the contexts within which policy and politics are made in various European countries. The result is that, to a considerable extent, immigration politics in Europe is 'channelled' by these national contexts and can be understood only if we pay attention to national particularities in each of our case countries, whether it be contrasting histories of colonialism and post-colonial immigration in Britain, France and the Netherlands, or the influence of economic informality in Italy and Spain.

National particularities are a necessary component, but are insufficient to provide a comprehensive analysis. To make this point, we distinguished between 'horizontal' and 'vertical' elements of convergence. The former can be thought of as the sharing of ideas and information between European countries that can lead to new ways of doing things, as has been the case with 'civic integration'. The latter is more focused on the EU's role as a transmitter of ideas, particularly although not only through the process of EU enlargement.

This does also raise the more basic question of the meaning of convergence. It would be highly unlikely that we would see convergence in the form of iden-tikit immigration and immigrant policies in all European countries. In fact, this is so wildly improbable that it can be discounted from the outset. But this is not the only way in which convergence could be assessed.

There are those who do identify convergence in immigration and immigrant policies. In Chapter 1 we analysed Freeman's (1995) argument that the dynamics of immigration policy in liberal democratic states will be convergent because of the forms of politics associated with immigration that favour particular groups of concentrated beneficiaries (such as business arguing for openness to labour migration). Others argue that there is convergence in the form of a 'gap' between restrictive rhetoric and the reality of continued immigration (Hollifield et al., 2014). These perspectives on convergence tend to focus on outcomes, but it is also equally relevant to focus on other issues, particularly the characteristics of the policy process, which is what Knill does when he defines convergence as:

> ... any increase in the similarity between one or more characteristics of a certain policy (e.g. policy objectives, policy instruments, policy settings) across a given set of political jurisdictions (supranational institutions, states, regions, local authorities) over a given period of time. Policy convergence thus describes the end result of a process of policy change over time towards some common point, regardless of the causal processes. (Knill, 2005: 768)

The result is that we may see convergence in objectives, instruments or settings, or some combination of all of these. These may arise from similar objectives, in the form of labour market or welfare state organisation, that drive similar patterns of behaviour, or they could arise from broader international pressures that induce convergence. Alternatively, we might see divergence in all of these areas with divergent objectives, instruments and policy settings. Another possibility mooted by Peixoto et al. (2012) is that we might see divisions within the EU between, for example, a 'Southern' immigration regime including countries such as Greece, Italy and Spain and other member states. Indeed, Peixoto et al. (2012) argue that divergence between South and North in the EU could mean that common EU policies are less likely. Analysis of responses to the Mediterranean crisis demonstrates the potential strength of this argument.

A search for evidence of cross-national convergence on immigration and migrant policies and politics requires looking across governance 'levels' to identify a range of possible outcomes that could include:

1. decreased variation between states that could arise as a result of the 'horizontal' sharing of ideas or the 'vertical' application of the EU's common legal framework and policy-making process;
2. 'catch up' by newer countries of immigration and newer EU member states in Central, Eastern and Southern Europe;
3. change in relation to an exemplary model that could, for example, be the requirement to adapt to the Schengen framework of border control;
4. convergence as a result of changes in country rankings that could occur as a result of benchmarking exercises.

If we take these as potential indicators of convergence then we can say that we have a more fine grained account of the scope for convergence in the EU that we could apply to objectives, instruments or policy settings while still accounting for elements of variation that are related to particular contexts. In such terms, we can conclude that there is evidence of convergence. This does not mean identikit European immigration policy and politics, but this book shows that the tools of comparative analysis can be applied to identify some similar patterns and trends and that the EU does play a key role in this.

Final reflections

The conclusions to this book cannot be conclusive because the issues that have been analysed will continue to evolve. We can't know exactly how they will develop because that would require predicting the future, which, at the very least, will be plagued by significant uncertainties. These uncertainties do not concern so much the fact that international migration will continue to be a key issue in international politics; this much, at least, is certain. What is far less certain is how states will respond to this uncertainty. To understand a little more about the context in which they will respond requires thinking about the drivers of migration and how they will evolve, and the drivers of migration politics and how they will evolve.

First, the key drivers of migration are relative inequalities of income and wealth as well as conflict either within or between countries. These are then mediated by the existence of social networks that can direct migration, as well as by demographic factors such as age and gender that can influence who moves. Finally, environmental factors such as land degradation can interact with these other factors to cause people to migrate (Black et al., 2011). Within the EU, free movement will be powerfully influenced by wealth and income levels, as well as by the ways in which the Euro crisis plays itself out. There is evidence of increased emigration from countries such as Greece, Italy and Spain with movement towards other EU member states such as Britain and Germany. Beyond the EU, it is fairly clear that these drivers will continue to exert powerful effects in a world that is plagued by inequalities and where conflicts bedevil areas such as the Middle East and North Africa. It is important to emphasise that this does not simply translate into migration pressure towards Europe as much of the resultant migration will be shorter moves to neighbouring states. One reason for this is that it is difficult to get into European countries. The deaths in the Mediterranean are indicators of the deadliness of Europe's borders as much as of their porousness.

The drivers of migration politics are, in some important ways, detached from the drivers of migration itself. As noted earlier, a key pattern across Europe is the rise of Eurosceptic parties that connect opposition to immigration with opposition to European integration. These parties do not form part of some cohesive bloc, but there are some important trends in European politics that explain their growth. One key aspect of such an explanation is the declining trust and confidence in political leaders and political institutions, with this lack of trust likely to be particularly evident in those who oppose immigration.

This creates a disjunction between the drivers of migration and the drivers of migration politics that is likely to present important challenges to political leaders in years to come. Developing a response to immigration is but one part of the challenge, another equally profound challenge is to respond to the disconnectedness between politicians and the people that is evident across Europe. If we move beyond this focus on European destination countries and the attendant bias that this implies, we can also see that how European leaders deal with immigration will have profoundly important consequences for countries of origin in the complex, inter-connected and necessarily international politics of immigration.

References

Acosta, D. and Geddes, A. (2013) 'The development, application and implications of an EU Rule of Law in the area of migration policy', *Journal of Common Market Studies*, 51(2): 179–93.

Adam, C. and Devillard, A. (2008) *Comparative Study of the Laws in the 27 EU Member States for Legal Migration*. Brussels: European Parliament.

Alexander, M. (2007) *Cities and Labour Immigration: Comparing Policy Responses in Amsterdam, Paris, Rome and Tel Aviv*. Ashgate, London.

Ålund, A. and Schierup, C.-U. (eds) (1993) *Paradoxes of Multiculturalism: Essays on Swedish Society*. Aldershot: Avebury.

Amiraux, V. and Simon, P. (2006) 'There are no minorities here: Cultures of scholarship and public debate on immigrants and integration in France', *International Journal of Comparative Sociology*, 47(3): 191–215.

Anderson, B. (2013) *Us and Them: The Dangerous Politics of Immigration Control*. Oxford: Oxford University Press.

Anderson, M. (1997) *Frontiers: Territory and State Formation in the Modern World*. Cambridge: Polity Press.

Andersson, R. (2014) *Illegality Inc.* Berkeley: University of California Press.

Andreas, P. (2000) *Border Games: Policing the US-Mexico Divide*. Ithaca, NY: Cornell University Press.

Arango, J. (2000) 'Becoming a country of immigration at the end of the twentieth century', in R. King, G. Lazaridis and C. Tsardanidis (eds), *Eldorado or Fortress? Migration in Southern Europe*. London: Macmillan, pp. 253–276.

Arango, J. (2013) *Exceptional in Europe? Spain's Experience with Immigration and Integration*. Washington DC: Migration Policy Institute.

Asscher, L. and Goodhart, D. (2013) 'Code Oranje voor vrij werkverkeer binnen EU', *De Volkskrant*, 17 August.

Aylott, N. (2015) *The Sweden Democrats: Ostracised and Energised*. London: Policy Network. Available at: http://policy-network.net/pno_detail.aspx?ID=4823&title=The-Sweden-Democrats-Ostracised-and-energised (accessed 19 June 2015).

Aylott, N. and Bolin, N. (2015) 'Polarising pluralism: The Swedish parliamentary election of September 2014', *West European Politics*, 38(3): 730–40.

Baganha, M. (2000) 'Immigrants social citizenship and labour market dynamics in Portugal', in M. Bommes and A. Geddes (eds.) *Immigration and Welfare: Challenging the Borders of the Welfare State*, London: Routledge, pp. 170–88.

Balch, A. (2010) *Managing Labour Migration in Europe: Ideas, Knowledge and Policy Change*. Manchester: Manchester University Press.

Baldwin-Edwards, M. (1997) 'The emerging European Union immigration regime: Some reflections on its implications for Southern Europe', *Journal of Ethnic and Migration Studies*, 35(4): 497–519.

Baldwin-Edwards, M. (2009) 'Greece', in M. Baldwin-Edwards and A. Kraler (eds), *REGINE: Regularisations in Europe*. Amsterdam: Amsterdam University Press.

Baltruks, D. (2015) 'The complementarity of the Irish and British Liberal market economies and skilled EU migration since 2004 compared to the Swedish coordinated market economy', *Journal of International Migration and Integration*, 25 August: 1–18.

Barroso, M. (2014) Speech given at LSE, London, 14 February. Available at: http://europa.eu/rapid/press-release_SPEECH-14-131_en.htm (accessed 13 April 2016).

Barry, B. (1996) 'Political theory old and new', in R. Goodin and H.-D. Klingemann (eds), *A New Handbook of Political Science*. Oxford: Oxford University Press.

Bauböck, R. (2003) 'Towards a political theory of migrant transnationalism', *International Migration Review*, 37(3): 700–23.

BBC (2015a) Theresa May pledges asylum reform and immigration crackdown, 6 October. Available at: www.bbc.co.uk/news/uk-politics-34450887 (accessed 1 March 2016).

BBC (2015b) Migrant crisis: Sweden doubles asylum seeker forecast, 22 October. Available at: www.bbc.co.uk/news/world-europe-34603796 (accessed 1 March 2016).

Bendel, P. (2014) 'Mainstreaming immigrant integration policy in Germany', in E. Collett et al. (eds), *Mainstreaming Immigrant Integration Policies*. Brussels: MPI.

Benhabib, S. (2002) *The Claims of Culture: Equality and Diversity in the Global Era*. Princeton, NJ: Princeton University Press.

Bertossi, C. (2001) *Les Frontières de la Citoyenneté en Europe: Nationalité, Résidence, Appartenance*. Paris: Editions L'Harmattan.

Bertossi, C. (2011) 'National models of integration in Europe: A comparative and critical analysis', *American Behavioral Scientist*, 55(12): 1561–80.

Black, R., Engbersen, G. and Okólski, M. (eds) (2010) *A Continent Moving West?: EU Enlargement and Labour Migration from Central and Eastern Europe*. Amsterdam: Amsterdam University Press.

Black, R., Adger, W.N., Arnell, N., Dercon, S., Geddes, A. and Thomas, D.S. (2011) 'The effect of environmental change on human migration', *Global Environmental Change*, 21: S3–S11.

Bleich, E. (2003) *Race Politics in Britain and France: Ideas and Policymaking since the 1960s*. Cambridge: Cambridge University Press.

Bolin, N., Lidén, G. and Nyhlén, J. (2014) 'Do anti-immigration parties matter? The case of the Sweden Democrats and local refugee policy', *Scandinavian Political Studies*, 37(3): 323–43.

Bommes, M. (2000) 'National welfare state, biography and migration: Labour migrants, ethnic Germans and the re-ascription of welfare state membership', in M. Bommes and A. Geddes (eds), *Immigration and Welfare: Challenging the Borders of the Welfare State*. London: Routledge, pp. 90–108.

Bommes, M. (2010) 'Migration research in Germany: The emergence of a generalised research field', in D. Thranhardt and M. Bommes (eds), *National Paradigms of Migration Research*. Osnabruck: IMIS Beitrage.

Bommes, M. and Geddes, A. (2000) *Immigration and Welfare: Challenging the Borders of the Welfare State*. London: Routledge.

Bonjour, S. (2009) *Grens en Gezin: Beleidsvorming Inzake Gezinsmigratie in Nederland, 1955–2005*. Amsterdam: Amsterdam University Press.

Bonjour, S. and Scholten, P. (2014) 'The Netherlands', in A. Triandafyllidou and R. Gropas (eds), *European Immigration: A Source Book*. Farnham: Ashgate, pp. 261–272.

Borevi, K. (2012) 'Sweden: The flagship of multiculturalism', in G. Brochmann and A. Hagelund (eds), *Immigration Policy and The Scandinavian Welfare State 1945–2010*. London: Palgrave Macmillan, pp. 25–96.

Boswell, C. (1999) 'The conflict between refugee rights and national interests: Background and policy strategies', *Refugee Survey Quarterly*, 18(2): 64–84.

Boswell, C. (2000) 'European values and the asylum crisis', *International Affairs*, 76(3): 537–57.

Boswell, C. and Geddes, A. (2011) *Migration and Mobility in the European Union*. London: Palgrave Macmillan.

Bowen, J. (2007a) 'A view from France on the internal complexity of national models', *Journal of Ethnic and Migration Studies*, 33(6): 1003–16.

Bowen, J. (2007b) *Why the French Don't Like Headscarves: Islam, the State, and Public Space*. New York: Princeton University Press.

Brochmann, G. (2014) 'Scandinavia', in J. Hollifield, P. Martin and P. Orrenius (eds), *Controlling Immigration: A Global Perspective* (3rd edn). Stanford, CA: Stanford University Press, pp. 281–301.

Brubaker, W.R. (1989) (ed.) *Immigration and the Politics of Citizenship in Europe and North America*. Lanham (MD): Rowman and Littlefield.

Brubaker, W.R. (1992) *Citizenship and Nationhood in France and Germany*. Cambridge, MA: Harvard University Press.

Brubaker, W.R. (1994) 'Commentary: Are immigration control efforts really failing?', in W. Cornelius, P. Martin and J. Hollifield (eds), *Controlling Immigration: A Global Perspective*. Stanford: Stanford University Press, pp. 227–31.

Brubaker, W.R. (2001) 'The return of assimilation: Changing perspectives on immigration and its sequels in France, Germany and the United States', *Ethnic and Racial Studies*, 24(4): 531–48.

Bucken-Knapp, G., Hinnfors, J. and Spehar, A. (2014) 'Political parties and migration policy puzzles: The European scene', *Comparative European Politics*, 12(6): 557–67.

Bürgin, A. (2012) 'European Commission's agency meets Ankara's agenda: Why Turkey is ready for a readmission agreement', *Journal of European Public Policy*, 19(6): 883–99.

Cahn, C. and Guild, E. (2010) *Recent Migration of Roma in Europe*. Strasbourg: Council of Europe.

Canek, M. and Cizinsky, P. (2011) 'The case of the Czech Republic', in G. Zincone, R. Penninx and M. Borkert (eds), *Migration Policymaking in Europe: The Dynamics of Actors and Contexts in Past and Present*. Amsterdam: Amsterdam University Press, pp. 327–346.

Carey, S. and Geddes, A. (2010) 'Less is more: Immigration and European integration at the 2010 general election', *Parliamentary Affairs*, 63(4): 849–65.

Carmel, E., Cerami, A. and Papadopoulos, T. (2011) *Migration and Welfare in the New Europe: Social Protection and the Challenges of Integration*. Bristol: Policy Press.

Carrera, S. and Guild, E. (2008) *The French Presidency's European Pact on Immigration and Asylum: Intergovernmentalism vs. Europeanisation?* Brussels: CEPS Policy Brief No. 170.

Carrera, S., Atger, A.F., Guild, E. and Kostakopoulou, T. (2011) *Labour Immigration Policy in the EU: A Renewed Agenda for Europe 2020*. Brussels: CEPS Policy Brief No. 240.

Carvalho, J. (2014) 'British and French policies towards high skilled immigration during the 2000s: Policy outplays politics or politics trumps policy?', *Ethnic and Racial Studies*, 37(13): 2361–78.

Carvalho, J. and Geddes, A. (2012) 'La politique d'immigration sous Sarkozy', in J. de Maillard and Y. Surel (eds), *Politiques Publiques, 3*. Paris: FNSP.

Castells, M. and Portes, A. (1989) 'World underneath: The origin, effects and dynamics of the informal economy', in A. Portes, M. Castells and L. Benton (eds), *The Informal Economy: Studies in Advanced and Less Developed Economies*. Baltimore, MD: Johns Hopkins University Press, pp. 11–40.

Castles, S. and Kosack, G. (1973) *Immigrant Workers and Class Structure in Western Europe*. Oxford: Oxford University Press.

Cerna, L. (2009) 'The varieties of high skilled immigration policies: Coalitions and policy outputs in advanced industrial countries', *Journal of European Public Policy*, 16(1): 144–61.

Cerna, L. (2013) 'Understanding the diversity of EU migration policy in practice: The implementation of the Blue Card initiative', *Policy Studies*, 34(2): 180–200.

Cernik, J. (2014) 'Czech Republic', in A. Triandafyllidou and R. Glopas (eds), *European Immigration: A Source Book*. Farnham: Ashgate, pp. 83–96.

COB (2014) *Burgerperspectieven 2014 – 2*. The Hague: COB.

Commission Nationale Consultative des Droits de l'Homme (2001) *Le Racisme e la Xénophobie*. Paris: CNCDH.

Commission of the European Communities (CEC) (2008) *Report from the Commission to the European Parliament and the Council on the Application of Directive 2003/86/EC on the Right to Family Reunification*, COM 2008 (610) final. Brussels: European Commission.

Commission of the European Communities (CEC) (2011) *The Global Approach to Migration and Mobility*, COM 2011(743) final. Brussels: European Commission.

Commission of the European Communities (CEC) (2013) *Fourth Annual Report on Immigration and Asylum*, COM 2013 (422) final. Brussels: European Commission.

Commission of the European Communities (CEC) (2015) *A European Agenda on Migration*, COM 2015 (240) final. Brussels: European Commission.

Commission of the European Communities (CEC) (2016) *Member States' Support to Emergency Relocation Mechanism. Communicated as of 4 January 2016*. Available at: http://ec.europa.eu/dgs/home-affairs/what-we-do/policies/european-agenda-migration/press-material/docs/state_of_play_-_relocation_en.pdf (accessed 1 March 2016).

Commission on Integration and Cohesion (CIC) (2007) *Our Shared Future*. London: CIC.

Consterdine, E. and Hampshire, J. (2014) 'Immigration policy under New Labour: Exploring a critical juncture', *British Politics*, 9(3): 275–96.

Cornelius, W. (1994) 'Spain: The uneasy transition from labor exporter to labor importer', in W. Cornelius, P. Martin and J. Hollifield (eds), *Controlling Immigration: A Global Perspective*. Stanford, CA: Stanford University Press, pp. 331–69.

Crossman, R. (1977) *The Diaries of a Cabinet Minister*. London: Hamilton.

CSO (2013) *Migracje Zagraniczne Ludności: Narodowy Spis Powszechny Ludności i Mieszkań 2011* (Population migration abroad: National Population Census 2011). Warsaw: Central Statistical Office. Available at: http://stat.gov.pl/spisy-powszechne/nsp-2011/nsp-2011-wyniki/migracje-zagraniczne-ludnosci-nsp-2011,13,1.html (accessed 13 April 2016).

Daily Telegraph (2013) Romanians' Presence in the United Kingdom and the Value of Free Movement of People, 21 February. Available at: www.telegraph.co.uk/news/uknews/law-and-order/9886338/Romanians-presence-in-the-United-Kingdom-and-the-value-of-free-movement-of-people.html (accessed 1 March 2016).

De Bruycker, P., Di Bartolomeo, A. and Fargues, P. (2013) *Migrants Smuggled by Sea to the EU: Facts, Laws and Policy Options*. Florence: European University Institute Migration Policy Centre.

De Haas, H. (2007) *The Myth of Invasion: Irregular Migration from West Africa to the Maghreb and the European Union*. Oxford: International Migration Institute.

De Zwart, F. (2012) 'Pitfalls of top-down identity designation: Ethno-statistics in the Netherlands', *Comparative European Politics*, 10(3): 301–18.

Deakin, N. (1964) *Colour and the British Electorate, 1964: Six Case Studies*. London: Pall Mall Press.

Der Spiegel (2010) Merkel's rhetoric in integration debate is inexcusable. Available at: www.spiegel.de/international/germany/the-world-from-berlin-merkel-s-rhetoric-in-integration-debate-is-inexcusable-a-723702.html (accessed 1 March 2016).

Dobson, J., Koser, K., McLaughlan, G. and Salt, J. (2001) *International Migration and the United Kingdom: Recent Patterns and Trends*. London: Home Office Research, Development and Statistics Directorate, Home Office.

Düvell, F. (2014) 'International relations and migration management: The case of Turkey', *Insight Turkey*, 16(1): 35–44.

Dyson, K. and Featherstone, K. (1996) 'Italy and EMU as a "Vincolo Esterno": Empowering the technocrats, transforming the state', *South European Society and Politics*, 1(2): 272–99.

Edelman, M. (1988) *Constructing the Political Spectacle*. Chicago: University of Chicago Press.

Einaudi, L. (2007) *Le Politiche Dell'immigrazione in Italia Dall'Unità a Oggi*. Bari: Laterza.

El-Enany, N. and Thielemann, E. (2011) 'The impact of EU asylum policy on national asylum regimes', in S. Wolff, F. Goudappel and J.W. de Zwaan (eds), *Freedom, Security and Justice after Lisbon and Stockholm*. Den Haag: Asser Institute. pp. 97–116.

Emilsson, H. (2014) *No Quick Fix: Policies to Support the Labor Market Integration of New Arrivals in Sweden*. Washington DC: Migration Policy Institute.

Engbersen, G., Okolski, M., Black, R. and Panţîru, C. (2010) 'Working out a way from east to west: EU enlargement and labour migration from Central and Eastern Europe', in R. Black, G. Engbersen, M. Okolski and C. Panţîru (eds), *A Continent Moving West? EU Enlargement and Labour Migration from Central and Eastern Europe*. Amsterdam University Press, Amsterdam, pp. 7–22.

Engbersen, G., Leerkes, A., Grabowska-Lusinska, I., Snel, E. and Burgers, J. (2013) 'A typology of labour migration. On the differential attachments of migrants from Central and Eastern Europe', *Journal of Ethnic and Migration Studies*, 39(6): 959–81.

Entzinger, H. (2003) 'The rise and fall of multiculturalism: The case of the Netherlands', in C. Joppke and E. Morawska (eds), *Toward Assimilation and Citizenship: Immigrants in Liberal Nation-states*. New York: Palgrave, pp. 59–86.

Entzinger, H. (2013) 'The growing gap between facts and discourse on immigrant integration in the Netherlands', *Identities*, 21(6): 693–707.

Escafre-Dublet, A. (2014) *Mainstreaming Immigrant Integration Policy in France*. Brussels: MPI.

Esser, H. and Korte, H. (1985) 'The policy of the Federal Republic of Germany', in T. Hammar (ed.), *European Immigration Policy: A Comparative Analysis*. Cambridge: Cambridge University Press, pp. 165–205.

EU Observer (2015) MEPs Challenge Orban's 'Horrible' Migration Survey, April 29. Available at: https://euobserver.com/beyond-brussels/128513.

Eurostat (2014) *Migration and Migrant Population Statistics*. Available at: http://ec.europa.eu/eurostat/statistics-explained/index.php/Migration_and_migrant_population_statistics (accessed 1 March 2016).

Eurostat (2015) *EU Citizenship – Statistics on Cross Border Activities*. Available at: http://ec.europa.eu/eurostat/statistics-explained/index.php/EU_citizenship_-_statistics_on_cross-border_activities#Foreigners_working_in_the_EU (accessed 1 March 2016).

Evans, G. and Chzhen, K. (2013) 'Explaining voters' defection from Labour over the 2005–10 electoral cycle: Leadership, economics and the rising importance of immigration', *Political Studies*, 61(1): 138–57.

Faist, T. (1994) 'How to define a foreigner: The symbolic politics of immigration in German partisan discourse', *West European Politics*, 17(2): 50–71.

Faist, T. (2000) *The Volume and Dynamics of International Migration and Transnational Social Spaces*. Oxford: Oxford University Press.

Faist, T. and Bauböck, R. (eds) (2010) *Diaspora and Transnationalism: Concepts, Theories and Methods*. Amsterdam: Amsterdam University Press.

Favell, A. (1998) *Philosophies of Integration: Immigration and the Idea of Citizenship in France and Britain*. Basingstoke: Macmillan.

Favell, A. and Hansen, R. (2002) 'Markets against politics: Migration, EU enlargement and the idea of Europe', *Journal of Ethnic and Migration Studies*, 28(4): 581–601.

Favell, A. and Recchi, E. (2011) 'Social mobility and spatial mobility', in A. Favell and V. Guiraudon (eds), *The Sociology of the European Union*. London: Palgrave Macmillan. pp. 50–75.

Feldblum, M. (1993) 'Paradoxes of ethnic politics: The case of Franco-Maghrebis in France', *Ethnic and Racial Studies*, 16(1): 52–74.

Feldblum, M. (1999) *Reconstructing Citizenship: The Politics of Nationality and Immigration Reform in Contemporary France*. Albany, NY: State University of New York Press.

Ferrera, M. (1996) 'The southern model of welfare in Social Europe', *Journal of European Social Policy*, 6(1): 17–37.

Financial Times (2014a) Study backs up business fears over UK migrant clampdown, 3 July. Available at: www.ft.com/cms/s/0/5325ada8-01f9-11e4-bb71-00144feab7de. html#axzz44rAaUgWT (accessed 13 April 2015).

Financial Times (2014b) The drain from Spain, 20 February. Available at: www.ft.com/cms/s/0/f7bdd5ce-995e-11e3-91cd-00144feab7de.html#axzz45hpqra3A (accessed 13 April 2016).

Financial Times (2015a) Outcast Sweden Democrats Ride a Wave of Popularity, 21 September. Available at: www.ft.com/cms/s/0/28a32d88-5e11-11e5-97e9-7f0b-f5e7177b.html#axzz3wIBDjo59 (accessed 1 March 2016).

Financial Times (2015b) UK Warned by East Europe not to Meddle with Migrant Rights, 11 May. Available at: www.ft.com/cms/s/0/e539afc6-f71e-11e4-99aa-00144feab7de. html#axzz3aVVkrUr6 (accessed 1 March 2016).

Financial Times (2016) Cologne Attacks Create a Defining Moment for German Tolerance, 11 January. Available at: www.ft.com/cms/s/0/3fb8df10-b7ab-11e5-b151-8e15c9a029fb.html#axzz3x93R7mGw (accessed 1 March 2016).

Finotelli, C. (2013) *Italy: Regional Dynamics and Centralistic Traditions*. Available at: www.researchgate.net/publication/259077081_Claudia_Finotelli_Italy_Regional_Dynamics_and_Centralistic_Traditions (accessed 19 June 2015).

Finotelli, C. and Arango, J. (2011) 'Regularisation of unauthorised immigrants in Italy and Spain: determinants and effects', *Documents d'anàlisi geogràfica, 57*(3): 495–515.

Finotelli, C. and Sciortino, G. (2009) 'The importance of being southern: The making of policies of immigration control in Italy', *European Journal of Migration and Law*, 11(2): 119–38.

Fondazione Migrantes (2014) *Rapporto: Italiani nel Mondo 2014*. Rome: Fondazione Migrantes.

Ford, R. and Goodwin, M. (2014) *Revolt on the Right: Explaining Support for the Radical Right in Britain*. London: Routledge.

Fox, J. (2013) 'The uses of racism: Whitewashing new Europeans in the UK', *Ethnic and Racial Studies*, 36(11): 1871–89.

Fredlund-Blomst, S. (2014) *Assessing Immigrant Integration in Sweden after the May 2013 Riots*. Washington DC: Migration Policy Institute.

Freeman, G. (1994) 'Britain: The deviant case', in W. Cornelius, P. Martin and J. Hollifield, *Controlling Immigration: A Global Perspective*. Stanford, CA: Stanford University Press. pp. 174–8.

Freeman, G. (1995) 'Modes of immigration politics in liberal states', *International Migration Review*, 29(3): 881–902.

Freeman, G. (1998) 'The decline of sovereignty? Politics and immigration restriction in liberal states', in C. Joppke (ed.), *Challenge to the Nation State: Immigration in Western Europe and the United States*. Oxford: Oxford University Press pp. 86–108.

Gallisot, R. (1989) 'Nationalité et Citoyenetté', *APRES-DEMAIN*, 286.

Garbaye, R. (2005) *Getting into Local Power: The Politics of Ethnic Minorities in British and French Cities*. Chichester: John Wiley & Sons.

Gaspard, F. (1995) *A Small City in France*. Cambridge, MA: Cambridge University Press.

Geddes, A. (2000) 'Denying access: Asylum seekers and welfare in the UK', in M. Bommes and A. Geddes, *Immigration and Welfare: Challenging the Borders of the Welfare State*. London: Routledge. pp. 134–47.

Geddes, A. (2005a) 'Getting the best of both worlds? Britain, the EU and migration policy', *International Affairs*, 81(4): 723–40.

Geddes, A. (2005b) 'Europe's border relationships and international migration relations', *Journal of Common Market Studies*, 43(4): 787–806.

Geddes, A. (2008a) *Immigration and European Integration: Beyond Fortress Europe?* Manchester: Manchester University Press.

Geddes, A. (2008b) 'Il rombo dei cannoni? Immigration and the centre-right in Italy', *Journal of European Public Policy*, 15(3): 349–66.

Geddes, A. and Guiarudon, V. (2004) 'Britain, France, and EU anti-discrimination policy: The emergence of an EU policy paradigm', *West European Politics*, 27(2): 334–53.

Geddes, A. and Taylor, A. (2013) 'How EU capacity bargains strengthen states: Migration and border security in South-East Europe', *West European Politics*, 36(1): 51–70.

Geddes, A. and Tonge, J. (2015) *Britain Votes 2015*. Oxford: Oxford University Press.

Gibney, M. (2008) 'Asylum and the expansion of deportation in the United Kingdom', *Government and Opposition*, 43(2): 146–67.

Ginsborg, P. (1990) *A History of Contemporary Italy: Society and Politics 1943–1988*. London: Penguin.

Gott, C., Loizillon, A., Portes, J., Price, R., Spencer, S., Srinivasan, V. and Willis, C. (2001) *Migration: An Economic and Social Analysis*. London: Home Office Research, Development and Statistics Directorate.

Goodman, S.W. (2010) 'Controlling immigration through language and country knowledge requirements', *West European Politics*, 32(1): 235–55.

Goodman, S.W. (2014) *Immigration and Membership Politics in Western Europe*. Cambridge: Cambridge University Press.

Gourevitch, P. (2015) 'Marine Le Pen's political patricide', *The New Yorker*, 14 April.

Grabbe, H. (2002) 'Europeanization goes east', in K. Featherstone and C. Radaelli (eds), *The Politics of Europeanisation*. Oxford: Oxford University Press.

Green, S. (2004) *The Politics of Exclusion: Institutions and Immigration Policy in Contemporary Germany*. Manchester: Manchester University Press.

Green, S. (2007) 'Divergent traditions, converging responses: Immigration and integration policy in the UK and Germany', *German Politics*, 16(1): 95–115.

Green, S. (2013) 'Germany: A changing country of immigration', *German Politics*, 22(3): 333–51.

Green Cowles, M., Caporaso, J. and Risse, T. (eds) (2000) *Transforming Europe: Europeanization and Domestic Change*. Ithaca, NY: Cornell University Press.

Green-Pedersen, C. and Odmalm, P. (2008) 'Going different ways? Right-wing parties and the immigrant issue in Denmark and Sweden', *Journal of European Public Policy*, 15(3): 367–81.

Guiraudon, V. (1998) *International Human Rights Norms and their Incorporation: The Protection of Aliens in Europe*, European Forum Working Paper EUF 98/04. Florence: European University Institute.

Guiraudon, V. (2000) *Les Politiques d'Immigration en Europe: Allemagne, France, Pays-Bas*. Paris: L'Harmattan.

Guiraudon, V., Phalet, K. and Ter Wal, J. (2005) 'Monitoring ethnic minorities in the Netherlands', *International Social Science Journal*, 57(183): 75–87.

Guttmann, A. (ed.) (1994) *Multiculturalism: Examining the Politics of Recognition*. Princeton: Princeton University Press.

Hall, P. (1986) *Governing the Economy: The Politics of State Intervention in Britain and France*. Oxford: Oxford University Press.

Hammar, T. (1985) *European Immigration Policy: A Comparative Study*. Cambridge: Cambridge University Press.

Hammar, T. (1990) *Democracy and the Nation State: Aliens, Denizens and Citizens in a World of International Migration*. Aldershot: Avebury.

Hammar, T. (1999) 'Closing the doors to the Swedish Welfare State', in G. Brochmann and T. Hammar, *Mechanisms of Immigration Control: A Comparative Analysis of European Regulatory Policies*. Oxford: Berg, pp. 169–202.

Hampshire, J. and Bale, T. (2015) 'New administration, new immigration regime: Do parties matter after all? A UK case study', *West European Politics*, 38(1): 145–66.

Hansen, R. (2000) *Immigration and Citizenship in Post-War Britain*. Oxford: Oxford University Press.

Hargreaves, A. (1995) *Immigration, 'Race' and Ethnicity in Contemporary France*. London: Routledge.

Haut Conseil à l'Intégration (HCI) (1991) *Pour un Modèle Français d'Intégration: Premier Rapport Annuel*. Paris: La Documentation Français.

HM Government (2010) *The Coalition: Our Programme for Government*. London: HMSO.

HM Government (2014) *Review of the Balance of Competencies between the UK and the EU: Asylum and Non-EU Migration*. London: HMSO.

Hinnfors, J., Spehar, A. and Bucken-Knapp, G. (2012) 'The missing factor: Why social democracy can lead to restrictive immigration policy', *Journal of European Public Policy*, 19(4): 585–603.

Hix, S. and Høyland, B. (2011) *The Political System of the European Union*. London: Palgrave Macmillan.

Hollifield, J. (1992) *Immigrants, Markets and States: The Political Economy of Post-War Europe*. Cambridge, MA: Harvard University Press.

Hollifield, J. (2000a) 'The politics of international migration: How can we bring the state back in?', in C. Brettel and J. Hollifield (eds), *Migration Theory: Talking Across Disciplines*. London: Routledge, pp. 137–86.

Hollifield, J. (2000b) 'Immigration and the politics of rights: The French case in comparative perspective', in M. Bommes and A. Geddes (eds), *Immigration and Welfare: Challenging the Borders of the Welfare State*. London: Routledge, pp. 109–33.

Hollifield, J. (2014) 'France', in J. Hollifield, P. Martin and P. Orrenius (eds), *Controlling Immigration: A Global Perspective* (3rd edn). Stanford, CA: Stanford University Press. pp. 157–87.

Hollifield, J., Martin, P. and Orrenius, P. (2014) *Controlling Immigration: A Global Perspective*, Stanford, CA: Stanford University Press.

Holmberg, S. (1999) 'Down and down we go: Political trust in Sweden', in P. Norris (ed.), *Critical Citizens: Global Support for Democratic Government*. Oxford: Oxford University Press, pp. 103–22.

Home Office (2001) *Community Cohesion: A Report of the Independent Review Team*. London: Home Office.

Hussey, A. (2014) *The French Intifada: The Long War between France and its Arabs*. London: Macmillan.

Honohan, I. (2009) 'Reconsidering the claim to family reunification in migration', *Political Studies*, 57(4): 768–87.

Ibrahimović, Z. (2014) *I am Zlatan: My Story On and Off the Field*. London: Random House.

İçduygu, A. and Kirişçi, K. (eds.) (2009) *Land of Diverse Migrations: Challenges of Emigration and Immigration in Turkey*, Istanbul: Bilgi University Press.

İçduygu, A. and Aksel, D. (2014) 'Two-to-tango in migration diplomacy: Negotiating readmission agreement between the EU and Turkey', *European Journal of Migration and Law*, 16(3): 337–63.

Iglicka, K. (2001a) *Poland's Post-War Dynamic of Migration*. Aldershot: Ashgate.

Iglicka, K. (2001b) 'Migration movements from and into Poland in the light of East–West European migration', *International Migration*, 39(1): 3–32.

Independent Commission on Migration (ICM) (2001) *Structuring Immigration, Fostering Integration*, report by the Independent Commission on Migration to Germany. Berlin: ICM.

International Organization for Migration (2016) *Missing Migrants Project. Mediterranean Update January 31 2015*. Available at: http://missingmigrants.iom.int/en/mediterranean-update-31-december-2015 (accessed 6 January 2015).

IPSOS MORI (2014) *Perceptions and Reality: Public Attitudes to Immigration*. London: IPSOS MORI Social Research Institute.

Iosifides, T. and King, R. (1998) 'Social spatial dynamics and the exclusion of three immigrant groups in the Athens conurbation', *South European Society and Politics*, 3(3): 205–29.

Ireland, P. (1997) 'Socialism, unification policy and the rise of racism in Eastern Germany', *International Migration Review*, 31(2): 541–68.

Ireland, P. (2004) *Becoming Europe: Immigration, Integration, and the Welfare State*. Pittsburgh: University of Pittsburgh Press.

Ivarsflaten, E. (2006) 'Reputational shields: Why most anti-immigrant parties failed in Western Europe, 1980–2005', paper presented to the Annual Meeting of the American Political Science Association, Philadelphia.

Jacobi, L. and C. Kluve (2006) Before and After the Hartz Reforms: The Performance of Active Labour Market Policy in Germany. IZA Discussion Paper Nr. 2100.

Jacobson, D. (1996) *Rights Across Borders: Immigration and the Decline of Citizenship*. Baltimore: Johns Hopkins University Press.

Jahn, A. and Straubhaar, T. (1998) 'A survey of the economics of illegal immigration', *South European Society and Politics*, 3(3): 16–42.

Joppke, C. (1997) 'Asylum and state sovereignty: A comparison of the United States, Germany and Britain', *Comparative Political Studies*, 30(3): 258–98.

Joppke, C. (1998) 'Why liberal states accept unwanted immigration', *World Politics*, 50(2): 266–93.

Joppke, C. (1999) *Immigration and the Nation State: The United States, Germany and Great Britain*. Oxford: Oxford University Press.

Joppke, C. (2007) 'Beyond national models: Civic integration policies for immigrants in Western Europe', *West European Politics*, 30(1): 1–22.

Joppke, C. (2009) *Veil: Mirror of Identity*. Cambridge: Polity.
Joppke, C. (2010) *Citizenship and Immigration*. Cambridge: Polity.
Jordan, B. and Düvell, F. (2002) *Irregular Migration: The Dilemmas of Transnational Mobility*. London: Edward Elgar.
Kahanec, M. (2012) 'Labour mobility in an enlarged European Union', in A.F. Constant and K.F. Zimmermann (eds), *International Handbook on the Economics of Migration*. Northampton: Edward Elgar. pp. 137–52.
Katz, R.S. and Mair, P. (1995) 'Changing models of party organization and party democracy: The emergence of the cartel party', *Party Politics*, 1(1): 5–28.
Kaunert, C., Occhipinti, J.D. and Léonard, S. (2014) 'Introduction: Supranational governance in the area of freedom, security and justice after the Stockholm Programme', *Cambridge Review of International Affairs*, 27(1): 39–47.
Kepinska, E. and Kindler, M. (2014) 'Poland', in A. Triandafyllidou and R. Gropas (eds), *European Immigration: A Source Book*. Farnham: Ashgate, pp. 273–86.
King, R. (2000) 'Southern Europe in the changing global map of migration', in R. King, G. Lazaridis and C. Tsardanidis (eds), *Eldorado or Fortress? Migration in Southern Europe*. London: Macmillan, pp. 3–26.
King, R., Iosifides, T. and Myrivili, L. (1998) 'A migrant's story: From Albania to Athens', *Journal of Ethnic and Migration Studies*, 24(1): 159–75.
Kirişçi, K. (2012) 'Turkey's new draft law on asylum: What to make of it?' in S. Paçacı Elitok and T. Straubhaar (eds), *Turkey, Migration and the EU: Potentials, Challenges and Opportunities*. Hamburg: Hamburg University Press, pp. 63–84.
Klusmeyer, D. and Papademetriou, D. (2009) *Immigration Policy in the Federal Republic of Germany: Negotiating Membership and Remaking the Nation*. Oxford: Berghahn Books.
Knill, C. (2005) 'Introduction: Cross-national policy convergence: Concepts, approaches and explanatory factors', *Journal of European Public Policy*, 12(5): 764–74.
Kofman, E. (1999) 'Female birds of passage a decade later', *International Migration Review*, 33(2): 269–99.
Koopmans, R. (2010) 'Trade-offs between equality and difference: Immigrant integration, multiculturalism and the welfare state in cross-national perspective', *Journal of Ethnic and Migration Studies*, 36(1): 1–26.
Korkut, U. (2014) 'The migration myth in the absence of immigrants: How does the conservative right in Hungary and Turkey grapple with immigration and quest', *Comparative European Politics*, 12(6): 620–636.
Kymlicka, W. (1995) *Multicultural Citizenship: A Liberal Theory of Minority Rights*. Oxford: Oxford University Press.
Lagerspetz, M. (2014) 'Estonia', in A. Triandafyllidou and R. Gropas (eds), *European Immigration: A Sourcebook*. Aldershot: Ashgate, pp. 188–198.
Lavenex, S. (1999) *Safe Third Countries: Extending the EU Asylum and Immigration Policies to Central and Eastern Europe*. Budapest: Central European University Press.
Lavenex, S. (2004) 'EU external governance in "wider Europe"', *Journal of European Public Policy*, 11(4): 680–700.
Lazaridis, G. (1996) 'Immigration to Greece: A critical evaluation of Greek policy', *Journal of Ethnic and Migration Studies*, 22(6): 335–48.
Lijphart, A. (1975) *The Politics of Accommodation: Pluralism and Democracy in the Netherlands*. Berkeley: University of California Press.
Linos, K. (2002) 'Understanding Greek immigration policy', in D. Keridis (ed.), *New Approaches to Balkan Studies*. Dulles, VA: Brasseys, pp. 309–44.
Livi Bacci, M. (ed.) (1972) *The Demographic and Social Pattern of Emigration from the Southern European Countries*. Rome: Università.

Lochak, D. (1989) 'Les minorités et le droit publique français: Du refus des différences à la gestion des différences', in A. Fenet and G. Soulier (eds), *Les Minorités et leurs Droits Depuis 1789*. Paris: L'Harmattan.

Lucassen, J. and Penninx, R (1997) *Newcomers: Immigrants and their Descendants in the Netherlands 1550–1995*. Amsterdam: Het Spinhuis.

Maas, W. (2007) *Creating European Citizens*. Lanham, MD: Rowman & Littlefield.

Maas, W. (2013) 'Equality and free movement of people: Citizenship and internal migration', in W. Mass (ed.), *Democratic Citizenship and the Free Movement of People*. Leiden: Martinus Nijhoff. pp. 9–30.

Mail on Sunday (2014) British values aren't optional, they're vital, 15 June. Available at: www.dailymail.co.uk/debate/article-265817/DAVID-CAMERON-British-values-arent-optional-theyre-vital-Thats-l-promote-EVERY-school-As-row-rages-Trojan-Horse-takeover-classrooms-Prime-Minister-delivers-uncompromising-pledge.html (accessed 13 April 2015).

Mann, M. (1995) 'A political theory of nationalism and its excesses', in S. Periwal (ed.), *Notions of Nationalism*. Budapest: Central European University Press, pp. 44–73.

Mann, M. (1999) 'The dark side of democracy: The modern tradition of ethnic and political cleansing', *New Left Review*, 235 (May–June).

Marshall, T.H. (1964) *Class, Citizenship and Social Development*. New York: Doubleday.

Martin, P. (2014) 'Germany', in J. Hollifield, P. Martin and P. Orrenius (eds), *Controlling Immigration: A Global Perspective* (3rd edn). Stanford: Stanford University Press. pp. 224–50.

Martiniez Viega, U. (1999) 'Immigrants in the Spanish labour market', *South European Society and Politics*, 3(3): 105–28.

Mattelart, T. and Hargreaves, A. (2014) 'Diversity policies, integration and internal security: The case of France', *Global Media and Communication*, 10(3): 275–87.

Maussen, M. (2012) 'Pillarization and Islam: Church-state traditions and Muslim claims for recognition in the Netherlands', *Comparative European Politics*, 10(3): 337–53.

McLaren, L. (2012) 'The cultural divide in Europe: Migration, multiculturalism, and political trust', *World Politics*, 64(2): 199–241.

Meijering, L. and Van Hoven, B. (2003) 'Imagining difference: the experiences of "transnational" Indian IT professionals in Germany', *Area*, 35(2): 174–82.

Memişoğlu, F. (2014) *Between the Legacy of Nation-State and Forces of Globalisation: Turkey's Management of Mixed Migration Flows*, Robert Schuman Centre for Advanced Studies Research Paper 2014/122.

Michalowski, I. (2010) 'Integration tests in Germany. A communitarian approach?', in R. Van Oers, E. Ersbøll and D. Kostakopoulou (eds), *A Re-definition of Belonging*. Brill: Leiden. pp. 185–210.

Migration News (2001a) Germany: Green Cards, Economy. Vol. 8, nr. 3 March.

Migration News (2001b) Germany: Schilly Proposal. Vol, 8: Nr. 9, 3 August.

Miles, R. (1993) *Racism after 'Race Relations'*. London: Psychology Press.

Miller, M. (1981) *Foreign Workers in Europe: An Emerging Political Force*. New York: Praeger.

Miller, M. (1989) 'Political participation and representation of non-citizens', in W. R. Brubaker (ed.) *Immigration and the Politics of Citizenship in Europe and North America*. Lanham (MD): University Press of America, pp. 129–44.

Mingione, E. and Quassoli, F. (2000) 'The participation of immigrants in the underground economy in Italy', in R. King, G. Lazaridis and C. Tsardanidis (eds), *Eldorado or Fortress? Migration in Southern Europe*. London: Macmillan, pp. 29–56.

Moch, L.P. (1992) *Moving Europeans: Migration in Western Europe since 1650*. Bloomington: Indiana University Press.

Modood, T. (2013) *Multiculturalism: A Civic Idea*. Cambridge: Polity Press.

Monar, J. (2001) 'The dynamics of justice and home affairs: Laboratories, driving factors and costs', *Journal of Common Market Studies*, 39(4): 747–64.

Monar, J. (2013) 'Justice and home affairs', *Journal of Common Market Studies*, 51(S1): 124–38.

Musch, E. (2011) *Integration durch Kosultation? Konsensbildung in der Migrations und Integrationspolitik in Deutschland und den Niederlanden*. Münster: Waxmann Verlag.

Noiriel, G. (1996) *The French Melting Pot: Immigration, Citizenship and National Identity*. Minneapolis: University of Minnesota Press.

Office for National Statistics (2013) Migration Statistics Quarterly Report, November 2013. London: ONS, www.ons.gov.uk/ons/dcp171778_335330.pdf (accessed 1 March 2016).

Okólski, M. (2001) 'Incomeplete migration: A new form of mobility in Central and Eastern Europe. The case of Polish and Ukrainian migrants', in C. Wallace and C. Stola (eds), *Patterns of Migration in Central Europe*. Basingstoke: Palgrave Macmillan, pp. 105–128.

Organisation for Economic Co-operation and Development (OECD) (2014) *International Migration Outlook 2014*. Paris: OECD.

Parekh, B. (2000) *Rethinking Multiculturalism*. London: Palgrave.

Park, A., Bryson, C. and Curtice, J. (eds) (2014) *British Social Attitudes: The 31st Report*. London: NatCen Social Research.

Parker, O. and López Catalán, O. (2012) 'Roma and the politics of EU Citizenship in France: Everyday security and resistance', *Journal of Common Market Studies*, 50(4): 379–95.

Pastore, F. (2001) *Reconciling the Prince's Two Arms. Internal and External Security Policy Co-ordination in the European Union*, Occasional Paper 30. Paris: Western European Union.

Paul, K. (1997) *Whitewashing Britain: Race and Citizenship in the Post-War Era*. Ithaca, NY: Cornell University Press.

Pawlak, M. (2014) 'Research-policy dialogues in Poland', in P. Scholten, H. Entzinger, R. Penninx and S. Verbeek (eds), *Integrating Immigrants in Europe*. Springer: Dordrecht, pp. 253–74.

Peixoto, J., Arango, J., Bonifazi, C., Finotelli, C., Sabino, C., Strozza, S. and Triandafyllidou, A. (2012) 'Immigrants, markets and policies in Southern Europe: The making of an immigration model?', in M. Okolski (ed.), *European Imigrations: Trends, Structures and Policy Implications*. Amsterdam: Amsterdam University Press.

Pew Research Centre (2014) 'In Europe sentiment against immigrants, minorities runs high', Washington DC: Pew Research Centre. Available at: www.pewresearch.org/fact-tank/2014/05/14/in-europe-sentiment-against-immigrants-minorities-runs-high/ (accessed 1 March 2016).

Phizacklea, A. (ed.) (1983) *One Way Ticket: Migration and Female Labour*. London: Routledge.

Pilkington, E. (1988) *Beyond the Mother Country: West Indians and the Notting Hill White Riots*. London: Tauris.

Pugliese, E. (1998) *Gli Immigrati in Italia* (5th edn). Rome: Laterza.

Rath, J. (1996) *Nederland en zijn Islam: Een Ontzuilende Samenleving Reageert op het Ontstaan van een Geloofsgemeenschap*. Amsterdam: Het Spinhuis.

Recchi, E. (2008) 'Cross state mobility in the EU: Trends, puzzles and consequences', *European Societies*, 10(2): 197–224.

Renan, E. (1882) *Qu'est ce qu'une Nation*, reprinted in *Qu'est ce qu'une Nation?* Paris: Presses Pocket (1992).

Reyneri, E. (1998) 'The role of the underground economy in irregular migration to Italy: Cause or effect?', *Journal of Ethnic and Migration Studies*, 24(2): 313–31.

Rich, P. (1986) 'Conservative ideology and race in modern British politics', in Z. Layton-Henry and P. Rich (eds), *Race, Government and Politics in Britain*. London: Macmillan, pp. 45–72.

Ripoll Servent, A. (2011) 'Co-decision in the European Parliament: Comparing rationalist and constructivist explanations of the Returns Directive', *Journal of Contemporary European Research*, 7(1): 3–22.

Rogers, R. (1985) *Guests Come to Stay: The Effects of Labour Migration on Sending and Receiving Countries*. Boulder, CO: Westview.

Roggeband, C. and Verloo, M. (2007) 'Dutch women are liberated, migrant women are a problem: The evolution of policy frames on gender and migration in the Netherlands, 1995–2005', *Social Policy & Administration*, 41(3): 271–88.

Rothstein, B. (1998) *Just Institutions Matter*. Cambridge: Cambridge University Press.

Ruggie, J. (1983) 'International regimes, transactions and change: Embedded liberalism in the post-war economic order', in S. Krasner (ed.), *International Regimes*. Ithaca, NY: Cornell University Press, pp. 195–232.

Ruhs, M. (2013) *The Price of Rights: Regulating International Labour Migration*. Princeton, NJ: Princeton University Press.

Sabbagh, D. and Peer, S. (2008) 'French color blindness in perspective: The controversy over "Statistiques Ethniques"', *French Politics, Culture & Society*, 26(1): 1–6.

Safran, W. (1985) 'The Mitterrand regime and its policies of ethno-cultural accommodation', *Comparative Political Studies*, 18(1): 41–63.

Saggar, S. and Somerville, W. (2012) *Building a British Model of Integration in an Era of Immigration: Policy Lessons for Government*. Washington DC: Migration Policy Institute.

Saraceno, C. (1994) 'The ambivalent familism of the Italian welfare state', *Social Politics*, 1(1): 60–82.

Sarrazin, T. (2010) *Deutschland schafft sich ab: Wie wir unser Land aufs Spiel setzen*. Berlin: DVA.

Sassen, S. (1998) 'The *de facto* transnationalizing of immigration policy', in C. Joppke (ed.), *Challenge to the Nation State: Immigration in Western Europe and the United States*. Oxford: Oxford University Press pp. 49–85.

Sassen, S. (1999) *Guests and Aliens*. New York: The New Press.

Schain, M. (1999) 'Minorities and immigrant incorporation in France: The state and the dynamics of multiculturalism', in C. Joppke and S. Lukes (eds), *Multicultural Questions*. Oxford: Oxford University Press, pp. 199–223.

Scheffer, P. (2000) 'Het multiculturele drama', *De Volkskrant*, 29 January.

Schneider, F. and Enste, D. (2013) *The Shadow Economy: An International Survey*. Cambridge: Cambridge University Press.

Schneider, J. and Scholten, P. (2015) 'Consultative commissions and the rethinking of integration policies in the Netherlands and Germany: The Blok Commission and the Süssmuth Commission compared', in P. Scholten, H. Entzinger, R. Penninx and S. Verbeek (eds), *Integrating Immigrants in Europe: Research-policy Dialogues*. Dordrecht: Springer, pp.77–98.

Scholten, P. (2011a) *Framing Immigrant Integration: Dutch Research-Policy Dialogues in Comparative Perspective*. Amsterdam: Amsterdam University Press.

Scholten, P. (2011b) 'Constructing Dutch immigrant policy. Research-policy relations and immigrant integration in the Netherlands', *British Journal of Politics and International Relations*, 13(1): 75–92.

Scholten, P. (2013) 'Agenda dynamics and the multi-level governance of migrant integration: The case of Dutch migrant integration policies', *Policy Sciences*, 46(3): 217–36.

Scholten, P. (2014) 'The multilevel dynamics of migrant integration policies in unitary states: The Netherlands and the United Kingdom', in E. Hepburn and R. Zapata-Barrero (eds.), *The Politics of Immigration in Multi-Level States: Governance and Political Parties*. Basingstoke: Palgrave Macmillan, pp. 150–74.

Scholten, P. and Timmermans, A. (2010) 'Setting the immigrant policy agenda: Expertise and politics in the Netherlands, France and the United Kingdom', *Journal of Comparative Policy Analysis*, 12(5): 527–44.

Scholten, P., Collet, L. and Petrovic, M. (2016) 'Mainstreaming migrant integration: A critical analysis of a new trend in integration governance', *International Review of Administrative Sciences*, published online first.

Scholten, P., Entzinger, H., Kofman, E., Hollomey, C. and Lechner, C. (2012) *Integration from Abroad? Perceptions and Impacts of Pre-Entry Tests for Third-Country Nationals*. Vienna: ICMPD.

Schönwälder, K. (2010) 'Integration policy and pluralism in a self-conscious country of immigration', in S. Vertovec and S. Wessendorf (eds), *The Multiculturalism Backlash: European Discourses, Policies and Practices*. London: Routledge, pp. 152–169.

Schuster, J. (1992) 'The state and post-war immigration into the Netherlands: The racialisation and assimilation of Indonesian Dutch', *European Journal of Intercultural Studies*, 3(1): 47–58.

Scientific Council for Government Policy (1989) *Allochtonenbeleid*. Den Haag: WRR.

Sciortino, G. (1999) 'Planning in the dark: The evolution of Italian immigration control', in G. Brochmann and T. Hammar (eds), *Mechanisms of Immigration Control: A Comparative Analysis of European Regulation Policies*. Oxford: Berg, pp. 233–60.

Sciortino, G. (2000) 'Towards a political sociology of entry policies: Conceptual problems and theoretical proposals', *Journal of Ethnic and Migration Studies*, 26(2): 213–28.

Simon, P. (2014) 'Contested citizenship in France: The Republican politics of identity and integration', in A. Cole, S. Meunier and V. Tiberj (eds), *Developments in French Politics*. Basingstoke: Palgrave Macmillan. pp. 203–17.

Simon, P. and Pala, V.S. (2010) 'We're not all multiculturalists yet', in S. Vertovec and S. Wessendorf (eds), *The Multiculturalism Backlash: European Discourses, Policies and Practices*. Abingdon: Routledge. pp. 92–110.

Slaughter, A.-M. (2009) *A New World Order*. Princeton, NJ: Princeton University Press.

Sniderman, P. and Hagendoorn, L. (2007) *When Ways of Life Collide: Multiculturalism and its Discontents in the Netherlands*. New York: Princeton University Press.

Soininen, M. (1999) 'The "Swedish Model" as an institutional framework for immigrant membership rights', *Journal of Ethnic and Migration Studies*, 25(4): 685–702.

Solé, C., Ribas, N., Bergali, V. and Parella, S. (1998) 'Irregular employment among migrants in Spanish cities', *Journal of Ethnic and Migration Studies*, 24(2): 336–46.

Somerville, W. and Goodman, S.W. (2010) 'The role of networks in the development of UK migration policy', *Political Studies*, 58(5): 951–70.

SOPEMI (2012) *International Migration Outlook 2012*. OECD, Paris.

Soysal, Y.N. (1994) *Limits to Citizenship: Migrants and Post-national Membership in Europe*. Chicago: Chicago University Press.

Spencer, S. (2011) *The Migration Debate*. Bristol: Policy Press.

Stigler, G. (1971) 'The theory of economic regulation', *Bell Journal of Economics and Management Science*, 2(2): 3–21.

Stone Sweet, A. and Sandholtz, W. (1997) 'European integration and supranational governance', *Journal of European Public Policy*, 4(3): 297–317.

Šūpule, I. (2014) 'Latvia', in A. Triandafyllidou and R. Gropas (eds), *European Immigration: A Sourcebook*. Aldershot: Ashgate, pp. 199–210.

Taguieff, P.-A. (1991) *Face au Racisme*. Paris: La Découverte.

Taylor, A., Geddes, A. and Lees, C. (2013) *The European Union and South East Europe: The Dynamics of Europeanization and Multilevel Governance*. London: Routledge.

Taylor, C. (1992) *Multiculturalism and the Politics of Recognition*. Princeton, NJ: Princeton University Press.

The Economist (1997) Nordic Eugenics: Here of all Places. August 27 1997. Available at: www.economist.com/node/155244 (accessed 1 March 2016).

The Guardian (2015) Refugee crisis: Germany creaks under strain of open door policy, 8 October. Available at: www.theguardian.com/world/2015/oct/08/refugee-crisis-germany-creaks-under-strain-of-open-door-policy (accessed 13 April 2016).

The Guardian (2016) Is the Schengen dream of Europe without borders becoming a thing of the past? January 6 2016. Available at: www.theguardian.com/world/2016/jan/05/is-the-schengen-dream-of-europe-without-borders-becoming-a-thing-of-the-past (accessed 1 March 2016).

Thränhardt, D. (1999) 'Germany's immigration policies and politics', in G. Brochmann and T. Hammar (eds), *Mechanisms of Immigration Control: A Comparative Analysis of European Regulation Policies*. Oxford: Berg, pp. 29–58.

Tolay, J. (2012) 'Turkey's "Critical Europeanization": Evidence from Turkey's Immigration Policies', in S. Elitok and T. Straubhaar (eds), *Turkey, Migration and the EU: Potentials, Challenges and Opportunities*, Hamburg: Hamburg University Press, pp. 39–62.

Toth, J. and Sik, E. (2014) 'Hungary', in A. Triandafyllidou and R. Glopas (eds), *European Immigration: A Source Book*. Farnham: Ashgate, pp. 173–84.

Triadafilopoulos, T. (2012) *Becoming Multicultural: Immigration and the Politics of Membership in Canada and Germany*. Vancouver: UBC Press.

Triandafyllidou, A. (2000) 'Racists? Us? Are you Joking? The Discourse of Social Exclusion of Immigrants in Greece and Italy', in R. King, G. Lazaridis and C. Tsardanidis (eds), *Eldorado or Fortress? Migration in Southern Europe*. London: Macmillan, pp. 186–206.

Triandafyllidou, A. (2014) 'Greek migration policy in the 2010s: Europeanization tensions at a time of crisis', *Journal of European Integration*, 36(4): 409–25.

Triandafyllidou, A. and Gropas, R. (2014) '"Voting with their feet": Highly skilled emigrants from Southern Europe', *American Behavioral Scientist*, 27 May.

Triandafyllidou, A. and Ambrosini, M. (2011) 'Irregular immigration control in Italy and Greece: Strong fencing and weak gate-keeping serving the labour market', *European Journal of Migration and Law*, 13(3): 251–73.

Tribalat, M. (1995) *Faire France: Une Grande Enquete sur les Immigrés et leurs Enfants*. Paris: La Decouverte.

United Nations Population Fund (UNFPA) (2015) *Topics: Migration*. Available at www.unfpa.org/migration (accessed 12 November 2015).

Van Amersfoort, H. and Van Niekerk, M. (2006) 'Immigration as a colonial inheritance: Post-colonial immigrants in the Netherlands, 1945–2002', *Journal of Ethnic and Migration Studies*, 32(3): 323–46.

Vargas-Silva, C. (2011) *Long-Term International Migration Flows to and from the UK*. Oxford: Migration Observatory, University of Oxford.

Vertovec, S. (2007) 'Superdiversity and its implications', *Ethnic and Racial Studies*, 30(6): 1024–54.

Villard, F. and Sayegh, P.Y. (2013) 'Redefining a (mono)cultural nation: Political discourse against multiculturalism in contemporary France', in R. Taras (ed.), *Challenging Multiculturalism*. Edinburgh: Edinburgh University Press, pp. 236–56.

Vink, M. (2007) 'Dutch "Multiculturalism" beyond the pillarisation myth', *Political Studies Review*, 5(3): 337–50.

Wallace, C. (2002) 'Opening and closing borders: Migration and mobility in East-Central Europe', *Journal of Ethnic and Migration Studies*, 28(4): 603–25.

Wasmer, M. (2013) 'Public debate and public opinion on multiculturalism in Germany', in R. Taras (ed.), *Challenging Multiculturalism*. Edinburgh: Edinburgh University Press. pp. 163–89.

Weil, P. (1991) *La France et ses Etrangers: L'aventure d'une Politique de l'Immigration 1938–1991*. Paris: Calmann-Levy.

Weil, P. (1994) 'Commentary: from hidden consensus to hidden divergence', in W. Cornelius, P. Martin and J. Hollifield (eds), *Controlling Immigration. A Global Perspective*. Stanford, CA: Stanford University Press.

Weil, P. (1997) *Mission d'études des Legislations de la Nationalité et de L'immigration*. Paris: La Documentation Français.

Weil, P. and Crowley, J. (1994) 'Integration in theory and practice: A comparison of France and Britain', *West European Politics*, 17(2): 110–26.

Weinar, A. (2006) *Europeizacja Polskiej Polityki Wobec Cudzoziemców 1990–2003*. Warsaw: Scholar.

Weinar, A. (2010) 'Instrumentalizing diasporas for development: International and European policy discourses', in R. Bauböck and T. Faist (eds), *Diaspora and Transnationalism: Concepts, Theories and Methods*. Amsterdam: Amsterdam University Press, pp. 73–90.

Wieviorka, M. (1991) *La France Raciste*. Paris: Fayard.

Wihtol de Wenden, C. (1988) *Les Immigrés et La Politique*. Paris: Presse de la Fondation Nationale des Sciences Politiques.

Wihtol de Wenden, C. (1994) 'The French response to the asylum seeker influx', *The Annals of the American Academy of Social and Political Sciences*, Special Edition, Mark Miller (ed.), Strategies for Immigration Control in Liberal Societies, vol. 534, July.

Wihtol de Wenden, C. (2014) 'France', in A. Triandafyllidou and R. Gopas (eds), *European Immigration: A Source Book*. Farnham: Ashgate, pp. 135–46.

Zincone, G. (1999) 'Illegality, enlightenment and ambiguity: A hot Italian recipe', *South European Society and Politics*, 3(3): 45–82.

Zolberg, A. (1989) 'The next waves: Migration theory for a changing world', *International Migration Review*, 23(3): 403–30.

Index

Figures and Tables are indicated by page numbers in **bold** print.